Preserving Ethnicity through Religion in America

# Preserving Ethnicity through Religion in America

## Korean Protestants and Indian Hindus across Generations

*Pyong Gap Min*

NEW YORK UNIVERSITY PRESS

New York and London

NEW YORK UNIVERSITY PRESS
New York and London
www.nyupress.org

Library of Congress Cataloging-in-Publication Data

Min, Pyong Gap, 1942–
Preserving ethnicity through religion in America : Korean Protestants
and Indian Hindus across generations / Pyong Gap Min.
p. cm.
Includes bibliographical references and index.
ISBN-13: 978-0-8147-9585-9 (cl : alk. paper)
ISBN-10: 0-8147-9585-4 (cl : alk. paper)
ISBN-13: 978-0-8147-9586-6 (pbk. : alk. paper)
ISBN-10: 0-8147-9586-2 (pbk. : alk. paper)
1. Ethnicity—Religious aspects. 2. Ethnicity—United States.
3. Identification (Religion) 4. Immigrants—United States—
Religious life. 5. Emigration and immigration—Religious aspects.
6. Minorities—Religious life. 7. Minorities—United States. I. Title.
BL65.E75M56     2010
200.8900973—dc22          2009042909

New York University Press books are printed on acid-free paper,
and their binding materials are chosen for strength and durability.
We strive to use environmentally responsible suppliers and materials
to the greatest extent possible in publishing our books.

Manufactured in the United States of America
c  10 9 8 7 6 5 4 3 2 1
p  10 9 8 7 6 5 4 3 2 1

# Contents

# Acknowledgments

THIS IS PROBABLY the most difficult book project I have ever undertaken, and the ten years that have gone into the effort indicate the great difficulty. It would have been absolutely impossible for me to finish it without the support, encouragement, and assistance that I have received from many organizations and people. I cannot possibly list all those who have helped me over a long period of time. But I can express something of the special debt I owe to the following people and organizations.

Starting with organizations, a fellowship from the Social Science Research Council and a grant from the Center for Immigration, Ethnicity, and Citizenship at New School University allowed me to take a sabbatical leave to collect personal interview data from fifty-nine Korean Protestant and sixty-five Indian Hindu immigrants. Grants from the PSC-CUNY, the Asian and Asian American Research Institute, and a FIPSE Faculty/Mentor project enabled me to hire research assistants to interview Korean Protestant immigrants and second-generation Korean Protestants and Indian Hindus. A grant from the PSC-CUNY also enabled me to visit Seoul to collect statistics on Protestant churches in Korea. The Queens College Presidential in-Residence Release-Time Award gave me release time to write some of the book chapters. A grant from the National Science Foundation allowed me to collect survey data on Korean and Indian immigrants' pre- and postmigrant religious affiliations and frequency of participation in religious institutions. Finally, a visiting scholar fellowship from Russell Sage Foundation gave me more time to revise some of the book chapters and update the literature.

Several graduate students conducted personal interviews with Korean Protestant and Indian Hindu immigrants and second-generation members, which were used as key data sources for this book. Hara Behk, Ho Su Kim, Kathy Kim, Young Oak Kim, and Ju Mun Oh interviewed the Korean informants, and Aarti Bhanot, Vasudha Gandhi, Krittika Ghosh, and Suman Saran interviewed the Indian informants. Another Korean interviewer and two Indian interviewers, as well as the just-named interviewers, played an important role in collecting data central to this book. Three Queens College Korean students, He Huang, Sang Ho Kim, and Young Oak Kim, helped me analyze the survey data and create the maps used in chapters 2 and 3. Dae Young Kim generously allowed me to use his dissertation data regarding religious affiliation and participation in religious institutions of 1.5- and second-generation Korean Americans.

I owe special thanks to Dr. Uma Mysorekar, president of the Hindu Temple Society of North America, and Padmanabhan Ganapathy, its public relations officer. They spent a great deal of time introducing the temple's various activities and responding to my repeated questions. Their kindness and cooperation made my ethnographic research at the temple less difficult than I had expected. In particular, Padmanabhan Ganapathy served as my major source of information, not only about his temple, but also about Hindu religious practices in general. I also owe a debt of gratitude to Rev. Jae Hong Han, senior pastor of the Shin Kwang Church of New York, for his exceptional kindness in giving me information about his church history and activities and contacts with other church members. Four other members of the Shin Kwang Church of New York—Keun Ok Kim, Ok Ja Park, Jae Hong Lim, and Esther Bong Ho Min—helped me with information about the church's sociocultural activities and organizational structure.

Several Indian friends taught me how Hindus and other Indian religious groups practice their religions at religious organizations and at home, as well as telling me their religious history in India. Madhulika Khandelwal, Ravi Kurkarni, Vinit Parmar, Parmatma Saran, Rupam Saran, Harvachan Singh, and Christine Varghese deserve special mention. Parmatma Saran was most helpful to my book project in teaching and showing me religious rituals practiced at home and in reading the entire manuscript. Many Korean pastors and church members—Won Tae Cha, Seong Gyu Hwang, Do In Joung, Chung Kuk Kim, Hyung Hoon Kim, Incha Kim, Nam Gon Kim, and David M. Lee—also gave me information about Korean church denominations and the historical development of Christianity in Korea.

Portions of chapters 3 and 4 are revisions of my article "Underrepresentation of Women in Church Leadership in the Korean Immigrant Community in the U.S.," *Journal for the Scientific Study of Religion* 46 (2008):255–42. Portions of chapter 6 appeared as "Religion and Maintenance of Ethnicity among Immigrants: A Comparison of Indian Hindus and Korean Protestants," in *Immigrant Faiths: Transforming Religious Life in America*, edited by Karen Leonard, Alex Stepick, Manuel Vasquez, and Jennifer Holdaway (Lanham, MD: Rowman & Littlefield, 2006), 99–122. Portions of chapter 7 appeared in a different form, written with Dae Young Kim, as "The Intergenerational Transmission of Religion and Culture among Korean Protestant Immigrants," in *Sociology of Religion* 66:263–82.

I gave talks based on data used in this book at New York University, New School University, Georgia State University, Smith College, Ithaca College, Queens College, the Graduate Center of CUNY, New York Theological Seminary, New Brunswick Theological Seminary, California State University at Los Angeles, Chonnam University, and Korea University. My conversations with many faculty members and students at these presentations sharpened my thoughts about major research issues in this book and improved its overall quality. I would like to express my sincere thanks to those who raised critical questions about my arguments and the overall direction of inquiry in my book.

Two anonymous reviewers of my book manuscript for New York University Press provided useful comments and constructive criticisms. Their challenging criticisms helped me strengthen some of my arguments, which I appreciate. Jennifer Hammer, an acquiring editor of New York University Press, accepted my book manuscript enthusiastically from the beginning and offered useful suggestions to make the book more accessible to lay readers. Her initial excitement about the book manuscript led me to believe that my ten years of hard work had been worthwhile. I would also like to express thanks to Despina Papazoglou Gimbel, the managing editor of NYU Press, for editing and processing the manuscript quickly.

A book project of this scope could not have been completed without support from my colleagues in the Department of Sociology, Queens College. Charles Smith, Dean Savage, and Andrew Beveridge have served as the chairpersons for the department for the past ten years, and I thank them for their efforts to facilitate my research. In particular, Dean Savage's assignment of my office in the sociology research area, away from the departmental office, enabled me to do my research with little interruption. The friendship with and support of many other colleagues in the sociology department, including Alem Habtu, Sophia Catsambis, Carmenza Gallo, and Joyce Tang, also helped me in my research. In addition, the exceptional kindness shown by two former (Lily Lindross and Robert Pisano) and current (Carol Goldberg and Sandra Dolberry) secretaries of the sociology department made my research activities more enjoyable and less stressful. Although Mehdi Bozorgmehr teaches at City College and the Graduate Center of CUNY, not at Queens College, he is a sociologist with whom I have maintained the closest personal relationship since we met in 1986 at UCLA. I feel lucky to have such a wonderful person as a friend in both my personal and academic life.

As my life partner, Young Oak was deeply involved in this book project in its early stage, collecting and analyzing data. She listened to me patiently about the progress of the book, and I appreciate her patience and support from the beginning to the end of the book project. I know my preoccupation with academic research has given me little time for my three children, Jay, Michael, and Tony. Even so, they supported my research. In particular, Jay, our oldest son, has been a strong supporter of my academic life.

Finally, I thank the nearly 250 anonymous Korean Protestant and Indian Hindu informants who agreed to be interviewed. Without their willingness to share their personal stories about their religious practices and identity, I would not have been able to write this book.

# Introduction

PETER PARK IS a 28-year-old, 1.5-generation Korean who works as an assistant salesman. He immigrated to New York City at the age of 8, accompanied by his mother. Although his mother was a Buddhist in Korea, she chose to attend a Korean immigrant church in New York so as to give her children the opportunity to meet other Korean children. As a young adult, Peter attends, twice a week, an English-language Korean evangelical church in New York City for 1.5- and second-generation Korean adults. Because he belongs to the church's praise team, he spends eight hours at his church on Saturday and ten hours on Sunday. He prays every night before going to bed and reads the Bible almost every night. Peter also sings one or more gospel songs and listens to Christian music almost every night at home, and he belongs to a twenty-member, second-generation Korean ministry organization that leads praise songs for local church retreats, which he attends twice a week.

When asked about the importance of a second-generation Korean church in maintaining Korean cultural traditions through various programs, Peter remarked, "I never thought about it, but I don't think it's necessary. It's not the church's responsibility. The church is some place you grow spiritually, and there are other centers that have those Korean programs. It's not the church's responsibility." When asked how important his Christian religion was to his identity, compared with his Korean background, he commented, "My religion is more important than being Korean because being Korean tells me what nationality I am, but being a Christian tells me who I am, meaning that I am the child of God."

Rani Ambany is a 32-year-old female, single Indian pediatrician. She was born in India to Hindu parents and immigrated with them to Detroit at the age of 3. During her childhood, she went to temple with her parents about three times a month and once attended a Hindu dance-music class offered by the temple. She said her parents took her to temple mainly for "exposure to Indian culture because at that time the temple was the only place to expose Asian Indians to Indian culture and community." She recalled that her mother prayed every day at home and performed major *pujas* (the devotional act of offering flowers and food to a sacred image) six or seven times a year. Rani often participated in family *pujas*. Her parents celebrated three major Hindu holidays each year, including Diwali (a major Hindu festival), which includes vegetarian food.

As a young adult, however, Rani attends temple only about three times a year, usually when she visits her parents in Arlington, Texas. Although she has neither a family shrine nor any religious decoration in her Manhattan studio apartment, she prays in the morning about three times a week. Her mother told her that she did not need a family shrine because "God is in your mind and heart." Rani does not celebrate any Hindu holidays; she simply says "Happy Diwali" on the phone to her parents in Arlington on the most important Hindu religious holiday. When asked to reflect on the importance of Hinduism compared with her national background to her personal identity, Rani replied, "I am Indian American first, and being Hindu means a lot for my Indian identity." Responding affirmatively to whether her "practice of Hinduism symbolizes her Indian identity," she noted, "I practice Hinduism because it reinforces my identity, makes me believe who I am." Whereas Rani's Hindu religion enhances her Indian ethnic identity, Peter's strong commitment to Christianity seems to weaken his Korean ethnic identity.

These are not isolated stories of two individuals. Peter's active religious practices both in church and at home, combined with his weak Korean identity, typify 1.5- and second-generation Korean evangelical Christians. Rani's moderate embrace of Hinduism, with its positive effect on her Indian identity and heritage, also is typical of most younger-generation Indian Hindus. The traditional literature on religion and ethnicity, largely based on studies of Christian immigrant groups at the turn of the twentieth century, emphasized religious rituals, especially those practiced in congregations, as the major mechanism for preserving ethnic culture and identity. By every measure, Peter and other younger-generation Korean evangelical Christians are more religious than Rani and other younger-generation Indian Hindus. In particular, Korean evangelical Christians participate far more actively in religious institutions than Indian Hindus do. Thus the traditional literature might lead us to believe that owing to their stronger religious involvement, younger-generation Korean evangelical Christians should have a stronger ethnic identity than their Indian Hindu counterparts do. Ironically, however, these Koreans' very strong commitment to Christian values weakens their Korean ethnic identity, and Indian Hindus' generally moderate embrace of Hinduism tends to enhance their Indian identity and ethnic heritage. For many beginning researchers of immigrants' religious practices, as well as lay readers, this relationship between religion and ethnicity for the two Asian groups is paradoxical.[1] I hope to resolve this paradox by comparing Korean Protestants and Indian Hindus in New York City.

## Theoretical Background

Scholars of the earlier European Christian immigrant groups emphasized participation in congregations as the main mechanism for ethnicity. Indeed, participation in a religious institution did help members of immigrant/ethnic groups preserve their ethnicity by maintaining their ethnic social networks and supporting their ethnic culture and identity. These early researchers, however, overlooked the importance of religion to the home country. When members of an immigrant/ethnic group practice their native religion, they are better able to preserve their ethnicity through religion because their religious rituals are tied to elements of their ethnic culture. For example, the Amish and Jews have been more successful than other white ethnic groups in preserving their ethnic culture and identity mainly because of the strong association between their religious rituals and their ethnic culture (Hammond 1988).

Religious groups use both participation in religious institutions and the association between religious rituals and ethnic culture to preserve their ethnicity. But because of their different styles of worship and different levels of nativity of religion to particular groups, some groups depend on one mechanism more than the other. Accordingly, to examine the two different ways of preserving ethnicity through religion, we need to compare two groups that represent the salient cases of using one or the other of the mechanisms for ethnic retention.

Large numbers of Koreans and Asian Indians have immigrated to the United States since the enforcement of the 1965 liberalized immigration law. Korean Protestant and Indian Hindu immigrants represent two extreme cases of using mainly one or the other religious mechanism for ethnic preservation. Most Korean immigrants are known to be affiliated with Korean Protestant churches and to participate exceptionally often in ethnic congregations (Hurh and Kim 1990; Kim and Kim 2001; Min 1992). But Protestantism is a Western religion brought to Korea by American missionaries at the turn of the twentieth century and popularized only over the last forty years. In 1962, Protestants constituted only 2.8 percent of the population in South Korea (Park and Cho 1995, 119). Along with the development of capitalism in South Korea, its Protestant population increased to 16 percent in 1985 (Korea National Statistical Office 1992, 300), 18 percent in 1999 (Korea National Statistical Office 2002, 538), and then 20 percent in 2003.

Protestants still are a numerically minority population in South Korea, where they are outnumbered by Buddhists (25% in 2003) by a significant margin. In its adaptation to Korean society, Protestantism has incorporated some Korean cultural traditions, especially Confucian and shamanistic elements (Baker 1997b; A. Kim 2000). But it has not incorporated elements of Korean folk culture, like foods, holidays, dance, music, weddings, and funerals. Accordingly, Korean Protestant immigrants cannot preserve their Korean culture and identity simply by practicing Christian faith and rituals. They can, however, maintain their Korean ethnicity by increasing their coethnic fellowship and practicing Korean culture, especially Confucian cultural traditions, through their active participation in Korean churches.

By contrast, for Indian immigrants Hinduism is a religion that originated in their home country and is still practiced by the vast majority of the Indian population. More significantly, it has incorporated much of the local culture in its rituals in different parts of India (Davis 1995). Thus, Indian national and local cultural traditions—language, values, foods, dress, holidays, weddings, and funerals—have become part of the Hindu faith and rituals: "Hinduism makes no clear distinction between sacred and secular activities and spheres" (Kurien 2007, 39). Indian Hindu immigrants can therefore preserve their ethnic/subethnic cultural traditions and identity simply by practicing religious faith and rituals at home. Studies of Hindu immigrants and their religious practices (Fenton 1988, 52–77; Joshi 2007; Khandelwal 2002, 79–80; Kurien 1998, 2007; Mazumdar and Mazumdar 2003; Williams 1988, 42–47, 1992) indicate that family worship is the primary way of transmitting their religious beliefs and rituals and Indian culture.

Indian Hindu immigrants in the United States do go to temple, but most of them attend services only a few or several times a year, usually on important religious holidays (Fenton 1988, 171–92; Gupta 2003; Kurien 1998, 2007; Min 2000; Williams 1988, 56–63). These studies show that even their moderate participation in a temple does contribute to their ethnic preservation, mainly because the religious beliefs and rituals practiced there symbolize Indian culture and identity. Some Hindu immigrants participate in medium-size regular (usually monthly) meetings (*satsang*) for *puja* consisting of prayers, chanting and singing, while others take their children to small-group educational classes, called *bala vihars* (Kurien 2002, 2007). No doubt, the development of these congregational forms of Hindu religious practices and educational programs was motivated by a desire to transmit Indian cultural traditions as much as spiritual traditions.

The weak linkage between Korean Christianity and Korean folk culture does not mean that all Korean churches in the United States minimize Korean cultural traditions in their worship services and other sociocultural activities. As several studies show (Dearman 1982; Hurh and Kim 1990; Kim 1981; Kim and Kim 2001; Min 1992), Korean Protestant immigrants do maintain high levels of ethnic fellowship and ethnic retention, albeit within their own generation, through their exceptionally frequent participation in Korean churches. Indeed, Korean immigrant churches have become the most important Korean community centers. As we will see, second-generation Korean mainline churches contain more Korean cultural elements than do Korean evangelical churches. Although Protestantism is not as widespread in Japan as in Korea, in the first half of the twentieth century, second-generation Japanese churches and Christian organizations in California, almost all mainline, were greatly concerned with racial and other community issues (Yoo 2000, 63–64).

The other important theoretical issue that explains why religious commitment enhances the ethnic identity of Hindu immigrants in the United States but weakens it for Korean immigrants is the strong effect of American evangelical Christianity on 1.5- and second-generation Korean Protestants. Korean evangelical congregations, comprising a vast majority of Korean English-language congregations, have been strongly influenced by American evangelical worship styles and sociocultural activities (Alumkal 1999, 2003; Chai 1998; Jeung 2005; S. Park 2001). This transformation of Korean immigrant ethnic churches into more or less race-blind evangelical churches for younger-generation Koreans indicates the strong influence of the evangelical movement in the United States after 1965. In the 1960s and 1970s when the contemporary immigration streams started, conservative evangelical denominations and evangelical Christians continued to grow in the United States with a concomitant decline of mainline denominations and mainline Christians (Hunter 1987, 23; Marsden 1991, 63; Smith 1998; Warner 1988, 22). Second-generation Korean Protestants were influenced by the American evangelical movement especially in their college years, through the evangelical campus ministry (R. Kim 2006). Researchers of the earlier white Catholic, Eastern Orthodox, and Protestant ethnic groups observed strong ethnic elements in second- and third-generation congregations partly because Catholic and Eastern Orthodox churches were not strongly influenced by the evangelical movement at that time.

## The Main Objectives of This Book

The New York / New Jersey area is an ideal place for a comparative study of Indian and Korean immigrants because it has large numbers of both groups. According to the 2000 U.S. census, approximately 400,000 single-race Indian Americans live in the New York / New Jersey / Long Island Consolidated Metropolitan Statistical Area, comprising the second largest Asian group after Chinese Americans. With approximately 171,000 single-race people of Korean ancestry in 2000, the Korean community in the New York / New Jersey metropolitan area is the second largest Korean community in the United States, following that in the Los Angeles metropolitan area. While the Chinese community in New York City has a long history dating back to 1880, both the Indian and Korean communities are largely the by-products of the post-1965 immigration waves.

This book has two main objectives. The first is to examine the different ways that Indian Hindu and Korean Protestant immigrants in New York preserve their ethnicity through religion. I originally began this research project looking at the preservation of ethnicity through religion among Indian Hindu and Korean Protestant immigrants, but soon I realized that data based on immigrant samples and immigrant religious institutions alone would not achieve my main objective. With the immigrant data sets I could show how the two Asian immigrant groups intend to use religion to preserve ethnicity. But I could not prove whether Indian Hindu or Korean Protestant immigrants were more successful in preserving their ethnicity through religion, because their success would be ultimately determined by the different degrees of intergenerational transmission. As noted earlier, Korean Protestant immigrants are as effective as Indian Hindu immigrants in preserving ethnicity through their religion within their own generation, albeit in different ways. To examine systematically the effects of religion on ethnicity for each group, I needed data based on second-generation Indian Hindus and Korean Protestants as well.

This meant that I needed to examine the intergenerational transmission of religion and ethnicity for both Indian and Korean groups. I subsequently collected data on the second generation for both groups in order to make the intergroup comparison between Korean Protestants and Indian Hindus more systematic. Accordingly, this book compares two Asian groups at one level and between generations for each Asian group at the other. As a result, I offer four comparisons: (1) between Indian Hindu and Korean Protestant immigrants, (2) between second-generation Indian Hindus and Korean Protestants, (3) between Indian Hindu immigrants and their second generation, and (4) between Korean Protestant immigrants and their second generation.

The second objective of this book is to examine the theological differences between evangelical Protestantism and Hinduism that have affected the intergenerational transmissions of religion and ethnic traditions through religion. Sociologists of religion, with some exceptions (Ebaugh and Chafetz 2000; Eid 2007; Kniss and Numrich 2007; Stevens 2004; Wuthnow 1995), have paid little attention to scriptures and theology, topics of great interest to religious scholars and theologians. Instead, they have focused on religious institutions, or what Warner (1998) called "faith communities." These sociologists usually analyze such communities' social, social service, cultural, economic, and other practical functions, following the Christian congregational model. Few sociological studies of contemporary immigrants' religious practices look at the role of theology in gender relations, the intergenerational transmission of religion, and other related issues (Ebaugh and Chafetz's *Religion and the New Immigrants* is an exception). As we will see, evangelical Christians have the highest level of what Donald Smith (1970, 175) calls "dogmatic authority" ("the degree of conviction that one's religion has the absolute truth") among all organized religious groups. Because of their great dogmatic authority, younger-generation Korean evangelical Christians tend to deemphasize the infusion of Korean culture into their worship services and other sociocultural activities in their congregation. Korean Protestant immigrants' strong belief in the absolute truth of their religion also leads them to consider transmitting their religion to their children as a life-or-death issue. In contrast, Indian Hindus' strong commitment to religious pluralism and tolerance stands at the other end of the dogmatic authority spectrum (D. Smith 1970, 175). This basic theological difference between evangelical Christianity and Hinduism significantly affects the ethnic identity, friendship patterns, and child socialization of Korean Protestant and Indian Hindu immigrants and their second generations.

First, I will clarify the concept of ethnicity in order to frame my comparison of Indian Hindus and Korean Protestants regarding the effects of religion on ethnicity. Milton Gordon (1964, 38) listed three major functional characteristics of the ethnic group:

> First, it [the ethnic group] serves psychologically as a source of group self-identification—the locus of the sense of intimate peoplehood—and second, it provides a patterned network of groups and institutions which allow an individual to confine his primary group relationships to his own ethnic group throughout all the stages of the life cycle. Its third functional characteristic is that it refracts the national cultural patterns of behavior and values through the prism of its own cultural heritage.

What Gordon considers to be three major functional characteristics of the ethnic group are the three major dimensions of ethnicity: (1) retention of ethnic subculture (cultural), (2) involvement in ethnic social networks (social), and (3) group self-identification (psychological). Other researchers (Hurh and Kim 1984, 78–82; Min 1992; Reitz 1980; Yinger 1994, 3–4) have also used ethnicity or ethnic attachment to indicate these three interrelated components of ethnic phenomena. Using this commonly used definition of ethnicity, this book examines how and to what extent participation in religious institutions and the practice of religious rituals at home contribute to one or more of the three components of ethnicity for Indian Hindus and Korean Protestants.

## The Significance of This Book

This book, first, demonstrates the limitations of the traditional literature on religion and ethnicity based on the earlier white ethnic groups. The traditional theoretical perspective overemphasizes mere participation in a congregation as the major mechanism for ethnic preservation and underestimates the positive effect on ethnic preservation of the association between religious rituals, more often practiced at home, and ethnic culture. To evaluate the importance of participation in a congregation and the association between religion and ethnicity for ethnic retention, I compared two religious groups, Indian Hindus and Korean Protestants, that represent the extreme cases of using one or the other mechanism. Moreover, since the positive effect of the association between religion and ethnicity on ethnic retention is more salient to the native Americans or those raised in America than for immigrants, an intergenerational comparison is necessary as well.

This book also looks at the importance of the theological difference between Korean evangelical Protestantism and Indian Hinduism in their transmission of religion and ethnicity through religion. The traditional social science literature on immigrants' religious practices does not look at the role of theology. This book, however, shows that Korean Protestants and Indian Hindus occupy the two extreme and opposite positions in the level of dogmatic authority and that this theological difference has significant effects on Korean Protestants' and Indian Hindus' religious and ethnic identities, child socialization patterns, and social networks. The final chapter offers a typology of the intergenerational transmission of religion and ethnicity through religion among several different contemporary immigrant religious groups.

Third, this book contributes to the literature on the intergenerational transmission of religion and ethnicity through religion for the post-1965 immigrant groups. Many studies have examined the religious experiences of contemporary immigrant groups (Carnes and Yang 2004a; Ebaugh and Chaffetz 2000; Guest 2003; Iwamura and Spickard 2003; Kurien 2007; Kwon, Kim, and Warner 2001; Min 1992; Min and J. Kim 2002; Suh 2004; Warner and Wittner 1998; Williams 1988; Yang 1999), and several studies have examined the ethnicity function of religion for different immigrant groups. But no researcher to date has systematically examined the intergenerational transmission of religion using empirical data on immigrants and their children, let alone the intergenerational transmission of ethnicity through religion.

Second-generation Korean evangelical Christians' religious practices have received more scholarly attention than any other second-generation Asian Americans' religious practices. Several pieces, including two books, that focus on second-generation Korean evangelical Christians have been recently published (Alumkal 1999, 2001, 2003; Chai 1998, 2001a, 2001b; Chong 1998; Ecklund 2005, 2006; H. Kim and Pyle 2004; R. Kim 2003, 2006; S. Kim 2008; Min and D. Kim 2005; S. Park 2001). Ecklund's book (2006) compares the patterns of civic participation of second-generation Korean Protestants affiliated with an ethnic church and those with a multiethnic church. Rebecca Kim's book (2006) also focuses on the ethnic elements of second-generation Korean evangelical congregations. But my book casts a wider net than Kim's book in examining second-generation Korean evangelical Christians and congregations and their ethnic components, by starting with evangelical Protestantism in South Korea and comparing Korean Protestant immigrants and congregations with second-generation Korean Protestants and congregations.

When I started this book project, many studies of Indian Hindu immigrants were available (Fenton 1988; Gupta 2003; Jacob and Thaku 2000; Kurien 1998, 1999; Williams 1988, 1992). No study of second-generation Indian Hindus' religious practices had been published, but as I was completing the book manuscript I found two books that shed light on second-generation Hindus. One is *A Place at the Multicultural Table: The Development of American Hinduism*, by Prema Kurien (2007), which is primarily about Hindu immigrants' religious practices, with one chapter on the Hindu Student Council at a university in California. The other book is *New Roots in American Sacred Ground: Religion, Race, and Ethnicity in Indian America*, by Khyati Y. Joshi (2007). This book examines the interrelationships among religion, race, and ethnicity among second-generation Indian Hindus, Muslims, and Sikhs based on forty-one personal interviews. By contrast, my book systematically examines intergenerational transmissions of religion and ethnicity through religions among Indian Americans using data based on immigrant and second-generation samples.

Fourth, this study is methodologically significant because it makes a two-way comparison, one an intergroup comparison and the other an intergenerational comparison, using multiple data sources. Most social science studies of contemporary immigrants' religious practices are case studies of a single group. A comparison of two or more groups and/or of the immigrants and their second generation enables us to test theoretically derived hypotheses, which is impossible with a case study.

Finally, my book draws on several data sources, including (1) a telephone survey of Indian and Korean immigrants in New York City, (2) ethnographic research at a Korean church and an Indian Hindu temple, (3) tape-recorded interviews with Indian Hindu and Korean Protestant immigrants, (4) a telephone survey of Korean English-language congregations, and (5) tape-recorded interviews with 1.5- and second-generation Indian Hindus and Korean Protestants.

## Research Methods

Traditional sociological studies of immigrant/ethnic groups' religious practices, largely based on white Judeo-Christian groups, used ethnographic research on one or more selected congregations as the major research method. Two major studies of contemporary immigrants' religious practices (Ebaugh and Chafetz 2000; Warner and Wittner 1998) also largely followed the congregational approach, although the study by Ebaugh and Chafetz (2000) offered information about "domestic religion" through personal interviews with members of religious institutions. According to Warner, it is quite natural that sociologists focus on the congregation because "religion as understood here exists in the form not of texts but of living communities" (Warner 1998, 9). Their concentration on congregations separates the sociological and other social science studies of religion from religious and theological studies.

Although the congregational approach has an advantage from a sociological point of view, if used alone, it can distort reality. Many of the studies previously cited showed that congregations or religious institutions help their participants preserve their cultural traditions and ethnic identity. If only a small proportion of members of a particular immigrant group participated in religious congregations, however, the overall effects of religious institutions on the group would be insignificant. Thus, to examine the ethnicity function of religious institutions systematically, we must use survey research to measure the religious affiliation and frequency of participation in religious institutions for a particular group. While substantial quantitative data on Korean immigrants' religious affiliation and frequency of participation in church are available (Hurh and Kim 1990; Kim and Kim 2001; Min 1992, 2000; Park et al. 1990), none of the studies of Indian Hindu immigrants' religious practices (Fenton 1988; Gupta 2003; Joshi 2007; Khandelwal 2002; Kurien 1998, 2002, 2007; Williams 1988) provides statistical information about their frequency of temple attendance. Moreover, as previously indicated, many non-Judeo Christian religious groups, including Indian Hindu immigrants, may be able to maintain their ethnic culture and identity by practicing religious faith and rituals at home. Therefore, it is important to obtain information about religious practices at home through tape-recorded interviews with the informants outside religious institutions.

As table 1.1 shows, I used all three types of data for a systematic comparison of Indian Hindu and Korean Protestant immigrants: (1) survey of 287 Indian and 277 Korean immigrants in New York City, (2) ethnographic research conducted in the Hindu Temple Society of North America and the Shin Kwang Church of New York, and (3) tape-recorded interviews with fifty-nine Indian Hindu immigrants and fifty-five Korean Protestant immigrants. Details about collecting the different types of data for Indian Hindu and Korean Protestant immigrants in this book are provided in appendix 1. In addition, I used the *Census of India 2001, Social Indicators*, the *2006 Churches Directory in Korea*, and the *2006 Korean Churches Directory of New York* for statistical information about Indian and Korean immigrants' religious distribution and the denominational affiliations of Korean immigrant churches. For information about Hindu rituals that are publicly recognized as the central aspect of Indian culture in the United States, I consulted many articles published in *India Abroad*, the most important weekly for Indian Americans. I also gained a great deal of information about Hindu religion and Hindu immigrant temples in the United States from websites.

**TABLE I.I**

*Research Techniques Used for Indian Hindu and Korean
Protestant Immigrants' Religious Practices and Ethnicity*

| Data Sources | Sampling Technique | Sample Size, Research Site, or Type of Data | |
|---|---|---|---|
| | | *Indian Hindus* | *Korean Protestants* |
| Survey | Surname sampling | 287 | 277 |
| Personal interviews | Snowball sampling | 59 | 56 |
| Ethnographic research | N/A | Ganesh Temple | Shin Kwang Church of New York |

**TABLE I.2**

*Research Techniques Used for 1.5- and Second-Generation Indian
Hindu and Korean Protestants' Religious Practices and Ethnicity*

| Research Technique | Sampling Technique | Sample Size | |
|---|---|---|---|
| | | *Korean Group* | *Indian Group* |
| Telephone survey of 1.5- and 2d-generation young adults | Kim sampling technique | 202 | N/A |
| Telephone survey of religious institutions | All 43 Korean English-language congregations (pastors) | 35 | N/A |
| Personal interviews with 1.5- and 2d-generation Korean Protestants and Indian Hindus | Snowball sampling | 66 | 55 |

Table 1.2 shows the three types of data I used to elucidate religious practices among younger-generation Korean Protestants in the New York / New Jersey area: (1) a survey of 1.5- and second-generation Korean young adults, (2) a survey of thirty-five Korean English-language congregations, and (3) tape-recorded interviews with sixty-six younger-generation Korean Protestants. Since the results of several ethnographic studies of second-generation Korean congregations are available (Alumkal 1999, 2001; Chai 1998, 2001a; Chong 1998; Ecklund 2006; H. Kim and Pyle 2004; R. Kim 2006), I instead surveyed Korean English-language congregations in the New York / New Jersey area. For 1.5- and second-

generation Indian Hindus, I used only one type of data, fifty-five personal interviews with 1.5- and second-generation Indian Hindu adults. I did not collect any other types of data—ethnographic or survey—on second-generation Hindu temples because no Hindu temple serves only second-generation Hindus.[2] But personal interviews with 1.5- and second-generation Indian Hindus shed light on their frequency of attendance at a Hindu temple.

Four separate data sets based on personal interviews with Indian and Korean immigrant and younger-generation informants comprise the most important data sets for this book. They provide qualitative information that conveys the nuanced meanings of the informants' religious practices. I used pseudonyms for my informants. I also used the results of personal interviews quantitatively by undertaking content analyses of responses to key questions. I had to use qualitative data quantitatively for intergroup and intergenerational comparisons. It is almost impossible to compare Korean Protestant and Indian Hindu immigrants or two second-generation groups, for example, in domestic religious practices without numerically comparing the two groups in daily prayers, reading scriptures, displaying religious decorations at home, and so forth. It also is almost impossible to examine the level of the intergenerational reduction or continuity in religious faith for each group without numerically showing the aforementioned domestic religious practices.

I also converted results of tape-recorded personal interviews into quantitative data because of my strong sociological conviction that qualitative data without some level of generalizability have a limited value. I do not think testing the level of statistical significance is meaningful when using data based on small, nonrandom samples. But if the informants were chosen to minimize selection bias, as I believe I did, I could generalize the findings to these groups using commonsense knowledge. For example, 74 percent of younger-generation Korean Protestant informants ($n = 66$), compared with only 38 percent of Korean Protestant immigrant informants ($n = 59$), cited being Christian as their primary identity. Based on this huge percentage differential, we can reasonably argue that the importance of religion to personal identity is significantly different for Korean immigrant and younger-generation Protestants.

I also used participant observations I made as an insider in the Korean community. I regularly attended a Korean church between 1988 and 1993, serving as the director of the church's Korean-language school for a few years. I also taught a course on Asian Americans for a group of Korean pastors enrolled in the doctor of ministry program at New York Theological Seminary between 1988 and 1992. In addition, I gave talks on Korean immigrant churches at several Korean churches in New York and other East Coast states. My conversations with many Korean pastors and church leaders and the observations I made in these contexts helped me better understand Korean immigrant churches.

I presented different chapters of this book in several conferences and colloquia organized in several schools and professional organizations. My conversations with the many students and faculty members I met at these talks helped me sharpen my thoughts and clarify some issues considered in this book.

## The Organization of This Book

Chapter 1 reviews the three theoretical perspectives for understanding the ethnic role of religion. Chapter 2 examines the religious landscapes in India and South Korea, and chapter 3 focuses on the religious affiliations of Indian and Korean immigrants in New York and their frequency of participation in religious institutions.

Chapter 4 examines the cultural and fellowship functions of Korean immigrant churches and other related topics in New York City based on the results of ethnographic research on the Shin Kwang Church of New York. Chapter 5 does the same for Indian Hindu temples based on ethnographic research on the Ganesh Temple. Chapter 6 compares Korean Protestant immigrants with Indian Hindus in their participation in religious institutions, family rituals, and identity and other related issues, using the results of two sets of interviews. Chapters 7 through 9 examine younger-generation Korean Protestants' and Indian Hindus' religious practices and their effects on ethnic preservation based on interview data. Chapter 7 examines the extent to which 1.5- and second-generation Indian Hindu and Korean Protestant adults participate in religious institutions and preserve ethnicity through their participation. Chapter 8 examines the extent to which religious practices at home by 1.5- and second-generation Koreans and Indians help preserve their ethnicity. Chapter 9 compares younger-generation Korean Protestants with Indian Hindus in the importance of religion to identity, socialization, and social relations and the selection of marital partners. Since the function of ethnicity for religion can ultimately be determined by the extent of intergenerational transmission of religion and ethnicity, these three chapters that focus on 1.5- and second-generation Indian Hindus and Korean Protestants are the key chapters. Chapter 10 summarizes this work's major findings and offers a typology of intergenerational transmission of religion and ethnicity through religion using seven contemporary immigrant-religious groups as examples.

# 1 Theoretical Frameworks

THREE MAJOR THEORETICAL perspectives are useful for comparing Korean Protestants and Indian Hindus in the intergenerational transmission of ethnicity through religion: (1) participation in congregations, (2) the association between religion and ethnicity, and (3) the theological difference between Korean evangelical Protestants and Indian Hindus in their acceptance of religious dogma. This chapter reviews the literature related to each theoretical perspective and discusses the implications of the theories for comparing the two groups.

## Participation in Congregations

An abundance of literature focuses on the earlier white immigrant and ethnic groups—Italian, Irish, German, Jewish, and Greek—stressing the positive effects of religion on ethnic preservation (Dolan 1985; Greeley 1972; Handlin 1979; Herberg 1960; Hirschman 2004; Ostergren 1981; Rosenberg 1985; Tomasi and Engel 1971; Warner 1994; Warner and Srole 1945). Because Christian immigrant groups and their descendants practiced their religion mainly through participation in congregations, the traditional literature emphasized this as the major mechanism for preserving ethnicity.

For example, in their classic book on white ethnic groups, Warner and Srole (1945, 160) pointed out that "the church was the first line of defense behind which these immigrants could organize themselves and with which they could preserve their group, i.e., system, identity." Tomasi and Engel (1971, 186) made a similar comment with regard to Italian Catholic parishes: "The network of Italian parishes functioned to maintain the ethnic personality by organizing the ethnic group around the familiar religious and cultural symbols and behavioral modes of the fatherland." Referring to "an explosion of congregations" in the United States in the nineteenth century, Ammerman (2001, 1) also made nearly the same observation: "By creating congregations—in cities and on the frontier— Americans embodied the cultural and religious values they cherished in ongoing institutions, structures that gave those values and traditions a place to thrive." Regarding the role of white immigrant churches in preserving ethnic culture, Stout also observed, "The church service became a symbolic rite of affirmation to one's ethnic association and a vehicle for preserving the ethnic language. Schools were established under the aegis of the church and efforts were made to inculcate the group with ethnic values and faith in the ethnic heritage" (Stout 1975, 207).

The previous review of the literature shows the strong emphasis on participation in a congregation as the major mechanism for the preservation of ethnicity by the studies of the earlier white immigrant groups. Following the same theoretical tradition, many studies of post-1965 immigrant groups emphasize the role of participation in religious institutions in preserving ethnicity (Bankston and Zhou 1995; Ebaugh and Chafetz 2000, 393–96; Fenton 1988; Gupta 2003; Hurh and Kim 1990; Kim and Kim 2001; Kurien 1998, 2002; Lin 1996; Min 1992; Numrich 1996; Warner 1994; Warner and Wittner 1998; Williams 1988; Yang 1999; Yang and Ebaugh 2001a, 2001b; Yu 2001). For example, based on survey data regarding Vietnamese high school students, Bankston and Zhou (1995) concluded, "Religious participation consistently makes a greater contribution to ethnic identification than any of the family or individual characteristics examined, except for recency for arrival." Regarding the ethnicity function of an Argentine immigrant church in Houston, Cook commented (2000, 183), "Iglesia Cristina Evangélica provides a social space where Argentine immigrants meet and interact on a regular basis, and the outcome of these exchanges is that Argentine ethnicity is maintained and reproduced."

Today's immigrants include many people of non-Judeo Christian faiths— Muslims, Buddhists, Hindus, and Sikhs—who did not take the congregational approach to their religious practices in their home countries. Partly influenced by Christian religions in the United States and partly to meet their own practical needs, non–Judeo Christian immigrants do participate in formal religious institutions, though less frequently than Judeo-Christian immigrants do. Researchers have indicated non-Christian immigrant groups' adoption of the Christian congregational model as one of the major transformations of their religious practices (Ebaugh and Chafetz 2000; Warner and Wittner 1998; Yang and Ebaugh 2001a). Many studies also show that these non-Judeo Christian immigrant groups use their religious institutions to maintain their ethnic traditions. For example, in his study of a Chinese Buddhist temple in Los Angeles, Lin (1996, 113) said, "Hsi Lai temple offers Mandarin, Taiwanese, and Cantonese classes, mainly to 1.5 and second generation Chinese Americans. Special classes on Chinese culture are offered as well, including Chinese art, folk dance, music, cooking, and tai-chi classes that help over-seas Chinese to keep in touch with their ancestral roots."

While contemporary non-Protestant immigrant groups, including Catholic groups, usually do not have separate religious organizations for second-generation members (Crane 2003; Ebaugh and Chafetz 2000), Korean and other East Asian Protestants have established ethnic or Pan–East Asian English-language congregations for 1.5-, second-, and third-generation members (Alumkal 1999,

2001, 2003; Chai 1998, 2001a, 2005; Ecklund 2006; Jeung 2005; R. Kim 2004, 2006; S. Kim 2008; Min and D. Kim 2005). A number of second-generation Korean Protestant scholars have studied second-generation Korean congregations, particularly Korean English-language evangelical congregations, emphasizing the differences between Korean immigrant and second-generation congregations in congregational culture.

Some of these studies indicate that because of their experiences with racial prejudice and discrimination, most second-generation Korean Protestants feel comfortable participating in Korean ethnic congregations that contribute to recreated Korean ethnicity (Chong 1998; R. Kim 2006; H. Kim and Pyle 2004; S. Kim 2008). For example, in the first social science study of a second-generation Korean congregation, Chong claimed that "Christianity in the Korean-American community, more specifically conservative/evangelical Protestantism, plays a powerful role in the construction, support, and reinforcement of Korean ethnic identity/boundary in second-generation members" (Chong 1998, 26–27). In her study of Korean American evangelicals on campus, Rebecca Kim (2006) shows that their individual desire for community and propensity for homophily (love of the same) and imposed racial and ethnic categorizations in the larger society have led Korean American Christian students to join Korean ethnic campus ministries rather than multiracial or white ministries. She asserts that microlevel conditions interact with macrolevel structures to crease a kind of "emergent ethnicity" in younger-generation Korean campus minorities. Based on her ethnographic research in Korean English-language congregations in Los Angeles, Sharon Kim (2008, 169) argues that second-generation Korean Americans have created "their own hybrid religious institutions" that radically differ from both white American churches and their parents' immigrant churches. Like Rebecca Kim, Sharon Kim emphasizes second-generation Koreans' sense of racial marginalization as the main reason that they prefer to attend Korean congregations instead of white American churches.

## The Association between Religion and Ethnicity and "Domestic Religion"

Another important religious mechanism for preserving ethnicity is the close association between religion and ethnicity in "ethno-religious" groups. In their discussion of the relationship between religion and ethnicity, Hammond and Warner (1993) offer three patterns. First, the relationship remains strongest when religion is the principal foundation of ethnicity. Hammond and Warner use the Amish, Jews, Hutterites, and Mormons as examples of groups with the strongest relationship and call this pattern *ethnic fusion*.

Among white ethnic groups, the Amish have been most successful in retaining their cultural traditions and identity, mainly because their religious values and rituals and ethnic cultural traditions correspond perfectly. Jewish Americans, too, have been more successful in retaining their ethnic traditions than other white ethnic groups, because their religious values and rituals also represent Jewish culture and identity (Hammond 1988; Hammond and Warner 1993), although their historical experience with discrimination all over the world also is an important source of Jewish ethnic identity. Both groups' religious values and rituals are closely intertwined with elements of their ethnic culture, such as food, holidays, music, dance, weddings, funerals, and other ethnic customs.

What Hammond and Warner did not point out is that the Amish, Jews, and others have been able to maintain their ethnic traditions to a far greater extent through religious practices at home and small-group community settings than through participation in congregations. Although the Amish community, school, and church have contributed to their preservation of religious and ethnic traditions, the Amish "family has remained the smallest and strongest unit of Amish culture, the central social institution" (Huntington 1998, 451). The synagogue has become a community center for Jews, but only a small fraction of Jewish Americans participates in it regularly. For example, according to an analysis of the 2001 National Jewish Population Survey, 46 percent of Jewish Americans are affiliated with a synagogue, and only 27 percent of them attend Jewish religious services monthly or more often (United Jewish Communities 2004, 7). Passover dinner, Shabbat candles, and kosher food are important elements of ethnicity for Jews, and they usually celebrate or perform these rituals with their families. Both the Amish religion and Judaism include more religious rituals involving elements of their folk cultures, such as dietary rules, holidays, weddings, and funerals, than Protestantism does. Since these religions evolved in their homeland over a long period of time by incorporating the local cultures, it is not surprising that they include more family and community rituals than Protestantism does.

To Hammond and Warner (1993), the second closest relationship between religion and ethnicity is when religion, along with language and geographical origin, becomes one of the major foundations of ethnicity, such as in the Greek or Russian Orthodox and the Dutch Reformed churches. In this relationship, ethnic identity enhances religious identity more than the other way around (Hammond and Warner 1993, 59). But with their highly nationalistic religious practices, Greek, Russian, and Hungarian Orthodox immigrants and ethnic groups also have a huge advantage over other Christian groups in preserving ethnic traditions through religion. They, too, perform their religious rituals and practices intertwined with ethnic traditions more often at home than in churches. For example, Gasi (2000, 156) reported that virtually all Greek homes have an "*iconostast*," an area that displays two or three icons, that are first blessed in the church, and an oil-burning candle. Not all members go through the process of blessing their icons, or burning the oil-candle, but there is no Greek American home that does not have one or two icons of their favorite saints or the Virgins.

Hammond and Warner's (1993) third, and weakest, relationship between religion and ethnicity can be found in many white ethnic groups that are linked to a religious tradition but share it with other ethnic groups. White Catholics—Polish, Irish, and Italian—and white Protestants —Danish, Norwegian, and Swedish Lutherans—are good examples. In this pattern, the linkage between religion and ethnicity is weak because a few or several national-origin groups share the same religious tradition. But because Polish, Irish, and Italian Catholic groups brought with them such strong national religious traditions when they immigrated (Greeley 1972, 119), they may have been more successful than other white ethnic groups in preserving ethnic traditions, mainly through their religious practices. And they practice their religious rituals, such as religious holidays, dances, weddings, and funerals, more frequently with family and/or in the community than in churches (Greeley 1971, 1972; Waters 1990).

Today's Asian immigrant groups have transplanted their traditional non-Christian religions—Buddhism, Hinduism, Sikhism, and Islam—which are inseparably linked to their regional, national, and/or local cultural traditions and identity, to their new, predominantly Christian, country. Asian Buddhist and Indian Hindu temples also contribute to ethnic preservation through language and other ethnic cultural programs in religious institutions (Fenton 1988; Huynh 2000; Yu 2001). These Asian, non-Christian religious institutions enhance the participants' ethnicity mainly because the physical characteristics of the temples and the religious faith and rituals practiced there symbolize their ethnic culture and identity. Herberg pointed out that white immigrant groups use their religion to maintain their cultural traditions and identity, especially because religious pluralism in the United States allows them to do so (Herberg 1960, 27–28). American multiculturalism in the post–civil rights era even encourages minority and immigrant groups to use their religion to mark their ethnic culture and identity. Thus Asian Buddhists and Indian Hindus offer their religious institutions and religious rituals to the American public as representing their "authentic" ethnic culture and different from the American Christian culture.

A number of studies show that Asian non-Christian immigrant groups have effectively used the close association between their religions and ethnic cultural traditions, and the differences between their non-Christian and American Christian religions, to enhance their ethnic identity (Chen 2002; Gupta 2003; Kurien

1998; Suh 2003, 2004; Williams 1988). For example, in her comparative study of a Taiwanese Buddhist temple and a Taiwanese evangelical church, Carolyn Chen (2002, 233) made the following observation:

> At the same time that their religious difference prevents Dharma Light [a Taiwanese Buddhist temple] from being truly "American," in the age of multiculturalism, the presence of "just enough difference" becomes the ticket to recognition and possible acceptance. By virtue of the association of Buddhism with the Far East and Christianity with the West, the Buddhists, rather than the Christians, are the ones to be recruited and courted as the Chinese representatives at the multicultural table.

Sharon Suh (2003, 181) made a similar observation about a Korean Buddhist temple: "Many male members of Sa Chal [a Korean Buddhist temple in Los Angeles] further claim that by remaining Buddhist in the U.S. they remain more loyal and more "authentic" Koreans—in contrast to their male counterparts in the Korean American Christian church."

These non-Christian Asian immigrant groups practice their religions through rituals in the family or small groups more often than do American Protestants. The reason is that like Judaism, these non-Christian religions, with a long history in Asian countries, have incorporated many rituals closely tied to ethnic food, holidays, life-cycle events, music, and dance. Accordingly, studies of Asian Hindu or Buddhist immigrants have paid special attention to "domestic religion" and "family shrines" (Ebaugh and Chafetz 2000, 391–93; Guest 2003; Huynh 2000, 50–51; Joshi 2007; Kurien 2007; Mazumdar and Mazumdar 2003).

Partly because of their Christian and partly because of their sociological bias, earlier studies of immigrant/ethnic religions looked exclusively at religious institutions as sites for religious practice.[1] But after 1965, the influx of Asian non-Christian and Latino/Caribbean Catholic immigrant groups has forced researchers to study religious practices at home, even those of white Christian immigrant groups. Catholics perform more rituals at home and in the community than Protestants do. Furthermore, various third-world versions of Catholicism feature more family and community rituals closely intertwined with their folk culture than does American Catholicism, as Roman Catholicism since the Vatican II (the Second Ecumenical Council of the Vatican) has allowed its missionaries to propagate the religion without destroying the local culture.[2] The mass migration of Catholics from Latin America, the Caribbean, and Asia also has led to the spread of Voodoo and other syncretic family and small-group rituals, combining Catholic beliefs and local folk culture, in American cities (Guest 2003; McAlister 1998; Orsi 1996; San Buenoventura 2002; Stepick 1998, 86–92; Stevens-Arroyo and Diaz-Stevens 1994; Sullivan 2000; Tweed 1997; Wellmeier 1998). In her introduction to an edited volume on Latino "popular religiosity," Ana Maria Diaz-

Stevens (1994, 19) claims, "Undeniably, Latinos have appropriated the notion and expression of popular religiosity as a defining characteristic of our religious experience in this country."

McAlister (1998) illustrated how Haitian Catholic immigrants in New York simultaneously employ the religious languages of both Roman Catholicism and Voodou, the Haitian (African) folk religious tradition, with family rituals performed in Haitian immigrant homes representing the Voodoo tradition (McAlister 1998, 144):

> Like the Chicana/o case, the Haitian home altar can be seen as an alternative sacred space controlled primarily by women. Prayer is offered according to the codes of Haitian religious culture, and dedicated to the spiritual work necessary to maintain relationships with the spiritual energy of both the saints and the *iwa*.

The fusion of Spanish Catholicism with the home-based rituals of the African folk tradition is also conspicuous among Cuban Catholic refugees. In his study of a Cuban Catholic shrine in Miami, Thomas Tweed (1997) exposes the struggles between the religion prescribed by Roman Catholicism and that practiced by many Cuban refugee devotees, emerging in rituals associated with the annual festival on September 8 (Tweed 1997, 53–54).

Asian Catholic immigrants also combine more ethnic-specific home rituals than do their white American counterparts (Guest 2003; Sullivan 2000, 259–71). Both Vietnam and Korea have been strongly influenced by Confucianism. Studies reveal that many Vietnamese and Korean Catholic immigrants also practice ancestor worship, an important component of Confucianism (Min 2004; Sullivan 2000, 259). Many Filipino Catholics also are part of an ethnic network of families that house, for a week, images of the Virgin. Sullivan (2000, 270) describes how it works: "Together with other compatriots, host families gather in prayer to welcome Mary into her new temporary abode. While she resides with a family, it prays together each evening before the image, thereby promoting family unity."

In an article entitled "Religion and Ethnicity among New Immigrants," Yang and Ebaugh (2001a) compared a Taiwanese Buddhist temple and a Taiwanese Christian church in Houston in the same way that Chen and Suh compared the two religious institutions of Taiwanese or Korean immigrants. In their conclusion, they state that the majority-minority status in both the host and the home country should be considered as predictive of variations in patterns of immigrant congregations' adaptations. The major findings from these studies suggest that the non-Christian immigrant groups who enjoyed the majority religious status in their home countries but who have minority religious status in the United States benefit from using their religion for preserving ethnic culture and identity, for two reasons. First, particular non-Christian religions represent their cultural and philosophical traditions of their home countries. Second, their "very un-Americanness constitutes an attraction to some native-born Americans who seek alternative beliefs" (Yang and Ebaugh 2001a, 7)

Not all groups with majority religious status in their home countries benefit equally from using religion to preserve their ethnicity. As Hammond and Warner (1993) pointed out, whether a particular religious group has originated from a single country or from several different countries should be considered as affecting the level of the association between religion and ethnicity. Buddhist immigrants come from many Asian countries, such as Thailand, China, and Sri Lanka (Prebish and Tanaka 1998). Consequently, although Thai immigrants come from a heavily Buddhist country, they cannot find a near-perfect association between being a Buddhist and being a Thai. Muslim immigrants have even more diverse origins than do Buddhist immigrants, as they come from all parts of the world (Haddad and Smith 1994). Thus, even though most Muslim immigrants come from heavily Muslim countries, they are likely to find a big gap between their religious and ethnic identities in the United States. Accordingly, U.S. mosques usually provide ethnically mixed services (Abusharaf 1998; Badr 2000). This suggests that even very religious Muslim immigrants may not be able to use their religion to preserve their country-of-origin ethnic identity, even though being a Muslim may be the core of that identity (see Peek 2005).

Because of their majority status in their home country and their single-country origin, Indian Hindu immigrants have an extremely high level of association between religion and ethnic culture/identity. Although India is a multireligious secular country, Hindus make up about 80 percent of the Indian population. Thus Indian Hindus do not have the near perfect association between religion and ethnicity that Jewish Americans and the Amish do. But Hinduism is India's oldest and an indigenous religion, reflected by the fact that India's Hindu Family Act defines a Hindu as anyone who belongs to a Hindu denomination, as well as any other person living in India who is not a member of a nonindigenous religion in India (Islam, Christianity, Zoroastrianism, and Judaism)[3] (Kurien 2007, 20). As a result, Hinduism has had a stronger effect on Indian culture and thought than any other Indian philosophy and religion. In addition, the vast majority of Hindu immigrants to the United States come from India, and nearly all come from a South Asian country (Nepal and Bangladesh are the other countries with a large Hindu population). Many Caribbean Indians are Hindus of Indian ancestry. Consequently, Hinduism represents Indian or South Asian culture and identity better than the Greek Orthodox religion represents Greek culture and identity. As several scholars noted (Bhardwaj and Rao 1998; Fenton 1988; Gupta 2003; Kurien 1998, 2007), Indian immigrants established their place in the American multicultural table by building Hindu temples, even though Indian Hindus practice their religion mainly through family rituals. As Mazumdar and Mazumdar (2003, 153) stated, "Hindu families attribute religious meanings to families placing religious objects on their doors and walls, by creating a family shrine, and through daily rituals."

By contrast, Korean Protestantism represents the least association between religion and ethnicity of any religiously active immigrant group, substantially less than found in Hammond and Warner's third pattern in many white Catholic ethnic groups. Despite the current reputation of South Korea as the leader in world missionary activities, Protestantism has such a short history that its religious rituals have not incorporated elements of Korean folk culture, such as food, holidays, dance, music, weddings, and other life-cycle events.

While Korean Buddhism represents Korean and Asian cultural traditions fairly well, Protestantism in Korea symbolizes "Western" and "modern" things associated with modern Christian schools and modern hospitals. Both Korean Buddhists and Korean Catholics practice ancestor worship, the core of Confucian norms, albeit in a revised form, whereas Korean Protestants usually reject ancestor worship as "idol worship."

### Evangelical Christians' "Dogmatic Authority" and Emphasis on Universalistic Christian Values

Younger-generation Korean Protestants have not preserved their ethnicity through religion as well as younger-generation Indian Hindus have done, mainly because Korean Protestantism has not incorporated much Korean culture. Moreover, younger-generation Korean Protestants are at a disadvantage because of their religion's unique aspects. As many studies (Alumkal 1999, 2001; Chai 1998, 2001a; Ecklund 2006; R. Kim 2006; Min and D. Kim 2005; S. Park 2001) show, a predominant majority of younger-generation Korean Protestants and congregations are evangelical. Evangelical Christians accept the Bible's words as absolutely true (their inerrancy), accept salvation through faith in Jesus Christ, and emphasize evangelism (spreading the word of the God) as the central components of their Christian life (Hunter 1987, 59–63; C. Smith 1998). Because they regard the Bible as the foundation of Christian life and emphasize universalistic or global Christian values, they deemphasize ethnic culture in worship services and place priority on their Christian identity rather than their ethnic or racial identity.

In order to show how younger-generation Koreans' commitment to evangelical Christianity influences their personal identity, child socialization, social relations, and overall worldview compared with younger-generation Indians' embrace of Hinduism, we must consider what Donald Smith calls *dogmatic authority*. According to Smith (1970, 75), dogmatic authority indicates "the degree of conviction that one's religion has the absolute truth." Using three types of authority (dogmatic, directive, and institutional), he ranked authority for four major world religions: Catholicism, Islam, Hinduism, and Buddhism. For dogmatic authority, Catholicism and Islam had a value of 3; Buddhism, 1; and Hinduism, 0. Evangelical Christianity, which Smith did not rank, should have a higher value, 4 or 5, than either Catholicism or Islam. Catholicism currently is more liberal than it was in the 1970s and thus has less dogmatic authority than Smith gave it.[4] He correctly gave the lowest value to Hinduism (0) and the next-to-lowest value to Buddhism (1). Thus Hinduism and evangelical Christianity comprise the two extremes of dogmatic authority. In this book, the theological difference in dogmatic authority between Korean evangelical Protestantism and Hinduism is extremely important.

Evangelical Christianity started in the mid-eighteenth century in the United States and Great Britain. Although it was a large but disintegrating force in the United States in the first half of the twentieth century (Noll 2001, 15–17), it has grown rapidly since the early 1960s with a concomitant decline in mainline Protestantism (Hunter 1987, 6–7; Warner 1988). Furthermore, evangelical Protestantism has been more popular on than off college campuses (Busto 1996; Lowman 1983; Quebedeaux 1978), where parachurch evangelical organizations, such as Campus Crusade for Christ, the Intervarsity Christian Fellowship, and Navigators, have been very active.

Significantly, since the early 1970s, evangelical Protestantism has become especially popular among Asian American college students (Busto 1996; R. Kim 2006; Warner 1994). Several researchers have pointed out that in the late 1990s and early 2000s, Asian American students comprised the vast majority or at least the majority of members of parachurch evangelical organizations in nationally known colleges and universities and that Korean and Chinese students are most active in these organizations (Busto 1996; R. Kim 2006; S. Park 2001, 2004). Moreover, Korean and Chinese students are active in multiethnic evangelical organizations and have established a separate Pan-Asian (e.g., the Asian American Christian Fellowship) and ethnic fellowship organizations at many colleges and universities in the West and Northeast. Because of their majority religious status in the United States, Korean and other Asian American Christian college students have been greatly affected by campus evangelical missionary organizations. Historically, no other second-generation white Christian group has been affected by American Christian missionary organizations as much as Korean and other Asian evangelical college students.

Jeung's *Faithful Generations: Race and New Asian American Churches* (2005) is the only and most systematic study of Pan-Asian churches for second-generation Asian American Protestants. Based on his interviews with forty-four ministers of Chinese, Japanese, and Pan-Asian congregations and his ethnographic research on a mainline and an evangelical Pan-Asian church in the San Francisco Bay area, Jeung shows the differences in congregational subculture between mainline and evangelical Pan-Asian churches. Mainline pastors consider it important for Pan-Asian churches to address the racism and marginalization faced by Asian Americans in both the church and society in general. Recognizing the Eurocentric orientations of American Christianity, mainline pastors also emphasize integrating Asian cultural traditions with Christian rituals. By contrast, as Jeung's research reveals, evangelical ministers emphasize meeting their members' individual psychological and emotional needs and oppose Pan-Asian churches' concern with issues of racial justice. They also oppose infusing Asian cultural traditions into Christian rituals. As Jeung commented, "Asian American evangelicals adopt the identities and practices that assimilate them into the broader evangelical world and discourage them from maintaining certain traditional ways" (2005, 122).

A number of studies of Korean English-language congregations (Alumkal 1999, 2001; Chai 1998, 2001a; R. Kim 2004, 2006; Min and D. Kim 2005; S. Park 2001, 2004) provide findings consistent with Jeung's analysis. They found that the culture of Korean English-language congregations is very similar to that of Pan-Asian evangelical churches. That is, second-generation Korean churches, which are predominantly evangelical, are generally modeled on white American evangelical churches. Although most second-generation Christians feel comfortable attending a Korean church, they put priority on the gospel and criticize Korean immigrant congregations for being too ethnic. These studies also indicate that second-generation Korean evangelicals accept being Christian as their primary identity and being Korean as their secondary identity. My data on second-generation Korean Christians and second-generation ethnic churches used in this book also strongly support these researchers' findings. One of the main theses of this book is that the great tensions between second-generation Korean evangelical Christians' religious and Korean ethnic identities have caused their strong Christian identity to weaken their Korean identity.

Although we have no empirical study of second-generation Indian Hindus, their emphasis on tolerance of other religions and rejection of proselytism helps us figure out how religion affects younger-generation Indian Hindus' identity, social boundaries, child socialization, and other worldviews in contrast to younger-generation Korean evangelical Protestants. As pointed out earlier, younger-generation Indian Hindus' embrace of some elements of Hinduism tends to enhance their Indian ethnic identity. But with the exception of a few very religious individuals, they do not hold their religious identity above their ethnic identity. In contrast, since younger-generation Korean evangelical Protestants organize their entire lives around Christian values, they are likely to limit their close friends and marital partners to Christians. But many younger-generation Indian Hindus, with their loose social boundaries, are able to make non-Hindu individuals into close friends and even marital partners without difficulty. Younger-generation Korean Christians' strong belief in salvation through Jesus Christ is likely to lead them to regard their children's religious socialization as a life-or-death issue. But younger-generation Indian Hindus' tolerance of religious pluralism and opposition to proselytism are likely to lead them to allow their children to choose their own religion.

Asian Christian immigrants, with the exception of Filipino immigrants, usually attend churches using their language and other ethnic cultural traditions (Chen 2002; Kim and Kim 2001; Kurien 2004; Min 1992; Yang 1999; Zhou, Bankston, and Kim 2002, 48–49).[5] But because of the language barrier and other cultural differences, U.S.-born second-generation Asian Americans often do not feel comfortable participating in their parents' ethnic congregations. Since they are not accepted as full American citizens because of their physical differences, they also do not feel comfortable attending predominantly white American churches (Jeung 2005, 38–40). These factors have contributed to the emergence of Pan-Asian Protestant churches in large Asian American centers like San Francisco and Los Angeles (Jeung 2005).[6] In Jeung's study, the vast majority of members of Pan-Asian churches are Chinese and Japanese Americans. In Los Angeles, the members are predominantly Chinese, Korean, and Japanese Americans. Although a significant number of younger-generation Indians are Protestants, they usually attend Indian ethnic churches rather than Pan-Asian churches (see chapter 3), because Indians do not share many cultural and physical characteristics with East Asians (see Min and C. Kim 2009). Since most of the members of what they call "Pan-Asian churches" are East Asians, it is better to refer to these churches as Pan–East Asian churches.

Despite the great differences in worship style and congregational culture of Korean immigrant and second-generation congregations, most second-generation Korean churches currently cannot be completely independent of immigrant churches because they are financially dependent on them. But as their members grow old enough to donate enough money to their churches, more and more second-generation Korean churches are likely to become independent of immigrant churches. As second-generation Korean churches become independent of immigrant churches, they may gradually turn into Pan-Asian or multiracial churches, because the latter follow evangelical theological principles and have advantages in growth and financial stability over ethnic churches (Chai 2005; Ecklund 2006; Min and D. Kim 2005).[7]

Since an increasing number of younger-generation Korean Protestants are likely to participate in Pan-Asian or multiracial congregations in the future, we need to clarify the ethnic phenomenon in Pan-Asian or multiracial congregations in which Koreans comprise a significant proportion of members. Jeung's analyses suggest that the emergence of Pan-Asian mainline Protestant churches is similar to the development of Asian Americans' panethnic racial solidarity that challenges white racism and discrimination (Espiritu 1992). They, however, show that the emergence of Pan-Asian evangelical churches is somewhat similar to the triple-melting-pot form of assimilation of white ethnic groups in the United States (Kennedy 1944), in that the salience of their religious identity and the weakening of their ethnic identity helped establish Pan-Asian religious institutions. Kennedy's creation of triple melting pots was made possible in the 1940s (Kennedy 1944) because third- and higher-generation European white ethnics had breached ethnic boundaries based on national origin but had maintained separate group boundaries based on religion.

Religion, along with national origin, language, and race, is a component of ethnicity. But Irish, Italian, and Polish Americans have a common religious identity but not a common ethnicity because the three groups do not share a sense of "peoplehood" associated with the same "ancestral homeland." I agree with many scholars (Gordon 1964, 23; Jaret 1995, 50; Schermerhorn 1970, 12) that the concept of peoplehood is central to ethnicity. If religious identity and the creation of one melting pot for white Catholics or Protestants contain an ethnic element, we should view it as a pan-ethnic formation based on religion rather than an ethnic formation. By contrast, we should consider the creation of a melting pot for Russian, Polish, and German Jews to be an ethnic rather than a panethnic phenomenon because it is based on both their common religious experience and their sense of peoplehood, closely related to their collective memory of Holocaust and their ancestral homeland, which was established in Israel in 1948 (Goren 1982, 108–10).

In this connection, I also would like to clarify what Will Herberg intended to emphasize and what he did not mean to emphasize in the following, frequently cited paragraph in his 1955 book, *Protestant—Catholic—Jew* (Herberg 1960, 27–28):

> Of the immigrant who came to this country it was expected that, sooner or later, either in his own person or through his children, he would give up virtually everything he had brought with him from "the old country"—his language, his nationality, his manner of life—and would adopt the ways of his new home. Within broad limits, however, his becoming an American did not involve his abandoning the old religion in favor of some native American substitute. Quite the contrary, not only was he expected to retain his old religion, as he was not expected to retain his old language or nationality, but such was the shape of America that it was largely in and through his religion that he, or rather his children and grandchildren, found an identifiable place in American life.

No doubt, Herberg meant to underscore that immigrants' religion survives much longer than national origin or language, especially because of the U.S. government's and American society's tolerance of different religions. Many researchers have also cited this paragraph to credit Herberg with emphasizing the ethnicity function of religion. But I contend that he did not mean to stress the ethnic role of religion, as the central theme of his book is to show the Americanization of Catholics, Protestants, and Jews by shedding their national traditions from Europe. His book also used the "triple melting pot thesis," in this case using the salience of religion, instead of intermarriage, to multigeneration white Americans. The salience of religion, instead of national origin, to third-generation Jewish Americans in the 1950s enhanced their Jewish ethnic identity because for them, religion and ethnicity overlap. But the ethnic identity of third-generation Italian and Polish Catholics who became American Catholics instead of remaining Italian and Polish Americans was weakened.

Accordingly, Korean evangelical Christianity's incorporation of Pan-Asian or multiracial evangelical Christianity is a process of pan-ethnic formation based on religion that has little to do with ethnic formation. Studies of younger-generation Muslims in the United States show that despite their various national origins, they generally have a strong religious identity and have close friendships with Muslims of different national origins (Leonard 2003; Peek 2005). For instance, Pakistani, Egyptian, and Nigerian Muslims form close friendships and date one another, which is a different form of panethnic formation based on religion, although their panethnic religious formation involves a higher level of reactive solidarity (Bozorgmehr and Bakalian 2005) than does a Pan-Asian evangelical Christian alliance. Second-generation evangelical Christians and Muslims establish panethnic religious congregations and boundaries across national origins more easily than do other second-generation religious groups because both are strongly committed to their universally applicable religious values.

# 2 Religions in India and South Korea

IMMIGRANTS' RELIGIOUS PRACTICES, like other aspects of their lives, have transnational components (Ebaugh and Chafetz 2000; Levitt 1999, 2001, 2007; Menjivar 2000). To better understand the relationships between immigrants' religion and ethnicity, we first examine the historical development and current distribution of Indians' and South Koreans' religions in their home countries. Although both countries are home to several religions, historically India has suffered far more social conflicts related to religious division than South Korea has, but more recently the emergence of strong evangelical Christians has contributed to some religious conflicts in South Korea.

## Religions in India

Table 2.1 shows the religious distribution of the Indian population, based on the Census of India, 2001. India has the second largest population in the world after China, with a population of nearly 1.02 billion in 2001. One noteworthy statistic is that less than 1 percent of Indians reported that they had no religion. The exceptionally low proportion of people with no religion was consistent in all twenty-eight states and union territories. No doubt, India is the world's most religious country.

Hindus made up 80.5 percent of the population in 2001, and Muslims, Christians, and Sikhs accounted for 13.4 percent, 2.3 percent, and 1.9 percent, respectively. Whereas the Hindu population decreased slightly from 83.4 percent in 1961, the proportion of Muslims rose sharply from 10.7 percent in the same year, mainly owing to their higher birthrate. Buddhism and Jainism, both of which have moderately influenced Hinduism, are India's other main minority religions. Six major religions, including Buddhism and Jainism, account for 99.3 percent of the country's religious adherents.

Table 2.2 shows that minority (non-Hindu) religions are highly concentrated in several states. West Bengal and three other states have much larger proportions of Muslims than does India as a whole. East Bengal, a heavily Muslim area, was incorporated into Pakistan in 1947 but later became a politically independent state, Bangladesh. West Bengal is included with India because the Hindus outnumber the Muslims by a large margin, although Muslims still are numerous. In Jammu and Kashmir, Muslims comprise about two-thirds of the population,

TABLE 2.1

*Distribution of Population by Religion in India, 2001*

| Religion | Number | Percent |
|---|---|---|
| Hindus | 827,578,868 | 80.5 |
| Muslims | 138,188,240 | 13.4 |
| Christians | 24,080,016 | 2.3 |
| Sikhs | 19,215,730 | 1.9 |
| Buddhists | 7,955,207 | 0.8 |
| Jains | 4,225,053 | 0.4 |
| Others | 6,639,626 | 0.6 |
| Religion not stated | 717,588 | 0.1 |
| Total population | 1,028,610,328 | 100.0 |

Source: Census of India, 2001 (http://www.censusindia.gov.in/Census_
And_You/religion.aspx).

with Hindus a numerical minority. These statistics reveal the reason for the frequent military conflicts between India and Pakistan in Kashmir.

Indian Christians are concentrated in four small northeastern states (Nagaland, Megahayaya, Minipur, and Mizoram) and two southwestern states (Kerala and Goa). The largest number of Indian Christians is in Kerala (about eight million), where they make up 19 percent of the population. Punjab is the only state in which Sikhs comprise the majority (about 60%) of the population. About 15 million Sikhs in Punjab account for more than three-fourths of all Sikhs (approximately 19 million) in India. Before Punjab was partitioned into two separate political entities, West Punjab into Pakistan and East Punjab into India in 1947, far more Muslims lived on the Indian side of Punjab than now. Also, many Muslims from East Punjab moved to Pakistan. Buddhists also are the majority in Sikkim and Arunachal Pradesh.

Unlike the world's other major religions, Hinduism has no overarching founding figure comparable to Jesus for Christianity or Muhammad for Islam. Nor does it have a single sacred text serving as a doctrinal point of reference, similar to the Bible or the Qur'an. The Vedas and the Bhagavad Gita are considered the most important sacred texts of Hinduism, and the Brahmanas, Upanishads, Ramayana, and Puranas also are regarded as its important sacred texts and/or epics (Michell 1988, 17). Hinduism evolved from a variety of cults and beliefs, some of which had their foundations in the Vedas associated with the Indo-Aryans who began to move to the Indus Valley around 2000 BCE (Davis 1995). Hinduism later added new layers by incorporating beliefs and rituals from other religions, especially from Buddhism and Jainism, which developed in India in the sixth century BCE. Most Buddhists and Jains, as well as Hindus, believe in incarnation and regard nonviolence as a key value. All three religions also use the term *dharma* as a central concept, although their definitions of it differ somewhat (Davis 1995, 21).

Moreover, because Hinduism's rituals have no single text or central hierarchy, it has developed into different forms in different Indian states by incorporating local cultures and beliefs. As a result, its diversity is greater than any other organized religion in regard to deities, sects, sacred texts, temples, and institutions (Williams 1988, 39). The development of particular Hindu sects, such as Swaminarayan Hinduism (Williams 1984), the Swadhyaya movement (Levitt 2007), and the International Society for Krishna Consciousness (Williams 1988, 130–37) adds to Hinduism's regional diversity. These three Hindu sects are highly organized and are similar to Christian churches in their congregational worship styles.

TABLE 2.2

*Self-Reported Religions (%) in Indian States, 2001*

| | Hinduism | Islam | Christianity | Sikhism | Buddhism | Jainism | Others | None |
|---|---|---|---|---|---|---|---|---|
| Whole country | 80.5 | 13.4 | 2.3 | 1.9 | 0.8 | 0.4 | 0.6 | 0.1 |
| West Bengal | 72.5 | **25.2** | 0.6 | 0.1 | 0.3 | 0.1 | 1.1 | 0.1 |
| Assam | 64.9 | **30.9** | 3.7 | 0.1 | 0.2 | 0.1 | 0.1 | 0.0 |
| Jammu and Kashmir | 29.6 | **67.0** | 0.2 | 2.0 | 1.1 | 0.0 | 0.0 | 0.1 |
| Kerala | 56.2 | **24.7** | **19.0** | 0.0 | 0.0 | 0.0 | 0.0 | 0.1 |
| Nagaland | 7.7 | 1.8 | **90.0** | 0.1 | 0.1 | 0.1 | 0.3 | 0.0 |
| Megahalaya | 13.3 | 4.3 | **70.3** | 0.1 | 0.2 | 0.0 | 11.5 | 0.3 |
| Mizoram | 3.6 | 1.1 | **87.0** | 0.0 | 7.9 | 0.0 | 0.3 | 0.1 |
| Goa | 65.8 | 6.8 | **26.7** | 0.1 | 0.0 | 0.1 | 0.0 | 0.5 |
| Punjab | 36.9 | 1.6 | 1.2 | **59.9** | 0.2 | 0.2 | 0.0 | 0.0 |
| Chandigarh | 78.6 | 3.9 | 0.8 | **16.1** | 0.1 | 0.3 | 0.0 | 0.2 |
| Sikkim | 60.9 | 1.4 | 6.7 | 0.2 | **28.1** | 0.0 | 2.4 | 0.0 |
| Arunachal Pradesh | 34.6 | 1.9 | **18.7** | 0.2 | **13.0** | 0.0 | **30.7** | 0.9 |

Source: Office of the Registrar General, India, "The First Report on Religion," *Census of India 2001*, September 2004 (http://www.censusindia.net/religiondata/index.html). Bold numbers indicate significant proportions of non-Hindu religious groups settled in particular states.

"Modern Hinduism," sometimes called "Neo-Hinduism," developed in India in the nineteenth and twentieth centuries largely through interactions with British colonialists and their Christian religion (King 1989; Kurien 2007). In fact, it was British colonialists in the nineteenth century who coined the term *Hinduism* to refer to the religion of India's indigenous people (King 1989, 78; Kurien 2007, 31). Their contact with Christianity in the nineteenth century led Hindu reformers to concentrate on the "unifying elements of the tradition which could be universalized and applied to people all over in India, as well as related to religion outside of it" (King 1989, 80, see also Frykenberg 1993, 549). Orally transmitted words from sages to their disciples, rather than written words, comprised the essential component of traditional Hinduism. Their encounter with Christianity, however, led Hindu reformers to emphasize the scriptural basis of Hinduism in the nineteenth century and after (King 1989).

Finally, King (1989, 82) points out that the Hindu reformers' encounter with Christianity led them to underscore Hinduism's monotheistic nature. Since Hindus worship different gods and goddesses, some people consider Hinduism a polytheistic religion, which Hindu leaders generally reject. The Hindu American Foundation, a nonprofit human rights organization for Hindu Americans, posted on its website a short article entitled "Introduction on Hinduism: Short Answers to Real Questions about Hinduism," which, among other things, explains why Hinduism is not a polytheistic religion.

> Hindus believe in one, all-pervasive supreme God, though He or She may be worshipped in different forms and different names. As such, Hinduism is monotheistic and henotheistic; monotheistic in its one God and henotheistic in that any one God can be worshipped without denying the existence of other Gods. And just as Hindus believe that Truth is one, called by many names, so too is God called by many names, be it, Krishna, Kali, Elohim, Jehova or Allah. (http://www. hinduamericanfoundation.org)

Islam is India's second most popular religion. Although Muslims (about 138 million) make up only 13 percent of the Indian population, India is the second most populous Muslim country in the world after Indonesia, which has more than 210 million Muslims. Islam was transported to the Indian subcontinent in the early eleventh century when the Islamic ruler Sultan Mahmud invaded northern India. Between 1200 and 1700, "rulers adhering to Islam prevailed in northern India" (Davis 1995, 32). The Muslim conquests of northern India led to the destruction of Hindu, Buddhist, and Jain temples, and often temples were converted into mosques (D. Smith 2003, 50–64). But "the south of India was not to experience Muslim rule until a much later period, when it had a less disrupting effect upon Hindu traditions" (Michell 1988, 18).

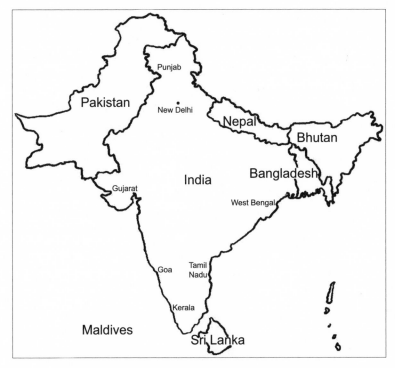

Map 2.1. South Asia

After it gained independence from Great Britain in 1947, India was partitioned into India and Pakistan. The area with a predominantly Hindu population became India, and the western and eastern parts, with largely Muslim populations, became Pakistan (see map 2.1). The partition forced many Hindus and Sikhs from Pakistan to move to India and many Muslims to move from India to Pakistan. Their movement was accompanied by intercommunal violence, during which about one million people were killed. Many Muslims elected to remain in India, however, when Prime Minister Jawaharlal Nehru (r. 1947–1964) promised to keep India a secular state.

The linguistic and other cultural differences between West (Urdu-speaking) and East Pakistan (Bengali-speaking) people and their physical separation led to conflicts between the two, and in 1971, in a war of liberation, East Pakistan seceded from Pakistan to form the new nation of Bangladesh. During the war of liberation, India supported East Pakistan (Bangladesh). As a result, India has maintained conflict-free, if not friendly, relations with Bangladesh, another Muslim country, but has had many conflicts, including military conflicts, with

Pakistan. Indeed, Hindus in both India and the United States accept Bangladesh Muslims more readily than they do Indian or Pakistani Muslims. Muslims make up about 95 percent of the population in Pakistan (Malik 1997, 678) and 83 percent in Bangladesh (Harris 1997, 58). Bangladesh also has many Hindus, and Nepal, another South Asian country, is heavily Hindu as well.

Sikhs are followers of its founder Guru Nanak, a saint who rejected both Hinduism and Islam in the fifteenth century, and his ten successors (gurus), covering about 170 years between 1539 and 1708. In the seventeenth century, the Sikhs had to fight against the Mogul administration to defend the Hindus and themselves (McLeod 1976). After a long period of political and military struggles, the Sikhs finally created a powerful kingdom in Punjab in the eighteenth century, but in the mid-nineteenth century, Great Britain annexed Punjab. The British recruited a large number of Sikhs into the army and the police, facilitating their mass migration throughout India and abroad to Great Britain, other British colonies, and the United States. In the early twentieth century, the majority of Indian immigrants in California were Sikhs, although white Americans commonly referred to them as "Hindus."

When the Sikh homeland in Punjab was partitioned into India and Pakistan in 1947, three million Sikhs moved from the Pakistan side of Punjab (West Punjab) to East Punjab. Thus the Sikhs also were uprooted, with many killed, during the bloody separation between India and Pakistan. With the establishment of the state of Punjab in 1966 by the Indian government, Punjabi Sikhs established the Golden Temple in Amritsar, Punjab, as their religious center. They made a number of demands to the Indian government for their religious, cultural, and economic autonomy in Punjab, often resorting to violent methods (Williams 1988, 78–79). In 1982, Prime Minister Indira Gandhi put Punjab under the rule of the central government, and two years later, in August 1984, she ordered the Indian army to occupy the Sikh Golden Temple. Many Sikhs who resisted, including Jarnail Singh Brindranwale, the Sikh opposition movement leader, were killed in the chaos. In retaliation, one of Prime Minister Gandhi's Sikh bodyguards assassinated her in October 1984. Hindu-led anti-Sikhs riots followed, leading to the death of a large number of Sikhs.

Both Sikhs and Hindus fought against British colonization and the Muslim invasion of India. Moreover, especially in Punjab, they shared many aspects of their religious doctrines, language, and social interactions (Khandelwal 2002, 75). For example, Sikhs celebrate Diwali, Hinduism's most important religious holiday. But because of the violent conflicts between the two groups over the 1984 military occupation of the Golden Temple, Sikhs both in India and in diasporic communities have strong religious, regional (Punjab), and political identities (Singh and Thandi 1999; Williams 1988, 78–81).

Even though Christians compose a small proportion (2.3%) of India's population, their number (24 million) is not negligible. Syrian Christians in Kerala also have a long history, dating back to the Apostle Thomas, one of Christ's twelve disciples, who traveled to India in 52 CE to preach the gospel of Jesus Christ and was martyred in 72 CE. Because Thomas's early Indian converts had been in contact with the church in Syria since the fourth century, St. Thomas Christians are also known as Syrian Orthodox Christians (Williams 1997). St. Francis Xavier and other Portuguese missionaries introduced Roman Catholicism to southern India in the mid-fifteenth century, and missionaries from several other countries, including Great Britain, brought Protestantism to India in the nineteenth and twentieth centuries. The different Protestant denominations, Syrian Orthodox Christianity, and Portuguese-influenced Catholicism all have developed different subgroups with separate hierarchies in India. The language and services of India's Christian churches that belong to the same denomination or subgroup also vary in different states. Thus Indian Christianity is diverse, a diversity that is reflected in Indian immigrant churches in the United States.

Jainism adds to India's religious diversity. Although Jains, numbering approximately 4.2 million in 2001 (see table 2.1), comprise less than half a percent of the population in India, they exercise a far greater influence than their number indicates in both India and the Indian community in the United States. Jains are concentrated in Gujarat and other northwestern (Rajasthan) and central states (Maharashtra). Jainism is as old as Hinduism. The term *Jain* refers to a follower of "a Jina," a perfected human being who teaches others the way to liberation from the suffering in this world's life (Seeling 1997, 485). Unlike Hindus who worship gods and goddesses, Jains worship Mahavira, the great hero who lived in India in the sixth century BCE, as well as the twenty-three other great teachers, the Tirthankaras, who reached perfection. But they share ritual practices with Hindus. For example, both Jains and Hindus perform *puja* (Seeling 1997). *Ahimsa* (nonviolence), the central value of Jainism, has had a strong influence on Hinduism, especially through Mahatma Gandhi. In addition, Jain immigrants share with Hindu immigrants the same language and province, and some Jain centers share religious space with Hindus in both India and the United States.

Owing to both historical conflicts between Hindus and Muslims on the Indian subcontinent and the current political and military conflicts between India and Pakistan, tensions and conflicts continue between Hindus and Muslims in India (Varshney 2002). These tensions worsened after the establishment of the Bharatiya Janata Party (BJP), the political wing of Hindu nationalism (Hindutva), in 1979. In December 1992, the BJP openly supported the demolition of a sixteenth-century Babre mosque in north India by Hindutva supporters, which, they claimed, had been built by a Muslim emperor on the site of a Ram Hindu temple (Marshall 2000, 159). The riots following the demolition of the mosque led to the killing of several thousand people, mostly Muslims. Then in 1998, the BJP came to power with its victory in the national elections and later controlled many state governments (Kurien 2001). The BJP's control of power in India raised the hopes of Hindu nationalists who want to make India a Hindu nation.

In the 2004 general election, however, the BJP lost control, leading to the creation of a coalition government led by the Congress Party and headed by Prime Minister Manmohan Singh, the first Sikh prime minister in Indian history.

In February 2002, a train car was set on fire by a mob of Muslims in Godhra, Gujarat, killing fifty-nine Hindus. The Godhra attack escalated into communal violence in central Gujarat, killing more than one thousand people, mostly Muslims, as well as the rape of and physical violence against many Muslims. Muslims have protested that the BJP-controlled Gujarat government made no effort to stop the rioters and that it has not taken any concrete action to punish them.

Because of their small number, Hindu nationalists do not perceive India's Christians to be as dangerous to the national unity as Muslims. In recent years, though, they, along with Western missionaries, have also been subjected to media attacks, physical violence, rape, and murder (Marshall 2000, 159–61). Because of their past and current conflicts with Hindus and one another, members of all three religious minority groups in India (Muslims, Christians, and Sikhs) have strong religious identities and maintain firm social boundaries. The fact that their religious names are unique to each religion strengthens their religious identities. Consequently, Indian Muslim, Sikh, and Christian immigrants find it difficult to change their religion because this involves changing the religious name that they use publicly. Interfaith marriages are difficult as well, even though the worshippers of all three minority religions, as well as Hindus, are more open to other religions than evangelical Christians are.

### Religions in South Korea

Table 2.3 provides data on religions in South Korea based on the Social Statistics Survey 2003. Fifty-four percent of the population (aged 15 and older) indicated a religion, with 25 percent of the respondents choosing Buddhism and 27 percent choosing either Protestantism (20%) or Catholicism (7%). Buddhism as a traditional religion gained popularity in rural areas, while the two Christian religions were more popular in urban areas. The difference between rural and urban has narrowed during recent years. Christians usually are better educated than the general population in South Korea, and Buddhists tend to be less educated (Korean Christian Institute for the Study of Justice and Development 1982, 49; W. Lee 2000, 76).

**TABLE 2.3**

*Growth of Religions (%) in South Korea*

| Year | Buddhism | Protestantism | Catholicism | Others | All Religions |
|------|----------|---------------|-------------|--------|---------------|
| 1962 | 2.6 | 2.8 | 2.2 | 1.8 | 9.7 |
| 1985 | 20.1 | 16.1 | 4.6 | 0.5 | 42.6 |
| 1999 | 26.3 | 18.6 | 7.0 | 1.8 | 53.6 |
| 2003 | 25.3 | 19.8 | 7.4 | 1.4 | 53.9 |

Sources: Adapted from Park and Cho 1995, table 2; and Korean National Statistical Office 2005, table 13-5.

Most South Korean farmers are Buddhists, and most professionals and business owners are Christians. Buddhism is more popular among elderly people, while the two Christian religions attract more younger people. In 2003, Protestants comprised about 27 percent of those aged 15 to 19 years, compared with 16 percent for Buddhists (Korea National Statistical Office 2005, 589). By contrast, Buddhists comprised 27 percent of the elderly population, compared with 16 percent for Protestants.

Buddhism was brought to Korea in 372 CE when King Sosurim of the kingdom of Koguryo welcomed Buddhist monks from China (Park 1982, 71). During the Koryŏ dynasty (918–1392 CE), it was adopted as the state religion when the kings tried to use it as a tool to strengthen their authority and protect the country from foreign invasions (Baker 1997b, 159). During the five centuries of the Chosŏn dynasty (1392–1910), Buddhism lost much of its official patronage when the new dynasty adopted Confucianism as the official political and social philosophy. In fact, the Chosŏn dynasty repressed Buddhism by levying taxes on land used for temples, abolishing examinations for the official appointment of monks, and barring monks from Seoul, the capital city. Buddhism was further repressed during the Japanese colonial rule (1910–1945), as the colonial government tried to repress all Korean religions, including Christianity. In 1962, Buddhists comprised only 2.6 percent of South Korea's population, but they, along with the Christians, have gradually increased their numbers, reaching 26 percent in 1999 (Korea National Statistical Office 2005, 589)and then declining slightly to 25 percent in 2003.

Buddhism came to have a powerful influence on Korean culture through painting, architecture, sculpture, poetry, and dance in all four dynasties. About one-third of objects officially recognized today by the Korean government as significant cultural treasures are paintings, statues, pagodas, bronze bells, and worship halls found in Buddhist temples or created by Buddhist monks (Baker 1997a, 163). Most of these Buddhist cultural treasures were made during the Silla

(57 BCE–935 CE) and Koryŏ (918–1392) dynasties, which testifies to a long history of Buddhism in Korea. Because of its long history and strong cultural influence in Korea, Buddhist immigrants in the United States regard Buddhism as representing Korean culture and traditions and Protestantism as an alien religion (Suh 2004).

American missionaries, mostly Presbyterian and Methodist, brought Protestantism to Korea in the 1880s by establishing Christian schools and hospitals, and Korean intellectuals brought Roman Catholicism to Korea from Western missionaries in China in the 1760s (K. Min 1988). It is important to note that "right from the beginning, the contact of Korea with Christianity began with an interest in Western culture, particularly its sciences, totally foreign to Korea" (C. Kim 1982, 117). Thus both Christian religions were more readily accepted in the northern part of Korea, where the Confucian cultural influence was weaker than in the southern part. But when the communist government was established in 1948 in North Korea, many Christians there fled to South Korea to avoid persecution (K. Min 1988, 453–54). Nevertheless, neither Christian religion was popular in South Korea until the late 1960s, because the Christian religious faiths and rituals collided with ancestor worship, the core of Confucian customs,[1] and because the Japanese colonial government banned Christianity during its occupation. In 1962, only 2.8 percent of South Koreans were Protestants and 2.2 percent were Catholic (Park and Cho 1995, 119).

South Korea's Christian population rose sharply over the next twenty-five years, with Protestants accounting for 16 percent and Catholics 5 percent in 1985 (Korea National Statistical Office 1992, 300). Three factors contributed to the rapid increase in South Korea's Christian, especially the Protestant, population between 1960 and 1985 (Baker 1997b, 191–92; Korean Christian Institute for Justice and Development 1982, 140–41). One factor was the need for communal bonds for urban migrants from rural areas who had lost their family and friendship ties. The period between 1960 and 1985 was the period of rapid urbanization in South Korea. Another factor contributing to the growth of South Korea's Protestant population was the Korean Protestants' proselytizing fervor. From the beginning, Korean Protestant churches were heavily evangelical and used the strategy of each church's self-propagation. The third reason for the rapid growth of the Christian population in South Korea was the identification of Christianity with modernity, leading to the establishment of many Christian schools, hospitals, and other Christian organizations, such as the YMCA and YWCA (C. Kim 1982). In the 1960s and 1970s when South Korea was rapidly urbanizing and industrializing, both Protestant and Catholic churches, but especially the former, actively recruited their members from urban residents through various social service, educational, and social programs. Since 1985, however, the growth

Map 2.2. Republic of Korea

of the Korean Christian population has been very slow, as the country's urbanization was mostly completed. In 2003, South Korea's Protestant and Catholic populations comprised 20 percent and 7 percent of the population, respectively, with Buddhists accounting for another 25 percent (see table 2.2).

Although both American Presbyterian and Methodist missionaries entered Korea at the end of the nineteenth century, Presbyterian churches have outnumbered Methodist churches in Korea by a large margin. In 1980, Presbyterian churches accounted for 64 percent of all Protestant churches in Korea, compared with 18 percent of Methodist churches (Min 1992). As table 2.3 shows, 71 percent of all South Korean churches in 2006 were Presbyterian, and only 12 percent were Methodist. South Korea also is home to significant numbers of Assemblies of God, Baptist, and Evangelical Holiness churches. The growth and dominance of Presbyterian churches is due to two related factors. First, American Presbyterian missionaries concentrated on evangelizing Koreans, whereas Methodist missionaries were equally concerned with providing social services such as schools and hospitals (K. Min 1988). Second, as a result of this difference in the beginning, Presbyterian denominations in Korea evolved into heavily evangelical denominations, whereas the Korean Methodist Church has become a liberal mainline denomination. The Korean Presbyterian Church's ninety-five denominations, with the exception of a small liberal denomination, concentrate on individual salvation and missionary activities, whereas the Korean Methodist Church pays enough attention to social issues (see table 2.4).

Other major Protestant denominations in Korea emphasize evangelism as the central aspect of Christian life, and as a result, the Protestant population has achieved a phenomenal growth in South Korea. More significantly, Korean Protestants have been actively involved in missionary activities in other countries over the last two decades. As of April 2007, about 15,000 Korean missionaries were working in 160 foreign countries, including China, India, the former Soviet Union, Latin America, Africa, and even Arab Muslim countries. They include about one thousand missionaries from Korea Campus Crusade for Christ (Hanguk Daehaksaeng Seon-gohoe) in countries from Asia to the Americas.[2] Only the United States has more foreign missionaries (46,000) than South Korea. Given that there are only about 10 million Protestants in South Korea, compared with more than 150 million Protestants in the United States, and that Protestantism has gained popularity in South Korea only over the last four decades, the sheer number of Korean missionaries working in foreign countries indicates their evangelist zeal.

Korean aid missionaries have dared to move into some dangerous Muslim countries, such as Iran, Iraq, and Afghanistan, confronting many fundamental-

**TABLE 2.4**

*Major Protestant Denominations in Korea (2006)*

| Denominations | Number of Churches | |
|---|---|---|
| PRESBYTERIAN DENOMINATIONS | 39,983 | (71%) |
| The General Assembly of Presbyterian Churches in Korea (Hapdong) | 10,717 | |
| The Presbyterian Church of Korea (Tonghap) | 7,153 | |
| The Presbyterian General Assembly in Korea (Hapdong Jungtong) | 2,772 | |
| **The Presbyterian Church in the Republic of Korea (Gijang)** | 1,600 | |
| 91 Other Denominations | 17,741 | |
| NON-PRESBYTERIAN DENOMINATIONS | 16,449 | (29%) |
| **The Korean Methodist Church** | 6,600 | |
| The Korea Evangelical Holiness Church | 3,553 | |
| The Association of Korean Baptist Churches | 2,545 | |
| The (Korean) Assemblies of God | 2,093 | |
| 36 Other Small Denominations | 1,458 | |
| ALL DENOMINATIONS | 56,432 | (100%) |

Sources: The Christian Council of Korea (The association of conservative Korean Protestant denominations), "Statistics on Member Denominations' Number Power," February 2006.
*Two denominations bolded are liberal denominations. These two and other smaller non-Presbyterian liberal denominations are affiliated with the Korean National Council of Churches (KNCC), which estimated (as of July 2006) the number of churches affiliated with each denomination.

ist Muslims who are more or less antagonistic to Christian missionaries. As a result, some of them have become victims of kidnapping and killing. In 2004, eight Korean missionaries in Iraq were kidnapped but later released after they pretended to be medical aid workers. In the same year, Sun-Il Kim, who went to Iraq for missionary work, was beheaded by a Muslim fundamentalist group. In July 2007, twenty-three Korean missionary workers entered Afghanistan despite the Korean government's warning. They were kidnapped by the Taliban, and two of them were shot to death. The Korean government used all its diplomatic channels to get the remaining twenty-one hostages released after six weeks of captivity (Choe 2007a).

Progressive-minded Koreans who were critical of Confucianism adopted Roman Catholicism spontaneously in the 1760s without the aid of any alien missionary or even priest. In order to receive the sacramental graces of salvation through the Roman Catholic Church, the Korean founders of Catholicism sent Seunghoon Lee to the Catholic church in Beijing, China. Lee became the first

Korean baptized as a Catholic (baptized in China in 1784) who preached the gospel of Catholicism in Korea (K. Min 1988, 61). The Catholic preaching that the savior of the world was God, instead of the king, and its rejection of ancestor worship challenged the core of the prevailing Confucian social and political ideology. For this reason, Lee and many other Korean pioneer Catholics suffered oppression by their families and the government, and ultimately persecutions by the latter until they were given religious freedom in the Korean-French Treaty of 1886 (A. Min 2008). In the first forty years of the nineteenth century, 113 Korean Catholics were reported to have been martyred (K. Min 1988, 83).

After Protestantism arrived in Korea at the end of the nineteenth century, Catholic and Protestant leaders competed to bring more Koreans to their churches. Since 1960, however, Protestantism has outstripped Catholicism, mainly because of its stronger evangelical orientation and partly because of its financial advantage in establishing various Christian organizations to meet the needs of the growing urban population. Despite their numerical and financial disadvantages, Catholic churches have been active in social concerns. Late Cardinal Soo-Hwan Kim was never afraid of criticizing the military government during the twenty-six years of military dictatorship between 1961 and 1987. In addition, Myongdong Sundang, Korea's largest Catholic parish, located in Seoul, used its building as a sanctuary for antigovernment demonstrators and labor protesters.

Catholicism in South Korea is more liberal than Protestantism, in regard to both social issues and theological position. For example, according to a 1997 poll conducted by Korea Gallup, 73 percent of Catholic respondents believed in Heaven after death, compared with 86 percent of Protestant respondents, with 60 percent attending services once a week or more, compared with 72 percent of Protestants (W. Lee 2000, 95, 97). More significantly, Korean Catholics are more open to other religions than Korean Protestants are, with 85 percent of Catholics, compared with 62 percent of Protestants, agreeing that "all religions, although they look different in religious doctrines, are the same or similar in telling the truth" (W. Lee 2000, 100).

Buddhism was invisible to urban dwellers in the 1960s and 1970s when the two Christian religions were actively recruiting urban residents. Temples were heavily concentrated in the mountains in rural areas, with little connection to city dwellers.[3] Accordingly, Koreans tended to identify Christianity with modernity and Buddhism with tradition (Baker 1997a, 165). Then, beginning in the 1970s, to compete successfully with Christian religions for the allegiance of city folk, Buddhist leaders tried to modernize their religion. The Chogye Order, the main Buddhist denomination in South Korea, established Buddhist proselytizing and meditation centers in condominium complexes and created social service programs in large cities. Urban Buddhists also modernized Buddhist music by setting *changbulga* (Buddhist hymns) to melodies borrowed from Christian hymns (Baker 1997a, 166; Chung 1982). Like Christian churches, Buddhist temples in large cities began to hold regular *bophe* (services) on Sundays. As a result, Buddhism is successfully competing with Christianity in attracting urban dwellers, especially young urban residents. Although Buddhism is slightly less popular than Christianity in urban areas, the proportion of Buddhists has increased throughout the nation similar to the increase of Christians over the last thirty-five years.

Although neither Confucianism nor shamanism is an organized religion, each has religious elements. Since both have strongly affected Korean culture and religion for many centuries, some background information about them is necessary. Confucianism, which originated in China, was introduced to Korea in the fourth century. It began to have a powerful cultural influence in Korea during the Chosŏn dynasty (1392–1910) when the government adopted it as a social, political, and economic philosophy. Confucianism has had a stronger influence on Korean culture than any other religion or philosophy. As practiced in Korea, Confucian values emphasized loyalty to the king, filial piety, strong family/kin ties, a patriarchal family order, and children's education as the main channel for social mobility (Park and Cho 1995; Peterson 1997). All these Confucian values, except the first, are related to establishing a good family order as a means of safeguarding social stability. "Filial piety" refers to children's obligations and devotion to their parents. Children are required to pay the highest respect to their parents not only during their lives but also after their deaths in the form of ancestor worship. Based on the Confucian belief in the existence of the soul after death, which is a religious element, sons observe a ritual mourning after a parent's death on the day he or she died, and younger generations of sons venerate their ancestors in the three preceding generations, usually on the lunar New Year and Chooseok (the Korean version of Thanksgiving Day).

Whereas Confucianism, Buddhism, and Christianity are foreign religions or philosophies introduced to Korea by elites, shamanism is the oldest belief system in Korea and a folk religion adopted and developed by laypeople. Of course, shamanistic folk religions have been popular not only in Korea but also in other East Asian countries, such as Taiwan and Japan (Caldarola 1982; Tamney 1993). It is difficult to generalize about the Korean form of shamanism because of regional variations, but it is centered on the *mudang* (shaman), a priestess who is believed to make contacts with gods or evil spirits through special ecstatic techniques and who thereafter performs ritual services for other people. Regardless of regional variations, "the main object of shamanistic ritual performance is the expulsion of misfortune and the calling for happiness, which includes good fortune, longevity, and wealth for family members" (K. Lee 1997, 127).

Shamanism was far more popular with farmers and lower-class people, especially in rural areas, than with middle-class people. Today, the cultural influence of shamanism in South Korea has diminished, under the impact of urbanization, technological advances, and the improvement of education. In particular, Park Chung-Hee, who headed Korea's military government in the early 1960s, discouraged shamanism, considering the superstitious religion to be a hindrance to modernizing South Korea. But many people in South Korea—whether shipowners, taxi drivers, or rich merchants—still have a shamanistic ritual performed regularly for good luck for their jobs/businesses, good health, or family prosperity. In fact, there is evidence that shamanism has enjoyed a revival during recent years (Choe 2007b).

In a religious survey conducted in 1962, more than 90 percent of the population in South Korea reported that they had no religion. It would be wrong to conclude from the results of this survey, however, that Koreans were not religious in the early 1960s. As noted earlier, Confucianism and shamanism had a stronger effect on laypeople's religious beliefs and culture in South Korea forty years ago than they do at present. Most people in South Korea seem to have held a religious belief associated with shamanism, Confucianism, or a combination of the two in the early 1960s and before. But as South Korea has become more and more urbanized, industrialized, and Westernized, with significant improvements in education since the early 1960s, the influence of more traditional religious beliefs associated with shamanism and/or Confucianism has been gradually weakened.[4] In contrast, the proportions of Koreans who chose Buddhism, Protestantism, and Catholicism greatly increased in the 1980s through the early 2000s, reaching about 54 percent in 2003.

In their adaptation to Korean society, all three religions have incorporated some elements of shamanism and Confucianism (Baker 1997b, 195; Yoon 2002, 102–3). Both Korean Buddhists and Catholics worship their ancestors, a principal Confucian norm, at home and in religious institutions. Although Korean Protestant churches do not practice ancestor worship, many Korean Protestants hold memorial services at home on the days that parents or ancestors died, a ritual borrowed from the Confucian ancestor worship. Moreover, some Korean Protestants worship their ancestors at home to fulfill their family obligations. For example, when a Korean Protestant woman marries a non-Protestant man, she will have to observe the ancestor-worship rituals practiced by her husband's family.[5]

In addition, it is important to note that Korean Protestantism, influenced by Confucianism, is more patriarchal than American Protestantism (Baker 1997b, 195; A. Kim 1996). Although women make up about 57 percent of Protestants in South Korea (Korea National Statistical Office 2002, 538), few serve as ordained ministers or hold leadership positions. Influenced by shamanism, both Korean Buddhists and Christians pray for good luck, good health, and prosperity (Baker 1997b, 194–95; Tamney 1993, 64). Owing to their common heritage of Confucian and shamanistic traditions and no history of religion-based conflict, Buddhists, Protestants, and Catholics in South Korea are flexible in accepting other religious groups or the other half of the population with no religion in terms of friendship and marriage. According to results of a 1997 survey, 16 percent of Korean adults who had a religion reported that they had converted from another religion to their current one (W. Lee 2000, 80). None of the three major religious groups in South Korea is large enough to be a numerically majority group, and no religious minority group in South Korea is subject to discrimination. Because of their cultural homogeneity, Koreans, regardless of their religious background, have a strong national identity but a weak religious identity. No Korean uses his or her religious name outside the religious organization, although Catholics usually use their religious names among their church members.

Korean Catholics are more liberal than Protestants, and approximately one-third to one-half of Korean Protestants are known to be strict evangelicals who reject other religions and try hard to evangelize other Koreans. Evangelical Protestants are known to have been responsible for the destruction of many Buddhist statues and many Buddhist stone pagodas in South Korea over the last two decades (W. Lee 2000, 242). In addition, many evangelical Protestants in South Korea maintain such strong social boundaries that they do not allow their children to marry non-Protestants. The somewhat "offensive hostile attitudes" of many Protestants toward Buddhists and the "defensive rejection" of Protestants by many Buddhists have contributed to recent religious conflicts in South Korea (W. Lee 2000, 250).[6] Finally, evangelical Protestants in South Korea have begun organizing themselves politically, with strong pro-American and anticommunist stances, thereby colliding with Korean nationalists who have become increasingly anti-American and tolerant of North Korea.

# 3 Korean and Indian Immigrants' Religious Affiliations and Participation in Religious Institutions

ONE OF THE chapters of the first major book on the Korean immigrant community in New York, by Illsoo Kim (1981) is devoted to Korean immigrant churches. At the beginning of the chapter, he summed up the importance of church to Korean immigrants (Kim 1981, 187):

> By opening membership to all segments of the population, the churches provide a grass roots base for common action. At least for members, the churches provide some degree of integration that does not exist in non-religious organizations. In the absence of a territorial base for a "natural" community, church activities are all the more self-consciously organized. Indeed, the church community has become the substitute for a territorial ethnic community, and thus the interplay between the minister and devoted professionals produces a leadership crucial to carrying out both religious and secular activities.

In a more recent monograph on the Asian Indian community in New York City, Madhulika Khandelwal (2002, 69) discusses various religious institutions:

> Because New York City enjoyed regular linkages to the home country, the Queens Indian population maintained intimate connections with religious resources and developments in South Asia: such items as religious statues, calendars, books, and ritual paraphernalia were readily available. The baggage of travelers arriving in New York City often included religious articles, not only for their own use but also to oblige requests from friends.

These two quotations indicate the importance of religious life to Korean and Indian immigrants in New York City. In fact, Koreans and Asian Indians are the two Asian immigrant groups most active in religious practices. This chapter looks at the immigration and settlement of Korean and Indian immigrants in New York City, their religious distributions in their home countries and here, and the frequency of their participation in religious institutions.

## Immigration and Settlement in New York City

Until the 1965 Immigration Act, few Koreans or Indians lived in the New York City area, but this changed after 1970. Table 3.1 shows the numbers of immigrants from India and Korea and the percentages of those who settled in New York and New Jersey between 1965 and 2004. The flow of Indian immigrants escalated in the early 1990s. Currently, approximately 60,000 Indians immigrate to the United States each year, more than from any other Asian country and the second largest number in the world after Mexico. The increased number of Indian immigrants since the early 1990s is due mainly to the Immigration Act of 1990, which raised the number of immigrants, especially professionals, to 140,000 each year (Rumbaut 1995, 7). Many Indian computer programmers, computer technologists, and engineers trained at technological institutes in India have been able to take advantage of the new law's preference for professional immigrants.

About 20 to 30 percent of Indian immigrants in the United States have settled in the New York / New Jersey area. In 1965, only a few Indian immigrants in New York were able to bring their family members with them. But after passage of the 1965 Immigration Act, the first wave of Indian immigrants settling in New York were mainly medical professionals, engineers and scientists, and their families (Saran 1985, 33). Many of these Indian professionals came to the United States as students and changed their status to that of permanent residents after they completed their graduate education here. At first, more Indian immigrants settled in New York City than in New Jersey. But since the late 1980s, the proportion of Indian immigrants in New Jersey has gradually risen, reaching 13 percent by 2005, whereas only 7 percent remained in New York State.

Table 3.1 also shows that in the 1970s and 1980s, more Koreans than Indians immigrated to the United States. In fact, in each year of the 1980s, more than 30,000 Koreans came, the third largest voluntary migrant group in the world, next to Mexico and the Philippines.

Strong political, economic, and military links between the United States and South Korea were the main reasons for the massive migration of Koreans to the United States. Many Korean women married to U.S. servicemen stationed in South Korea and many children adopted by American citizens accounted for a significant proportion of the Korean immigrants during this period. But the number of Korean immigrants began to drop sharply in the early 1990s, reaching its lowest level in the latter half of the 1990s, with an average of 15,000 per year. The improvement in economic conditions, the end of the 26-year-old military dictatorship in South Korea, and an easing of tensions between North and South Korea all contributed to the reduction of Korean immigration to the United States.

Table 3.1 shows that after 1965, about 20 percent of Korean immigrants to the United States settled in the New York / New Jersey area, with some fluctuations over the years. The first wave of post-1965 Korean immigrants in New York (those who acquired green cards before 1980) included large numbers of profes-

TABLE 3.1

*Annual Number of Immigrants from China, India, and Korea to
the United States and Percentage in New York and New Jersey by Five-Year Period*

| Five-Year Period | India | | | Korea | | |
|---|---|---|---|---|---|---|
| | U.S. Total | % in NY | % in NJ | U.S. Total | % in NY | % in NJ |
| 1965–1969 | 18,327 | N/A | NA | 17,869 | N/A | N/A |
| 1970–1974 | 67,253 | 25 | 9 | 92,745 | 12 | 4 |
| 1975–1979 | 92,334 | 19 | 10 | 148,645 | 9 | 3 |
| 1980–1984 | 116,282 | N/A | N/A | 162,178 | N/A | N/A |
| 1985–1989 | 137,499 | 15 | 12 | 175,803 | 11 | 4 |
| 1990–1994 | 187,528 | N/A | N/A | 112,215 | 14 | 6 |
| 1995–1999 | 184,397 | 12 | 12 | 75,579 | 12 | 8 |
| 2000–2004 | 303,785 | 7 | 13 | 89,871 | 9 | 7 |
| Total | 1,107,405 | — | — | 874,905 | — | — |

Source: Immigration and Naturalization Service 1965–1978, 1979–2004.

sionals, especially medical professionals, and foreign students who changed their status to that of permanent residents in the United States (D. Kim 2004; I. Kim 1981). Illsoo Kim estimated that between 1965 and 1977, approximately 13,000 Korean medical professionals—physicians, nurses, and pharmacists—immigrated to the United States directly from Korea or via Germany (I. Kim 1981, 148). With the passage of the 1976 Immigration Act, which made it more difficult for professionals to enter the country, the immigration of Korean medical professionals to the New York area dropped to an insignificant number. Then the flow of Korean immigrants resumed when the earlier immigrants became naturalized and brought their family members to join them. Like Indian immigrants, Korean immigrants in the New York / New Jersey area initially preferred New York City, especially Queens, where they established a Korean enclave in the Flushing/Bayside area. Then, similarly, the Korean migrants gradually moved from New York City to New Jersey, especially to Bergen County. Korean immigrants in Bergen Country established two suburban enclaves, in Fort Lee and Palisades Park. After the Los Angeles area, the New York / New Jersey has the second largest Korean population in the United States.

After four decades of massive in-migration, both the Indian and Korean populations have grown. In table 3.2, the IPUMS of the American Community Survey shows that in 2005, there were 2.3 million single-race Indians in the United States. As a legacy of British colonization, several million people of Indian ancestry took up

TABLE 3.2

Indian and Korean Populations in the United States and
the New York / New Jersey CMSA, 2005

| | United States | | NY/NJ CMSA | | B as of A |
|---|---|---|---|---|---|
| | Single Race (A) | Single Race and Multiracial | Single Race (B) | Single Race and Multiracial | |
| Indian | 2,309,322 | 2,433,597 | 522,981 | 545,133 | 23 |
| Korean | 1,261,226 | 1,374,879 | 195,395 | 200,664 | 16 |

Source: IPUMS of 2005 American Community Survey.

residence in Africa, the Caribbean, and other parts of the world. In particular, since the early 1980s, huge numbers of people of Indian ancestry in Guyana and other Caribbean countries remigrated to the United States, mostly to New York City, The nearly 523,000 Indian Americans settled in the New York / New Jersey metropolitan area in 2005 comprised 23 percent of the total Indian population, more Indian Americans than any other area in the United States. Other South Asians (Pakistanis, Bangladeshis, and Sri Lankans) are even more highly concentrated in the New York / New Jersey area than Indian Americans (Kibria 2006, 210).

Table 3.3 shows the educational levels of two Asian immigrant groups in the New York / New Jersey area based on the 5 percent Public Use Microdata Sample of the 2000 U.S. Census, compared with native-born non-Hispanic whites. White Americans in this area have more education than in the United States as a whole, with 43 percent (25 to 64 years old) completing four years of college, compared with only 30 percent of the total population. But Korean immigrants have a slightly higher college graduation rate than white Americans, and Indian immigrants have a much higher educational level. Impressively, about one-third of economically active Indian immigrants obtained a graduate degree. In 2000, 42 percent of Indian immigrants (25 to 64 years old) held professional and related positions, compared with 21 percent of Korean immigrants and 26 percent of native-born white Americans. Indian immigrants' exceptionally high educational level can be explained by the selective migration of highly educated elites in India. Looking at Indian immigrants' educational level by immigrant cohort, pre-1980 immigrants are more highly educated (64% graduating from college) than post-1990 immigrants (44%). Indian immigrants are fluent in English, of course, as almost all of them spoke it in India. About 90 percent of Indian immigrants reported in the 2000 census that they spoke English well or very well, compared with only 59 percent of Korean immigrants.

# Distribution of Korean Immigrants' Religions

Between 1903 and 1905, about 40 percent of the approximately 7,200 Korean immigrants were Protestants, and during the Japanese occupation of Korea (1910–1945), the majority of Korean students and political refugees in the United States also were Protestants (Lyu 1977; Patterson 1988). The Korean church was even more important to this earlier Korean immigrant community than to the present Korean immigrant community, as it was the only major Korean gathering place at that time. Moreover, the Korean church played the central role in the transnational Korean independence movement fighting against the Japanese colonization, sending large donations to the Korean provisional government in Shanghai (J. Kim 2002). Korean church leaders also used the Bible to attack Japan's colonization and justify their home country's political independence (Yoo 2010).

The Korean Church of New York (a Methodist church), established in 1921 and located near Columbia University in Manhattan, was one of the early Korean immigrant churches active in the independence movement (Korean Church of New York 1992). Because Korean Christians were the leaders of the independence movement during Japan's colonization of Korea, the active role of Korean immigrant churches in the anti-Japanese independence movement is not surprising.

Table 3.4 shows the self-reported religions of Korean immigrants in Korea before their migration to the United States and their current religion in New York City at the time of the interview. The table is based on a 2005 telephone survey of Korean immigrants using the Kim sample technique. The table reveals that about 60 percent of Korean immigrants in New York City were Christians in South

**TABLE 3.3**

*Educational Levels of Indian and Korean Immigrants 25 to 64 Years Old in the New York / New Jersey CMSA, 2000*

|  | High School | College | Advanced Degree | Total Population |
|---|---|---|---|---|
| Indian | 88% | 65% | 33% | 171,578[a] |
| Korean | 91% | 50% | 16% | 101,685 |
| Native-born Non-Hispanic white | 94% | 43% | 18% | 5,550,415 |

Source: U.S. Bureau of the Census, 5% Public Use Microdata Sample of 2000 Census.

Note: [a]Only Indian immigrants 25 to 64 years old were included for data analysis. Thus Indian immigrants from the Caribbean Islands with a much lower educational level than immigrants from India were eliminated.

TABLE 3.4

*Korean Immigrant Respondents' Self-Reported*
*Religions in Korea and New York (2005)*

| | In Korea | | In New York (Now) | |
| --- | --- | --- | --- | --- |
| | Number | % | Number | % |
| Protestantism | 133 | 48.0 | 162 | 58.5 |
| Catholicism | 35 | 12.6 | 39 | 14.1 |
| Buddhism | 36 | 13.0 | 22 | 7.9 |
| Other | 1 | 0.4 | 2 | 0.7 |
| None | 72 | 26.0 | 52 | 18.8 |
| Total | 277 | 100.0 | 277 | 100.0 |

Source: 2005 Survey of Chinese, Indian, and Korean Immigrants in
New York City.

Korea; with 48 percent being Protestants and 13 percent being Catholics. Given that Protestants and Catholics comprised 20 percent and 7 percent, respectively, of the population in South Korea in 2003 (see table 2.3), there are almost 2.5 times more Protestants among the Korean immigrants and almost twice as many Catholics as there are in Korea. These two Christian populations accounted for even smaller proportions of the population in Korea in the 1970s and 1980s, indicating that there were even more Protestants and Catholics among Korean immigrants than these figures indicate. By contrast, Korean immigrants who were Buddhists in Korea made up 13 percent of Korean immigrants in New York, about half the percentage of Buddhists in South Korea. Other survey studies found that about 55 to 60 percent of Korean immigrants attended either a Protestant or a Catholic church in South Korea (Hurh and Kim 1990; Min 2000; Park et. al. 1990).

Because of discrimination and even physical violence in their home country, minority religious groups are usually overrepresented among emigrants (Bozorgmehr and Sabagh 2000). Although Protestants and Catholics together make up a little more than one-fourth the population of South Korea, they can hardly be considered a minority group there. In fact, Christians, especially Protestants, currently have more influence in South Korea than Buddhists do, as they have a higher socioeconomic status and more financial resources, resulting in larger donations to religious institutions. Thus the minority-discrimination hypothesis is not helpful to understanding why more Christians in South Korea decide to move to the United States.

The overrepresentation of Christians among Korean immigrants in New York City, as well as in other Korean communities, and the severe underrepresentation of Buddhists can be explained by the following factors. First, most Korean immigrants have come from South Korea's urban and middle class, in which Christians are overrepresented. For example, a pre-departure survey of the 1986 cohort of Korean emigrants conducted in Seoul during their visa interview found that about 55 percent of the respondents resided in Seoul, even though only one-fourth of the total Korean population lives there (Park and Cho 1995, 31). That is, there are more Christians in Seoul and other large Korean cities. Second, more young people in Korea are Christians, and more Korean immigrants are younger. Third, aside from their class, urban or rural background, and age, Christians are more apt to immigrate to the United States than Buddhists or Confucians because the United States is known to be a Christian country.

Table 3.4 also shows that the number of Korean Protestant immigrants rose by 11 percent, from 48 percent in Korea to 59 percent in New York, and the number of Buddhist immigrants fell by 5 percent, from 13 percent to 8 percent. These figures suggest that since migrating, many Buddhist and atheist immigrants have converted to Protestantism. Because Korean Protestant churches serve a number of practical functions, such as orientation help for immigrants, fellowship, and Korean-language education, it is difficult for Korean immigrants, especially those Korean immigrants who came to the United States in the 1970s and earlier, to survive without participating in a Korean church (Hurh and Kim 1990; Kim and Kim 2001; Kwon et al. 1997; Min 1992). Even now, the Korean church still is the most important Korean ethnic organization providing social, social service, and cultural services, although many other nonreligious ethnic organizations now offer similar services.

While the provision by Korean churches of communal bonds has contributed to the increase in the Korean community's Christian population, the large number of Korean Protestant churches, caused by the oversupply of Korean pastors, also has contributed to the large increase in the number of Korean Protestant immigrants. The presence of many Korean Protestant churches is the main reason why they have been able to absorb far more non-Christian Korean immigrants than the Korean Catholic churches could, although both Korean Protestant and Catholic churches provide similar social, social service, and cultural services. The oversupply of ministers in Korea, caused by denominational schisms and the subsequent surplus of theological colleges in Korea, has contributed to oversupply of pastors in the Korean community in the United States, as well as in other overseas Korean communities (Han 1994).[1] The many Korean Protestant pastors have led to the exceptionally large number of Korean Protestant churches. A Korean pastor can easily start a new church with a small number of families, mostly his relatives and friends who have been attending another church, which in turn leads to the great number of Korean immigrant churches (Shin and Park 1988). To survive, each new church needs to attract more members, including non-Christian Koreans. Moreover, since most Korean Protestant churches emphasize evangelism as the central component of Christian life, they try to bring more and more non-Protestant Koreans to their churches. By contrast, most Korean Catholic churches are liberal and do not emphasize converting non-Catholics to Catholicism as an important aspect of Christian life. Moreover, Korean Catholic immigrants in New York can establish a new Korean Catholic community only with the approval of the Brooklyn and Manhattan dioceses. As a result, New York has no small Korean Catholic churches, which is another reason why Korean Catholic churches have been able to absorb only a small number of non-Christian Korean immigrants.

I should also note that Buddhists or atheists in Korea can convert to Protestantism or Catholicism rather easily, for the following two reasons. First, Koreans, unlike Asian Indians, have not experienced serious regional, political, or social conflicts caused by religion. Although many Buddhists are very critical of Korean Protestants' aggressive evangelizing efforts, they have not had gone to war with them. Second, Korean Protestants, Catholics, and Buddhists all share Confucian social norms and shamanistic beliefs (R. Kim 2006; Yoon 2002, 102–3). Many Korean Protestants or Catholics in both South Korea and the United States have Buddhist or atheist parents (Korean Christian Institute for the Study of Justice and Development 1982, 54), so some Korean immigrants are affiliated with both a Korean Christian church and a Buddhist temple (Kwon 2003).

## Religious Institutions in the Korean Community and Their Denominational Affiliations

### Protestant Churches

*The 2006 Korean Churches Directory of NY* lists 564 Korean Protestant churches located in the New York / New Jersey metropolitan area. Because some recently established Korean churches were not listed in the directory, the number may actually be close to 600. Nearly 600 churches serving the population of 200,000 Korean Americans in the New York / New Jersey area translate into one church for about every 330 Koreans. Sixty percent of the 200,000 Korean Americans in the New York / New Jersey area are Protestants, so the average membership of Korean Protestant churches is approximately 200. No other immigrant community in New York or in any other city has such a large number of religious organizations.

In addition, there are about forty other Korean Christian organizations and about thirty Korean Christian/theological schools in the New York / New Jersey area. Korean Christian organizations include the Council of Korean Churches of Greater New York, an umbrella organization of Korean churches in the area, and the Korean Youth Center of New York, a youth center established 1991 and run by the Council of Korean Churches. Both organizations have offices in the Korean business district in Flushing. The (Korean) YWCA of Queens (Young Women's Christian Association of Queens) is the oldest and the most important social service agency in the Korean community. It has a youth center, a school for the elderly, a Korean children's choir, and a Korean women's choir. Although the YWCA also serves non-Korean immigrants and their children in the neighborhood in Queens, as of 2004, more than 80 percent of its clients were Koreans.

About 130 Korean churches are located in Flushing and Bayside where Korean immigrants are heavily concentrated. Because many Korean churches have vans to pick up worshippers, Korean church buildings and church vans with Korean-language signs can be seen in almost every neighborhood in Flushing and Bayside. Even Korean immigrants in Long Island, Westchester, and many other suburban areas in New Jersey can find a Korean church not far from their home. The church vans pick up elderly Koreans and others who have no cars, making it easy for Korean immigrants, compared with Indian Hindu immigrants, to participate in Korean religious organizations.

According to table 3.5, exactly half of Korean immigrant churches in New York (282 to 564) are Presbyterian, fewer than in South Korea. But since almost all large Korean immigrant churches are Presbyterian churches, Presbyterians seem to comprise the majority of Korean Protestant immigrants in New York, much as in South Korea.[2] By number alone, Korean Presbyterian churches in the United States have an important position in the Presbyterian denomination in the United States, which is a small denomination relative to other Protestant denominations, such as the Methodists and Baptists. Methodist and Baptist churches are the second and third most popular denominations in New York's Korean community. Korean Protestant churches in this area also include many other denominations, including the Full Gospel, Assembly of God, Salvation Army, and Seventh Adventists. A Full Gospel church in Seoul (the Yoido Full Gospel Church), a Pentecostal church founded by its charismatic leader, Yong Ki Cho, is the largest church in the world, with about 70,000 members in 2000 (Cho 2002, 8). The Korean Full Gospel church in Flushing has about 4,000 members and was the largest Korean Protestant church in the New York / New Jersey area as of 2006.

Several scholars have studied the religious aspects of transnational linkages between home and host cities (Ebaugh and Chafetz 2000; Levitt 1999, 2001, 2007; McAlister 1998), but few studies of contemporary immigrant groups' religious practices have examined in detail immigrant churches' denominational linkages to churches in the home country (the exceptions are Levitt 2004 and Yang 2002). Whereas the denominational hierarchies of Catholic and even Eastern Ortho-

TABLE 3.5

*Denominational Affiliations of*
*Korean Immigrant Protestant Churches in Tristate Area*

|  | Number | % |
|---|---|---|
| PRESBYTERIAN CHURCHES | 282 | 50 |
| 1. KAPC (Korean American Presbyterian Church) | 85 | 16 |
| 2. KPCA (Korean Presbyterian Church in America) | 63 | 11 |
| 3. **PCUSA (United Presbyterian Church in the United States of America)** | 46 | 8 |
| 4. **RCA (Reformed Church in America)** | 16 | 3 |
| 5. **PCA (Presbyterian Church in America)** | 12 | 2 |
| 6. Other Korean Presbyterian denominations or denominations not reported | 60 | 11 |
| NON-PRESBYTERIAN CHURCHES | 281 | 50 |
| 1. **United Methodist Church (UMC)** | 50 | 9 |
| 2. Korean Methodist Church (KMC) | 23 | 4 |
| 3. **Assemblies of God (AG)** | 37 | 7 |
| 4. Korean Evangelical Holiness Church of America (KEHCA) | 22 | 4 |
| 5. **Southern Baptist Convention (SBC)** | 27 | 5 |
| 6. Other denominations, independent, or denomination not reported | 123 | 19 |
| ALL KOREAN IMMIGRANT PROTESTANT CHURCHES | 564 | 100 |

Source: Council of Korean Churches of Greater New York, *2006 Korean Churches Directory of New York.*

Note: American denominations are in boldface.

dox immigrant churches are automatically determined, the Protestant immigrant churches have more flexibility in deciding their denominations. Therefore, to understand the degree of continuation or transformation of homeland religious practices in the United States, we must examine how immigrant churches are linked to home-country denominations.

Table 3.5 provides information about the denominational affiliations of Korean immigrant churches in the tristate area (New York, New Jersey, and Connecticut) based on *The 2006 Korean Churches Directory of New York.* Eighty-five of the 282 Korean Presbyterian churches in the area (30%) are affiliated with KAPC (the Korean American Presbyterian Church). KAPC is an independent overseas

Korean denomination, established in 1978, that follows the theological line of the GAPCK, a very conservative and the largest Presbyterian denomination in Korea. In Korea, the senior pastor's theological school determines the church's denomination.[3] Since most of the KAPC's senior pastors graduated from the theological school in Korea established by the GAPCK, its independent denomination, the KAPC, follows the theological line of its mother association in Korea. The KAPC is the largest Presbyterian denomination in the Korean immigrant community in the United States. Another sixty-three Korean Presbyterian churches in New York are affiliated with the KPCA (the Korean Presbyterian Church in America), another Korean independent Presbyterian denomination. It is closely related to the PCK, the second largest Presbyterian denomination in Korea. It was established in 1976 by the Korean pastors in the United States who graduated from the PCK's Presbyterian Theological School in Korea.[4]

Forty-six Korean Presbyterian churches (16%) in the area are affiliated with the PCUSA (the Presbyterian Church in the United States of America), a mainline Presbyterian association, and sixteen Korean Presbyterian churches (6%) belong to the Reformed Church in America, a conservative Presbyterian association that originated in the Netherlands. Twelve Korean Presbyterian churches in New York are affiliated with the Presbyterian Churches in America, a very small and conservative U.S. Presbyterian association. Many other Korean Presbyterian churches in New York are affiliated with several small Presbyterian denominations in Korea.

Seventy-four Korean churches in the area are Methodist, 12 percent of all Korean churches. The majority of them (50/74 = 68%) are affiliated with the United Methodist Church, the major U.S. Methodist and a mainline denomination. The remaining Korean Methodist churches are affiliated with the Korean Methodist Church, the dominant Methodist denomination in South Korea. Korean Methodist churches in the United States affiliated with the KMC make up one of the denomination's special North American districts, which sends its delegates to the annual conference held in Korea. Many other Korean immigrant churches in New York are affiliated with several small Presbyterian denominations in Korea. Following the Korean tradition, all Korean Methodist immigrant churches have elders, although the United Methodist Church does not.

Thirty-seven Korean immigrant churches in New York are affiliated with the Assemblies of God (AG), a conservative U.S. denomination. Influenced by the Presbyterian Church, the KAG has an eldership system, which the AG does not, although it permits the system for Korean immigrant churches affiliated with the denomination. As a result, some Korean churches affiliated with the AG formally recognize elders, but others do not. About fifty other non-Presbyterian Korean churches in New York are affiliated with two other major conservative denominations, the Korean Evangelical Holiness Church of America (KEHCA) and the

Southern Baptist Convention (SBC). The KEHCA is another semi-independent Korean Protestant association that follows the theological line of the home denomination (KEHC). All Korean Baptist churches in New York are affiliated with the Southern Baptist Convention, a major U.S. denomination. The Association of Korean Baptist Churches (AKBC) in Korea has adopted the ordained-deacon system, comparable to the eldership system for Presbyterian churches, although some Baptist churches in Korea have elders.

I asked a few pastors of Korean Baptist and Assemblies of God churches with elders why their churches kept the eldership system in violation of the U.S. denominations' rules. They told me that without the eldership system they would have difficulty maintaining their churches. First, without formally recognizing the elder position, their churches could not attract new members who were already ordained as elders in Korea or Korean Presbyterian churches in the United States.[5] Second, they argued that through their strict adherence to Christian norms and rules, the elders could serve as role models for other church members. Third, and most important, without the elders' devotion to their churches in time and money, their churches could not function, much less grow. An analysis of data based on a national sample of Korean Presbyterians supports this explanation. Kim and Kim (2001) show that Korean elders attend church more frequently, spend more time on each Sunday service, and contribute more money than do nonelders.[6]

Most Korean immigrant churches in New York and in other Korean communities are theologically conservative evangelical churches. Evangelical Christians believe in the inerrancy of the Bible, the divinity and resurrection of Jesus Christ, and the importance of evangelism (Hunter 1983, 19–42). Korean Protestant immigrants and congregations also are theologically more conservative than American Protestants. In a survey of Korean pastors in Los Angeles conducted in the early 1980s, 56 percent of the sixty-four respondents described themselves as evangelical, and another 30 percent described themselves as conservative (Dearman 1982, 169). The heavily evangelical orientation of Korean Protestant immigrants is reflected, too, in their regular participation in a congregation as the essence of Christian life. The Korean immigrant churches affiliated with the three liberal denominations—the PCUSA, UMC, and KMC—are more liberal than the other Korean immigrant churches, even though some Korean churches affiliated with these liberal denominations and many of their members describe themselves as evangelical. For example, in the 1997/1998 Racial Ethnic Presbyterian Panel Studies, 26 percent of the Korean PCUSA church respondents agreed that "the Bible as the literally inerrant Word of God and a single guide for faith and secular matters," compared with about 10 percent of African American and white Presbyterians (Kim and Kim 2001, 86). Moreover, 60 percent of the Korean respondents cited as "essential" three items pertaining to their personal relations with God: "studying the Bible regularly," "spending time in prayer," and attending church regularly," the highest percentage of the four racial ethnic groups (Kim and Kim 2001, 86). Since Korean churches affiliated with the PCUSA are more liberal than most other Korean immigrant churches, Korean immigrant churches as a whole are more conservative and more evangelical than these statistics indicate.

The importance of Christians and Christian churches to New York's Korean community is made clear in the Korean ethnic media. The Korean Christian Broadcasting Network, an FM subcarrier radio station, was established in Manhattan in 1990 mainly for Christian missionary activities and is largely supported by donations from Korean Christian immigrants and Korean churches in the New York / New Jersey area. It airs Korean pastors' sermons and hymns, along with news and classical music, to an audience in the tristate area, twenty-four hours a day. Korean immigrants must buy a special receiver to listen to the subleased Christian station, and in 2000, approximately 40,000 Korean families in the tristate area subscribed to the station, which indicates the significance of Christianity to the Korean community. In addition, the Korean Christian TV System of New York, established in 1999, airs Korean pastors' sermons and choirs singing hymns for the Korean Christian population in the New York / New Jersey area through the main Korean cable channel (Channel 76) for one hour (11 to 12 pm) every night and for an additional hour on Friday (8 to 9 am) and Sunday (2 to 3 pm). The Korean cable channel (Channel 76) itself replays tapes of selected Korean churches' Sunday worship services for six hours on Sunday. The cable channel covers New York City, Bergen County in New Jersey, and Westchester County in New York. Many Korean churches pay fees to the Korean Christian radio and TV stations and the cable TV channel to publicize their pastors' sermons to the Korean Christian population.

### Catholic Churches

In January 2008, there were twenty-five Korean Catholic communities in the New York / New Jersey area. Only three—one in Flushing, another in the Bronx, and the third in Fort Lee, New Jersey—are physically independent Korean parishes, with the others being Korean Catholic communities within multiethnic Catholic parishes. In proportion to the Korean Catholic population, the number of Korean Catholic churches is much smaller than that of Korean Protestant churches. The reason is that while Korean Protestants can establish a church independent of the denominational hierarchy, Korean Catholics must have permission from the local Catholic diocese to start a parish or a Catholic community. Therefore, there is no small Korean Catholic community comparable in size to many small Korean churches. In fact, the largest Korean Christian church in New York is a Korean Catholic parish with about six thousand registered members.

In the "market" situation (Finker and Stark 1988, 1992), Korean Protestant churches compete with other churches to bring more Koreans to their churches through various programs. But Korean Catholic churches do not compete with other Korean Catholic churches. Korean Protestant churches, heavily evangelical, try to proselytize other Koreans partly for theological reasons and also to increase their revenues. Korean Protestant immigrants donate much money to their church, much more than white American Protestants and Korean Catholics do.

By contrast, Korean Catholic churches do not have to compete with other Korean churches because they send donations made by church members to the Brooklyn diocese, which pays their expenses, including the salaries for the priests and other staff members. Korean priests even encourage their members to attend mass in other Catholic congregations, including non-Korean congregations, when convenient. Thus Korean Catholic immigrants often go to other Korean Catholic churches for Sunday mass to meet their friends or relatives there. Unlike Korean Protestant churches, Korean Catholic churches do not publicize their own churches or the Korean Catholic community as a whole through either the media or their own newsletters. Nor do they use vans to pick up members from their homes.[7] Moreover, since they do not compete to bring in more members, Korean Catholic churches in New York spend more time engaging in various joint and cooperative activities. For example, each year Korean Catholics celebrate Korean Saints Day together in one church. In 1979 the largest Korean Catholic church in New York established a credit union, which has turned into a large banking system with eight full-time employees and assets of $8 million as of 2008. The approximately 3,500 members of the credit union include members of this church as well as those of other Korean Catholic communities. This kind of joint enterprise is unimaginable for Korean Protestant churches, each of which concentrates on its own programs to attract more members.

### Buddhist Temples

In the 1970s and 1980s, many Korean Buddhists in the New York / New Jersey area went to a Korean Protestant or a Korean Catholic church because there were few Korean temples. At that time, Korean Buddhists had difficulty establishing temples because of a shortage of priests, but since the early 1990s some Korean Buddhists have come to the United States to build temples for Korean immigrants. Also, a number of Korean priests who came to the United States for religious studies at universities on the East Coast served Korean temples in the area on the weekends. As a result, as of November 2004, the number of Korean

Buddhist temples in the New York / New Jersey area had increased to twenty-seven. All but two Korean Buddhist temples belong to the Chogye Order, the main Buddhist denomination in South Korea, and the other two are Won Buddhism, a Korean nationalist Buddhist denomination founded by Sot'aesan in South Korea in 1916 (B. Kim 2001).

As the number of Korean Buddhist temples rose, so did the number of Korean immigrants attending Korean temples. In some cases, Korean Buddhist immigrants who converted to Protestantism returned to Buddhism when they found a temple. Other Korean immigrants who attended a Korean Protestant church in South Korea and the United States converted to Buddhism for different reasons.[8]

Despite the significant increase in the number of Buddhist temples, many former Korean Buddhists continue to attend a Korean Protestant or a Catholic church, and still others do not belong to any religious institution. One main reason for the temples' difficulty in attracting Koreans is their location far from Korean enclaves. Most Korean temples are located in suburban New Jersey and upstate New York, fifteen or more miles away from Flushing and other Korean communities in Queens. The other reason is their lack of social services and secular educational programs for Korean immigrants and their children. Only two of the twenty-seven Korean Buddhist temples in the New York / New Jersey area have a Korean-language school, compared with more than one-fourth of the approximately six hundred Korean churches. Some Korean children of Buddhist immigrants also attend a Korean church to be with their Christian friends.

As previously pointed out, Buddhists in South Korea generally have a lower socioeconomic status than Christians. As a result of selective migration, however, Buddhists in the Korean immigrant community have a similar or even higher socioeconomic status than Christians (Hurh and Kim 1990; Kwon 2003). Members of Korean Buddhists temples in New Jersey and upstate New York include many Korean employees of overseas branches of major Korean firms, which are heavily concentrated in Bergen County, New Jersey. Women members of Korean immigrant temples outnumber men more than they do in Korean immigrant churches. The reason is that devotional work in a temple involving bowing down to the Buddha was traditionally considered women's work (Suh 2004, 136). In both South Korea and the United States, Korean women usually pray in and donate money to a temple for their husbands and children as well as themselves.

A Korean-language monthly magazine for Buddhists, entitled *Mizu Hyundae Bulgyo* (*Modern Buddhism in America*), has circulated in the New York area since 1989. Korean Buddhist leaders also started a Korean Buddhist television station in 2002, which airs a Buddhist program for one hour per week on Saturday between 8 and 9 in the morning on New York City's Korean cable television channel (Channel 76). Korean Buddhists in New York hold an annual parade in Manhattan on April 8 to celebrate Buddha's birthday. Many non-Korean Buddhists, including whites, march in the parade. Chinese Buddhists have a parade in Chinatown on the same day.[9]

One of the two Won Buddhism temples, Won Buddhism of America, located in Flushing, has about three hundred members. Founded in 1976, it has a *bophe* (worship service) every Sunday and a Korean school that is open for three hours on Saturday. More than a hundred children are registered in the Korean school each semester, which teaches the Korean language and history as well as *taekwondo* and *samulnori* (a traditional Korean dance/music). The principal indicated that even some Korean church members send their children to the Saturday Korean school. This temple holds a traditional Korean children's folk festival at Flushing Meadow Park on May 5 on Korea's Children's Day. It also opened a social service center in 2007, which offers English-language and yoga classes and translation and interpretation services for elderly Koreans.

### Indian Immigrants' Religious Affiliations

Table 3.6 shows Indian respondents' religions in India before their migration and in New York during the interview. The data on Hindus, Sikhs, and Jains are based on the results of a telephone survey of a random sample of twenty prominent Indian names listed in New York City's 2004 telephone directory. Most Sikh men have the surname Singh, meaning "lion," and most Sikh women's surname is Kaur, meaning "princess." The 2005 survey sample included two hundred Singh households, and thus fifty-one Indian Sikh respondents. The survey eliminated Indian Muslims and Christians because we could not separate the two groups' formal religious names from other Muslims or other people with Christian names. Using their own contacts, three Indian students interviewed forty-two Indian Muslims and thirty Indian Christians in the spring of 2006.

Because members of Indian religious minority groups do not have common Indian names, we could not determine Indian immigrants' religious affiliations using survey data based on an Indian surname-sampling technique. Thus, depending on which surnames we selected, we might have oversampled the members of a particular religious group. Consequently, the figures in table 3.6 cannot be used for Indian immigrants' religious affiliations in India and New York City, but they do tell us two important things about their religions.

First, almost all Indian immigrants have a religion. Even if we eliminate those Muslim and Christian respondents who were interviewed through personal con-

TABLE 3.6

Indian Immigrant Respondents' Self-Reported
Religions in India and New York

| | In India | | In New York | |
|---|---|---|---|---|
| | Number | % | Number | % |
| Hinduism | 148 | 53 | 147 | 53 |
| Sikhism | 51 | 18 | 50 | 18 |
| Jainism | 15 | 5 | 13 | 5 |
| Islam | 38 | 14 | 42 | 15 |
| Christianity | 25 | 9 | 25 | 9 |
| No religion | 2 | 1 | 2 | 1 |
| Total | 279 | 100 | 279 | 100 |

Source: 2005 and 2006 surveys of Chinese, Indian, and Korean
Immigrants in New York City.

tacts, all but two of the other respondents selected using the Indian surname
sampling subscribed to a religion in both India and New York City. The tendency
of almost all Indian immigrants to have a religion reflects the trend of the general
population in India (see table 2.1). According to table 3.1, 26 percent of Korean
immigrants in New York City did not have a religion in Korea, which dropped to
19 percent in New York.

Second, the data indicate that few Indian immigrants changed or dropped
their premigrant religion when they arrived in New York, in contrast to the many
Korean atheist or Buddhist immigrants who converted to Protestantism after
they migrated. Korean Buddhist or atheist immigrants can go to a Korean Protestant church with no difficulty because religion in Korea is not a marker of a subethnic boundary and because Korean Protestant churches actively try to recruit
non-Christian members. Indian immigrants, however, have difficulty converting
to other religions because for them it is like changing their family names. Moreover, Indian Hindus can remain Hindus, regardless of whether they are actively
religious, because the religious boundaries are very loose; they do not have to
make many commitments to remain Hindu. According to results of the 2007
U.S. Religious Landscape Survey, 84 percent of Hindus retained their childhood
religion, the highest retention rate among all major religious groups (Pew Forum
on Religion and Public Life 2008, 30). Second- and 1.5-generation Indian Hindus
accounted for most of the 16 percent of Hindu respondents who had converted
to other religions (8%) or had no religion.

In 2003, Gillemina Jasso, Douglass Massey, Mark Rosenzweig, and James Smith conducted a large survey of 8,573 new immigrants (Guillermina et al. 2003). The survey's data, which are publicly available, includes a large Indian subsample (752), and thus the findings give a fairly accurate picture of Indian immigrants' religious distribution. Table 3.7 is based on 720 Indian immigrants' responses to the religious affiliation question. About two-thirds of the Indian immigrant respondents reported that they were Hindus, a substantially smaller proportion than that in India (81% in 2001, as shown in table 2.1). Because minority groups are usually under greater pressure to leave their home countries, this significant drop in the Hindu immigrant population is not surprising.

Although Christians make up less than 2 percent of India's population (see table 2.1), about 12 percent of immigrants from India are Christian, mainly because of their higher educational level.[10] Nearly half of Indian Christian immigrants are Protestants. More Indian Christians than Hindus moved to the United States because they were subjected to minor discrimination in India and because they, especially Indian Christian women, had skills, such as medical skills, that were marketable in the United States (Kurien 1998). Another 12 percent of Indian respondents were Sikhs, who comprise less than 2 percent of the population in India (see table 2.1) but, like Christians, are overrepresented among Indian immigrants in the United States. Muslim immigrants from India accounted for only 5 percent of all Indian immigrants, compared with 13 percent of Muslims in the Indian population. By contrast, Jains comprise a much larger proportion of Indian immigrants (2%) than that of the population in India (0.4%). The sub-

TABLE 3.7

*Religious Affiliation of Indian Respondents in*
*2003 New Immigrant Survey*

| Religion | Number | % |
| --- | --- | --- |
| Hinduism | 487 | 67.6 |
| Christianity | 85 | 11.8 |
| Sikhism | 84 | 11.7 |
| Islam | 37 | 5.1 |
| Jainism | 12 | 1.7 |
| Buddhism | 2 | 0.3 |
| Other religion | 1 | 0.1 |
| No religion | 12 | 1.7 |
| Total | 720 | 100.0 |

Source: 2003 New Immigrant Survey conducted by Gillemina
Jasso, Douglass Massey, Mark Rosenzweig, and James Smith.

stantially lower-class background of Muslims and the much higher-class background of Jains than Hindus seem to explain their lower and higher proportions of Indian immigrants.[11]

Assuming that Hindus are 66 percent of the approximately 520,000 Indian Americans (the 2005 Current Population Survey) in the New York / New Jersey Metropolitan Area, about 343,000 Indian Hindus, including Caribbean Indian Hindus,[12] lived in the area in 2005. When Bangladeshi and Nepali Hindus are included, the total number of Hindus in the New York / New Jersey area may be as high as 350,000. The Council of Hindu Temples of North America lists thirty Hindu temples in New York and New Jersey in 2004, meaning one temple per 12,000 Hindus, compared with one Korean church per 200 Korean Protestant immigrants in the New York / New Jersey area. These Hindu temples (a small number) are concentrated in areas with a large Indian population, such as Flushing, Woodside / Jackson Heights, and Richmond Hill in New York, and Jersey City in New Jersey. Indian immigrants who do not live in Indian enclaves therefore must have to drive to a Hindu temple. Indeed, many Hindu immigrants complain that they cannot go to a temple frequently because none is close to their home.

Most Indian nurses are Christians, and because nursing is considered a lower-level profession in India, many nurses from Kerala and other southern states immigrated to the United States. They accounted for many of the foreign medical professionals who were admitted to meet the shortage of medical professionals in the United States in the late 1960s and 1970s (George 1998, 271; Williams 1988, 104). When they became naturalized citizens, the Keralan medical professionals and their spouses who came in the earlier period were able to bring their relatives to the United States, and many, like other Indian medical professionals, settled in New York City.

According to a few Indian Christian informants, there are more than two hundred Indian immigrant churches in New York City, Long Island / upstate New York, and New Jersey. These include churches under the aegis of the Indian Orthodox Church and St. Thomas Catholic Church, and various Protestant denominations, including the Assembly of God. Many Indian Protestant churches in New York are Pentecostal. Although the majority of Indian Protestant immigrants are Pentecostals or evangelicals, unlike Korean evangelical immigrants, they do not actively engage in evangelism. An Indian Protestant immigrant told me that Indian Protestants' sensitivity to Hindus' aversion to conversion and evangelical activities in India contributed to their inactivity in evangelism.

The Pentecostal Youth Fellowship of America is an active young Indian Pentecostal organization in the New York / New Jersey area. According to its website, forty-one Indian Pentecostal churches are associated with the organization.

As I discuss in chapter 7, younger Koreans in New York and other cities usually belong to English-language congregations in Korean immigrant churches, some of which are independent of immigrant churches and a few of which have turned into Pan-East Asian or multiracial congregations (Eckland 2006). Younger Indian Protestants, though, usually belong to Indian immigrant congregations that hold intergenerational English-language worship services.

Largely as a result of the British colonization of Punjab, Sikhs from Punjab established major diasporic communities in Africa, Great Britain, and North America in the nineteenth and twentieth centuries (Bhachu 1985; Singh and Thandi 1999), and most of the Indian immigrants in California in the early twentieth century were Sikh farmers (Gibson 1989; Jensen 1988, 41; Leonard 1992). Most of Sikh immigrants in New York City after 1965 came from Punjab, where Sikhs dominate the population. The anti-Sikh sentiment that followed their bloody attempt to establish an independent state in 1984 pushed many Sikhs to migrate to the United States. Assuming that Indian immigrants in New York contains the same proportion of Sikh immigrants (12%) as the Indian national sample, as of 2005 there were more than 60,000 Sikh immigrants (12 percent × 520,000 Indian immigrants) in the New York / New Jersey Metropolitan Area.

According to a Sikh American leader, a group of sixteen Sikh immigrants established a *gurdwara* (the Sikh version of a temple) using the basement of a Protestant church in Richmond Hill in 1969, and in 1971, they purchased an abandoned church for a *gurdwara*. In 1972, they established the Sikh Cultural Society, the first *gurdwara* in New York City, in Richmond Hill. This is the largest *gurdwara* in the area, with approximately 6,000 members. As of 2004, the New York / New Jersey Metropolitan Area had twelve other *gurdwaras*, including five in Queens and four in New Jersey. The Sikh leader told me that only about 20 percent of Sikh immigrants are orthodox Sikhs who strictly follow the religious rules, such as wearing a turban. The other 80 percent are liberal Sikhs who, like himself, do not wear a turban and do not comply with many other Sikh religious rules. He reported that all *gurdwaras* are controlled by orthodox Sikhs and that in many *gurdwaras*, there are some tensions between orthodox and liberal Sikhs. The association of *gurdwaras* in the New York / New Jersey area holds an annual Sikh parade in Manhattan in April, while the Sikh Cultural Society has its parade in Queens in November.

The New York / New Jersey Metropolitan Area is home to the greatest number of South Asian immigrants in the United States. Moreover, since about 5 percent of Indian immigrants and most of the Pakistani and Bangladeshi immigrants (95 percent and 83 percent, respectively) are Muslims, the New York / New Jersey area has the country's largest South Asian Muslim population, along with Los Angeles, Washington, and Detroit, which also has a high concentration of Muslim immigrants. The South Asian Muslim population in the New York area will continue to increase, as the immigration from Pakistan and Bangladesh to New York City has exploded in recent years.

According to my Bangladeshi research assistant, there were about 110 mosques in the New York / New Jersey area as of January 2003, with about half for South Asian Muslims. South Asian Muslims usually have interethnic services for all South Asian Muslims and often other Muslims as well. South Asian mosques usually use Urdu and English for communications and Arabic and English for their worship services. But several mosques are predominantly for Bangladeshi immigrants who speak Bengali instead of Urdu (Mohammad-Arif 2002, 148).

## Korean Immigrants' Frequency of Participation in Religious Institutions

According to the 1997/1998 Queens survey, only two of the 148 Korean Christian (one Protestant and the other Catholic) respondents reported attending a non-Korean church (Min 2000). Other survey studies conducted in large Korean communities indicate that almost all Korean Christians belong to a Korean congregation (Hurh and Kim 1990). One main reason for this is that because of the abundance of Korean Protestant pastors, there are more than enough Korean Protestant churches providing Korean immigrants with Korean-language services. Indeed, Korean Protestant churches offer all kinds of programs to attract Korean immigrants.

The other reason is that Koreans speak only one language and their regional differences in culture are almost insignificant (Min 1991, 2001). Not only Filipino and Indian immigrants, but also Chinese immigrants have different languages and places of origin (Min and Kim 2009). According to Fenggang Yang (1999), a Chinese American church in Washington, D.C., has difficulty with its services because of its members' multilingual background and differences in country of origin. But because they speak only one language, Korean immigrants can attend any Korean church and enjoy all kinds of social and cultural programs. And because most Korean immigrants have difficulty with English and every Korean immigrant church offers Korean-language services, it is understandable that Korean immigrants prefer Korean churches to non-Korean churches. Some Korean professional immigrants are fluent in English, but even they, with a few exceptions, attend a Korean church because it offers social services and sociocultural programs that a non-Korean church does not (Hurh and Kim 1990; I. Kim 1981; Kim and Kim 2001; Min 1992).

Korean Christian immigrants in the United States are interesting to researchers not only because almost all of them are affiliated with a Korean church but

TABLE 3.8

*Korean Immigrant Respondents' Frequency of
Participation in Religious Institution*

| | Few Times a Week or Less | Once Every Two Weeks or Less | About Every Week | Twice or More a Week | Total |
|---|---|---|---|---|---|
| Protestants | 8 (5%) | 8 (5%) | 87 (54) | 59 (36%) | 162 (100%) |
| Catholics | 4 (10%) | 5 (13%) | 23 (59%) | 7 (18%) | 39 (100.0) |
| Buddhists and others | 11 (46%) | 7 (29%) | 4 (17%) | 2 (8%) | 24 (100%) |
| Total | 23 (10%) | 20 (9%) | 114 (51%) | 68 (30%) | 225 (100.0%) |

Source: 2005 survey of Chinese, Indian, and Korean immigrants in New York City.

also because they attend services very frequently. Table 3.8 shows the frequency of Korean immigrants' participation in religious institutions based on the results of the 2005 New York City survey. Ninety percent of Korean Protestant immigrants go to church at least once a week, with 36 percent going twice or more. Interviews with fifty-six Korean Protestant immigrants revealed a similarly frequent attendance rate, with 90 percent of them going to church at least once a week and 36 percent twice or more a week. Eight of them (14%) said that they went to church almost every morning. According to table 3.8, 77 percent of Korean Catholic immigrants go to church at least once a week, slightly less frequently than Korean Protestants, but far more frequently than American Catholics in general. By contrast, only 25 percent of Buddhist respondents reported going to temple every week.

Korean Protestant immigrants' exceptionally frequent church attendance becomes clearer when compared with that of other non-Korean Protestant groups in the United States. According to the 1997–1999 Racial and Ethnic Presbyterian Panel Studies, 78 percent of Korean Presbyterian respondents attended Sunday worship services every week, compared with 28 percent of white Americans, 34 percent of African Americans, and 49 percent of Latino Presbyterians (Kim and Kim 2001, 82). The 77 percent weekly attendance rate of Korean Catholic immigrants also is much higher than that of American Catholics. The results of a 2004 national survey by the Center for Applied Research in the Apostolate show that only 28 percent of U.S. Catholics went to church at least once a week (Goodstein 2004; see also Gillis 2003, 44).

Previous studies emphasized the psychological and social needs of Korean Protestant immigrants for regular attendance at an ethnic church (Hurh and Kim 1990; Kim and Kim 2001; Min 1992, 2000; Warner 1993, 1062). According to this interpretation, Korean immigrants go to church so often in order to fulfill their psychological needs deriving from their downward social mobility and to fulfill their practical needs for communal bonds and social services. This explanation, based only on Korean immigrants' psychological and social needs, is not logical because other Asian Christian immigrant groups with similar adjustment difficulties go to church much less frequently than Koreans do. For example, according to results of the same 2005 survey of Chinese immigrants in New York City, only about 45 percent of Chinese Christian immigrants attended church once a week or more often.

The results of my interviews with Korean Christian immigrants do not support the view that they go to church more often in the United States than they did in South Korea mainly because of their adjustment difficulties. I asked forty-one of the fifty-six Korean Protestant respondents who were Christians in Korea about their attendance at services in both South Korea and the United States. Forty-two percent of them went to church more often here, and 26 percent went less often, with the remainder (26%) attending with the same frequency. Those who attended services here less frequently pointed to long hours of work as the main reason for their inability to attend church as often as they did in Korea. Yet most of those who went to church more frequently here were older respondents who had lived here for a long time. Thus, their more frequent attendance at church services seems to have been caused mainly by their growing older rather than by their immigration situation.

In addition, as we have seen, Protestant churches in Korea emphasize going to church as the central component of Christian life. Pastors in Korean immigrant churches, mostly educated and trained in Korea, likewise emphasize regular attendance at church, following the Korean tradition. Results of the Social Statistics Survey 1991, conducted in Korea based on a national sample, reveal that 76 percent of Protestants aged 15 and older in South Korea went to church at least once a week and that 35 percent went twice or more a week (Korea National Statistical Office 1992, 301). The results of the same social survey in Korea also show that 60 percent of Catholics went to church at least once a week and 19 percent went twice or more (Korea National Statistical Office 1992, 301). The results of survey studies of Korean Christian immigrants, including my 2005 survey in New York City, show slightly more frequent attendance rates than those for Christians in Korea, probably because the samples did not include children and adolescents. Thus Korean Protestant and Catholic immigrants' exceptionally frequent attendance at church services reflects more on their religious practices in South Korea than on their adaptation to the immigration situation. Being more liberal in both theology and social issues, Korean Catholics go to church less frequently than do Korean Protestants in both South Korea and the United States. But their attendance rate is very high compared with U.S. Catholics, who are far more congregationally oriented than Catholics in South and Central America.

The exceptionally high rate of Korean Protestants' church attendance in both South Korea and the United States is closely related to their strong belief that regular attendance is essential to being a real Christian. In the 1997–1999 Racial Ethnic Panel Studies, 67 percent of the Korean Presbyterian respondents regarded "attending church regularly" as essential to a good Christian life (Kim and Kim 2001, 82). Much lower proportions of white (32%), African American (39%), and Latino (52%) Presbyterian respondents considered regular church attendance to be essential to a Christian life. The results of my interviews with Korean Protestant immigrants and pastors strongly supported their conviction that regular attendance is essential to being a good Christian. Referring to the results of the 1997–1999 Racial and Ethnic Panel Survey, I told a small group of Korean Protestant immigrants that more than two-thirds of white American Christians believe they can be good Christians without going in church regularly. I then asked them whether they agreed, and all but one strongly disagreed to the view. Choong Sik Kim, a Korean Presbyterian elder in his sixties, made the following comment:

> White American Christians misinterpret the Bible. According to the Bible, we Christians should make God happy by regularly holding services in a congregation. In a communist country they have no freedom to have an open religious meeting. Therefore, people in a communist country may be able to become good Christians by practicing religion at home without regularly participating in a congregation. But we who live in the United States have no excuse for not participating in a congregation regularly because we have full religious freedom here.

## Indian Immigrants' Participation in Religious Institutions

As expected, Indian Hindu respondents were found to participate in temple activities much less frequently than Korean Protestants did. Only 35 percent of the Hindu respondents to the 2005 survey reported that they went to temple at least once a week, while two-thirds said they attended from a few times a year to once every two weeks. The results of interviews with the fifty-nine Hindu informants conducted in 2001 show an even lower rate, with 24 percent of them going to temple at least once a week. Most Indian Hindus visit a temple a few or several times a year, whenever the religious organization has a cultural function. Most

**TABLE 3.9**

*Indian Immigrant Respondents' Frequency of*
*Participation in Religious Institutions*

| | Few Times a Year or Less | Once Every Two Weeks or Less | About Every Week | Twice or More a Week | Total |
|---|---|---|---|---|---|
| Hindus | 39 (27%) | 56 (38%) | 47 (32%) | 5 (3%) | 147 (100%) |
| Indians with other religions[a] | 11 (9%) | 30 (23%) | 49 (38%) | 38 (30%) | 128 (100%) |
| Total | 50 (18%) | 86 (31%) | 96 (35%) | 43 (16%) | 275 (100%) |

Source: 2005–2006 surveys of Chinese, Indian, and Korean Immigrants in New York City.

Note: [a]Indian respondents with other religions are Sikhs, Muslims, Christians, and Jains.

Indian Hindus believe they can practice their religion at home without going to temple regularly, as reflected by the popular phrase "god is everywhere."

Some Hindus, however, maintained that they could concentrate on their worship better in a temple than at home. For example, Raj Mohan, a 34-year-old Hindu accountant who had lived in the United States for four years, stated,

Q: What are the important reasons you go to temple regularly?

R: For a religious purpose, that is, for peace of mind.

Q: Don't you think you can practice religion at home, too?

R: Of course, I can. But by going to a temple, you can concentrate on your prayer. It is similar to going to a theater to watch movies. We can watch movies at home, but we have to answer the phone, talk with children, and so forth. So we cannot concentrate on watching movies. We can have *pujas* and meditation at home, but many things can disrupt our concentration.

Table 3.9 also shows that non-Hindu Indian respondents, consisting of Sikhs, Muslims, Christians, and Jains, go to a religious institution far more frequently than do Indian Hindus. Sixty-eight percent of them went to the institution at least once a week, with 30 percent going twice or more. As Williams (1988) pointed out, Indian Sikhs and Jains, as well as Indian Christian and Muslim immigrants, use a more congregational style of worship services on Sunday. Their religious institutions also are more similar to American Christian churches than to Indian Hindu temples in that they put more emphasis on fellowship and social services.

Several scholars have suggested that to preserve their ethnicity through religion, Indian Hindu immigrants have become more religious in the United States than they were in India (Carnes and Yang 2004b, 2; Kurien 1998, 2002, 102; Warner 1993, 1062; Williams 1988, 11, 28). No doubt, religion has new meanings for Indian immigrants as well as for other immigrant groups in their new society. Indeed, many Indian immigrants take their children to temple to teach them Indian religious and cultural traditions. In India, Hindu parents do not need to do this because their children can easily learn the Hindu faith and rituals in religious schools and from the media and many other organizations. Indian Hindu immigrants are more conscious of their being Hindu in the United States than in India, with their attendance at temple having a different meaning here.

However, Indian Hindu immigrants' "becoming more religious," in the form of their increased attendance rate at temple, is not supported by results of my interviews. Instead, I found that Indian Hindu immigrants visited a temple in India far more often than they do here. Twenty-seven percent of my Indian Hindu informants reported that they went to temple in India at least once a day, with 42 percent going it at least twice a week. Their two reasons why they could not go as often here as in India were their long hours of work here and the distance of a Hindu temple from their homes. It is easy to visit a temple in India because, as one Hindu woman in her fifties said, "It is located in almost every neighborhood." When I asked how often he visited temple in India compared with here, a Hindu man in his forties, who had come from Tamil Nadu three years earlier, observed,

> In India, I went to temple very often, usually twice or three times a week. It is easy to visit temple there because there are plenty of temples in India, many small temples and some large temples. But I cannot visit temple often here because there are not many temples close to my home. I visit this temple once a year on an important holiday. I cannot come here very often because I live in New Jersey, 65 miles away from this temple. I visit another temple in New Jersey, closer to my home, usually once a month.

To have confidence in the finding regarding Indian Hindus' more frequent visits to temple in India than here, I asked several Hindu priests about it, and they confirmed that Hindus go to temple far more frequently in India than in the United States, mainly because they have easy access to temples there.

Asian Buddhist immigrants also go to temple less frequently than they did in their home countries mainly because there are not many temples here. For example, Chen pointed out that half her Buddhist respondents reduced the number of their temple visits after immigrating because of the temple's greater distance from their home (Chen 2008, 87). The results of a survey study of Muslim immigrants from Iran show that their religious observance as a whole was reduced owing to their "lack of time" and a "facility too far" in the United States (Bozorgmehr and

Sabagh 2000, 174; Sabagh and Bozorgmehr 1994). Iranian Muslim immigrants are a special case because as secular Muslims they chose to immigrate to the United States to escape Iran's Muslim fundamentalist government. As the least observant Muslims in their home country, they would be even less observant in the United States, where it is even more difficult to observe Islamic rituals. But their "lack of time" due to overwork and a "facility too far" here also contributed to their extremely low rate of religious observance (only 5% of the respondents).

# 4  Ethnographic Research on the Shin Kwang Korean Church

IN 1989, I conducted a survey study of the social functions of 131 Korean immigrant churches in New York City. Based on the results, I concluded that Korean immigrant churches play a central role in enhancing Korean immigrants' ethnicity by facilitating their ethnic fellowship and preservation of their cultural traditions (Min 1992). In this chapter I examine the ethnicity functions of Korean immigrant churches based on ethnographic research on the Shin Kwang Church of New York.

## History, Location, and Structure

The Shin Kwang Church of New York opened its doors in October 1985 with a worship service for about thirty Korean immigrants at a park in Yonkers, New York. The church was soon relocated to Queens, an area where many Korean immigrants lived. The church first used a gymnasium in Corona and then rented a white American church in Flushing. In 1989, it bought the land on which it built the current church, the northern end of downtown Bayside. The building was completed in 1992, and the church's twenty-year anniversary was celebrated in 2005 with many activities. The first floor of the approximately 35,000-square-foot building has a huge worship hall and several rooms for the Sunday school, the youth group, and other educational programs, including kindergarten. The basement has a kitchen and a large cafeteria called a *chingyosil* (friendship room). The second floor has several offices and a gymnasium. The third floor houses the senior pastor's office and a few guest rooms for visiting pastors. In addition to the senior pastor, the church has four associate pastors, two of whom are part time, as well as a part-time evangelical pastor (*jondosa*). The church's kindergarten has four full-time teachers.

Most of the members of the Shin Kwang Church are from Bayside and the adjacent northeastern Queens suburban neighborhoods of Little Neck, Oakland Gardens, and Douglaston. These neighborhoods are predominantly white, middle-class neighborhoods with a large Asian immigrant population. In 2000, Asian Americans made up 27 percent ($n = 30,786$) of the population (116,404) of Queens Community District 11, which encompasses these northeastern Queens neighborhoods (New York City Department of City Planning 2004). In 2000, the 23,000 Chinese Americans were the largest Asian American population in this area, and Korean Americans were the second largest group.

This area attracts Chinese and Korean immigrants because it is more suburban than Flushing but close (10 minutes' drive) to the Asian enclaves in Flushing and because it is in New York City's best school district. Many Koreans who live in this area originally settled in Flushing and western Queens and moved here because of its good schools. Over the past ten years, a Korean business district has grown up in downtown Bayside, stretching about four to six blocks in four directions at the intersection of Bell Boulevard and Northern Boulevard. Korean churches have proliferated in Bayside over the past twenty years, many of them moving from Flushing and western Queens. The 2006 (Korean) Churches Directory of New York listed twenty-six churches in Bayside, eight of them opening after 2003.

Most Korean Presbyterian churches in New York are affiliated with two independent Korean denominations that adhere to the theology of the two major Presbyterian denominations in Korea. The Shin Kwang Church, however, is one of the sixteen Korean Presbyterian churches in New York affiliated with the Reformed Church in America, a conservative Presbyterian denomination that originated in the Netherlands and emphasizes John Calvin's theological principles. Even though this church is affiliated with an American Presbyterian denomination, the senior pastor agreed that it is influenced more by the two conservative Presbyterian denominations in Korea. It is a typical Korean evangelical church. According to a church pamphlet, "Our church believes in the inerrancy of the 66 chapters of the Bible, the trinity, and our salvation through our belief in the crucification [sic] of Jesus Christ."

The *danghe* (consistory), which consists of the senior pastor and twelve elders, makes all the important decisions, including hiring the associate pastors. In this way, elders, who retain their position until retirement, exercise a great deal of power and authority in this church. This also is true of most other Korean immigrant churches in the United States, reflecting the strong influence of Korea's Presbyterian churches. Korean immigrant evangelical churches usually are dominated by the senior pastor, with most of the elders supporting him. Thus lay control is weaker in most Korean immigrant churches than in white American churches. But because of his particularly democratic personality, the senior pastor seems to exercise less power and authority at the Shin Kwang Church than at most other conservative Korean immigrant Presbyterian churches.

The Shin Kwang Church begins the main service on Sunday at 11 am, which approximately 350 to 400 adults attend. Approximately 200 adolescents, children, and kindergarteners/preschoolers attend the concurrent services. The church has three additional services on Sunday and two other meetings on weekdays. In addition, the Shin Kwang Church, like most other Korean churches, holds a prayer meeting at 6 am every day. The church operates five buses and five minivans to pick up elderly and other members without cars throughout New York City and Long Island on Sundays, Wednesdays, and Fridays. Several members volunteer to drive these ten church vehicles. Finally, the church operates a kindergarten that is open from Monday through Friday.

The Reverend Jae Hong Han, the senior pastor, is in his early sixties. He attended an undergraduate theological school in Korea,[1] but in 1971, before finishing, he came to the United States and completed his undergraduate education at the Moody Bible Institute. Rev. Han received his master of divinity degree from New Brunswick Theological Seminary in New Jersey and then began a doctor of ministry program in San Francisco. In 1978, before he finished, he accepted a position as a pastor in a Korean immigrant church in San Francisco, and in 1983 he came to New York City to serve as an associate pastor at another Korean church before he became the senior pastor at the Shin Kwang Church.

When I met him for the first time for an interview, Rev. Han described himself as "theologically conservative" but "open-minded in everyday life." After talking with him several times, I realized that this accurately describes both his theological/ministry position and his personality. Theologically conservative, he emphasizes attending services a few times a week, reading the Bible regularly, and evangelizing other people as the necessary tasks of good Christians. As noted earlier, the church holds three more services in addition to the Sunday's main service for adult members. The church has three Bible study meetings, one of which is at 1:30 pm on Sunday. In order to encourage church members, it awards certificates to those members who have read the entire Bible or at least thirteen chapters each month. The church supports Korean missionaries in foreign countries and also has sent its own members abroad for short-term missionary activities. Even though these practices reflect Rev. Han's conservative theological position and evangelical orientation, he is a nice, humble person available to meet with any church member at any time. Because of his informal personality, he is highly respected by his church members.

## Programs and Activities for Fellowship and Ethnic Networks

A number of studies suggest that participation in Korean immigrant churches contributes to Korean ethnicity by increasing ethnic fellowship and networks among church members (Hurh and Kim 1990; I. Kim 1981, 187–207; Kim and Kim 2001; Min 1991, 1992). Ethnographic research on the Shin Kwang Church confirms most of these findings.

A small church consisting of a few dozen families offers its members an opportunity for face-to-face, familylike interactions, which is why the Korean immigrant community has so many small churches (I. Kim 1981; Min 1992). As Illsoo Kim (1981, 198) pointed out, there is a strong connection between the small size of Korean churches and their extended-family function:

> One of the main functions of Korean churches is to provide church members with a "family" atmosphere, which presupposes a small congregation in which everyone knows everyone else and everyone else's business. Through church-centered activities Korean immigrants attempt to cope with their overwhelming sense of alienation from the larger society. The search for a pseudo extended-family through church communities has also caused an increase in the number of small churches.

Compared with small churches, large and even medium-size churches have disadvantages in offering members fellowship and ethnic networks (Min 1992). But the Shin Kwang Church, like other large and medium-size Korean churches, has created mechanisms to enhance fellowship, friendships networks, and familylike ties among church members. At the end of each year, the church gives a copy of the church directory for the coming year to each family. Along with other basic information about the church, the directory includes the home and business phone numbers, addresses, and names of all family members. At the end of Sunday's main worship service, the senior pastor announces important information about the church members, such as weddings, the birth of a new baby, a serious illness, the opening of a business, and a fifty-year wedding anniversary. This information also is included in the weekly report given to each participant on the following Sunday. New members are introduced on their first day at church, and their pictures are posted on the wall near the church's dining hall.

The church provides three services for Korean immigrants on Sunday, beginning at 9 am, 11 am, and 4:30 pm. Approximately 350 to 400 members attend the main, 11 am, service, while about 60 members, mostly teachers of infant and kindergarten groups, Sunday schools, and youth groups (whose services also start at 11 am) and other members who cannot attend the 11 am service, go to the 9 am service. Approximately 90 members, mostly the elders and deacons who attend the main service in the morning, also attend the 4 pm service because they are very religious. In fact, the senior pastor believes that all elders and deacons should attend the Sunday afternoon service, and many also go to the Bible study meeting between 1 and 2 pm and the prayer meeting at 3 pm. The church also offers an English-language service at 1 pm on Sunday for 1.5- and second-generation young adults. About 40 people attend that service. The church has two other meetings in addition to Sunday services: a one-hour service between 8:30 and 9:30 on Wednesday (with about 50 attending) and a prayer meeting at 8:30 on Friday (about 40). Most of those at the Friday prayer meeting stay for

Members of the Shin Kwang Church of New York enjoy fellowship over lunch in the fellowship room after Sunday's main service.

one and a half hours, but some stay longer, with a few or several participants even spending the night in the church. In addition, this church, like most other Korean churches, holds a prayer meeting at 6 am every morning, which about 40 members attend.

The majority of church members attend the church once a week, the Sunday's main service, but many others come twice or more, interacting with other members for several hours weekly. But since most of them also spend long hours at work, they have little time to meet other, nonchurch, Korean friends, which probably strengthens their fellowship and ethnic networks with their church members. The church's free lunch service also enhances the members' fellowship and friendship networks. Church members voluntarily pay for the Sunday lunch on a rotating basis, while the three women's missionary groups rotate in preparing lunch in the cafeteria. The senior pastor reported that more than three hundred members eat lunch at the church every Sunday,[2] which means that most of the attendants at the 11 am service and their children enjoy fellowship over lunch after the service.[3] The lunch always features Korean dishes, with *kimchi* and a beef and radish soup and often Korean rice cakes and other traditional foods donated by a church member who had a wedding, birthday party, or other family event on the preceding Saturday. Adult members usually eat lunch with their spouses and close friends, and the children eat with their own friends.

While eating lunch, the church members usually talk about what happened over the past week. The senior pastor told me that according to the Bible, providing fellowship for members is one of the five major missions of a Christian church (the other four are worship, education, evangelism, and service to others). During the lunch hour, he moves around the cafeteria, shaking hands with members and asking them about what they did during the past week. He is the last person to eat lunch. Because of his kind personality, he is very popular among church members, which is one of the main reasons for the church's growth.

The church's large gymnasium, open seven days a week, has basketball and volleyball courts and five ping-pong tables. Many young members play basketball or ping-pong in the church's gymnasium after Sunday lunch, some playing until the afternoon service. Several groups of church members regularly play basketball, volleyball, or badminton at the church, on either Tuesday or Thursday evening, when the church does not have an extra worship service.

The church divides its members into seven missionary groups by age and sex (women 30 to 39 years old, men 30 to 39 years old, women 40 to 49 years old, men 40 to 49 years old, members 50 to 59 years old, members 60 to 69 years old, and members 70 or older). Each missionary group holds a meeting every month at the church, which most of its members attend. Many members also participate in a few particular missionary activities organized by each missionary group each year, such as visiting the homeless in Harlem and a Korean elderly center on Long Island. Most adult members also belong to one or more of the ten committees, each of which has twenty members. Many of them spend a great deal of time at church performing their assigned jobs, interacting with committee members every week. In addition, more than fifty members belong to the church's two choirs, spending two extra hours each Sunday—one hour before the main service and another hour after it—practicing. In November and December, they come to the church even more often to prepare concerts for Thanksgiving and Christmas.

Their participation in weekly or monthly committee/group meetings and involvement in their activities enhance their fellowship and personal networks. Since members of each organization work for common goals and have extended formal and informal social interactions, they easily make friends with one another. For example, Kyong Man Hurh, a middle-aged Korean man who transferred from another church three years earlier, said that as a result of his active participation in church activities, about 60 percent of his close friends are members of this church. He is the chairperson of the 50-to-59 missionary group and a member of the choir for the main service. In addition, he attends the Wednesday service and the Friday prayer meeting. He plays golf every Thursday with five or six close friends, all of whom belong to the 50-to-59 missionary group. After playing golf, they usually eat at a Korean restaurant. He enjoys eating with his church members, especially because as "good Christians," they share his policy of not drinking beer or other liquor. Hurh also plays golf every other Saturday, and a few of the golfing partners belong to his church's choir.

Han, another middle-aged man who had attended the church for fifteen years, told me that all of his five best friends were members of his church. Serving both as a deacon and the chairperson of the committee that welcomes new church members, he spends 7.5 hours (between 10 am and 5:30 pm) at the church every Sunday, in addition to two hours driving from his Long Island home to the church. But he finds time to play golf on Sunday between 7 and 8 am with his church friends who belong to the same missionary group (men 40 to 49 years old). When I asked him whether sharing religious faith made it easier to make friends with his church members, he agreed:

> Religious faith facilitates my friendship with our church members. For as sincere Christians we try to maintain our conducts within a certain moral boundary. Even many members of other Korean churches drink liquor and go to *noraebang* (singing places). But we accept our pastor's admonition that faithful Christians should refrain from drinking and entertainment.

He said that his wife was also in an intensive, informal friendship network of women from the same missionary group (women 40 to 49 years old).

The church's other activities that encourage members' fellowship are a family retreat in July, one-day athletic activities for all members, and *hyodo kwankwang* ("filial tours" for elderly members). The pastor told me that although the four-day retreat in upstate New York in July strengthens friendship among church members, the percentage of members who go to the retreat has fallen to only 20 percent. On Memorial Day, the church stages a full-day athletic competition for fellowship enhancement in Cunningham Park in Bayside. On that day, church members, divided into small groups, have a traditional Korean barbecue prepared by the church and compete in various athletic activities. This church, as well as many other Korean churches, arranges formal "filial tours" for elderly members, usually organized and paid for by the younger members. Park *halmoni* (Korean for "grandmother"), a 73-year-old woman who immigrated from Korea in 1987, shared her thoughts about the "filial tours":

> We [elderly members of the church] usually take two out-of-the city trips in spring and fall. One or more church members, often anonymously, cover our travel expenses. This fall about twenty elderly people, mostly women, went to Evergreen Farm in New Jersey on a church bus. On our way to the farm, we played a Bible game and sang hymns. An elder bought box lunches for all of us. At the farm, we bought apples, pears, potatoes, peas, and bean paste. We had a lot of fun.

Providing filial tours is only one of the many ways the church offers fellowship and friendship networks for elderly members. Korean immigrant churches, including the Shin Kwang Church, play a significant role in the successful adjustment of Korean elderly immigrants, especially women (Min 1998, chap. 6). Park *halmoni* said that the elderly women at her church often meet at private homes and Korean bakeries. Whenever a member of her missionary group (those 70 and older) moves to a new apartment, members visit her home with gifts of plants and picture frames. In return, the host woman's children serve dinner for the visitors with food ordered from Korean *janchijip*.[4] The elderly female members also have a year-end party, rotating every year at a private home. Park *halmoni* also noted that many of her church friends visit her apartment almost every week during the day when her daughter and son-in-law are at work.

Living in Flushing, which has about 110 Korean churches and many Korean ethnic organizations, Park *halmoni* also takes advantage of elderly programs established by other Korean Christian organizations. On Tuesday, she attends the elderly school (*noin daehak*) established by the (Korean) YWCA of Queens in Flushing.[5] The school has a morning program between 9:30 and 12:10 on Tuesday, which offers an English-language class and an elective course (dance, drawing, computer skills, or Korean language). After the formal program, most of the thirty Korean elderly students eat lunch together for $2. Park *halmoni* and many other women students belong to Evergreen Elderly Choir, one of the YWCA of Queens's two Korean choirs. After lunch, they practice for one and a half hours. Several times a year, she and other members of the choir perform at concerts in the Korean community. After choir practice at the YWCA, Park *halmoni* and her friends often visit a Korean bakery in Flushing to chat over tea and Korean cakes. On Wednesdays Park *halmoni* attends another elderly school at a Korean church in Flushing. This school also provides English-language and music/dance classes for three hours in the morning. Several other Korean churches in New York have elderly schools or social service programs for elderly Koreans.

The Shin Kwang Church's most important service is an opportunity for face-to-face, small-group interactions through the *gooyok yebae* (district services) or "cell ministry" (see Ebaugh and Chafetz 2000, 360–61; Kwon, Ebaugh, and Hagan 1997; Min 1992). The *gooyok yebae*, widely performed in Korean immigrant churches in the United States, is a practice brought from South Korea, a system of dividing church members based on their area or neighborhood of residence for local, small-group meetings.[6] Both Protestant and Catholic churches in South Korea have district services.[7] District services are especially helpful in the Korean immigrant community because Korean Christians usually do not attend the neighborhood church. According to the results of the 1997–1999 Presbyterian Race and Ethnic Panel Studies, half the Korean Presbyterian respondents lived ten or more miles from their church. In contrast, half of all other groups (white, African American, and Latino) attended a church within three miles of their homes (see Kim and Kim 2001, 79–80).[8] Pastors in Korean immigrant churches use district services mainly as a means of attracting and retaining church members. But they also help form Korean immigrants' friendship networks.

The Shin Kwang Church has divided its members into thirty-two districts, each consisting of six to eight households. They usually hold a two-hour district meeting at a district member's home once a month between 8 and 10 pm under the guidance of the elder assigned to that district and the head of the district. Usually about four or five families come. After a short (20-minute) service, the families eat dinner together, usually prepared by the host family but sometimes a potluck. They enjoy talking about their children's education, businesses, politics in Korea, and other matters of mutual interest. New immigrant families receive help from the head and other members of the district in adjusting to American society.

The members of each district often become close friends, and because they often bring their children to the district service, they often become friends, too. A 49-year-old woman who served as the head of a district and ran a nail salon on Long Island summarized her monthly district meetings:

> Four of the seven families that belong to our district always participate in the monthly district meeting. One family has moved out, and another family does not attend church any longer. I don't know why the other one family does not participate. We hold the district meeting Monday, Tuesday, or Thursday evening, when we do not go to church. My mother not only prepares dinner for the district meeting in my home but also helps two other families prepare dinners for the district meetings because we all work until late. It is convenient for my mother to help two other families because they are in the same apartment complex.
>
> We start the district service around 8:30 with a worship service. We have a forty-minute full-worship service, a much longer service than most other districts. Not only adults, but also our children participate in every district service. My son attended until he went to college. For the service, we have a long prayer by the representative, read a phrase from the Bible and discuss it together, and sing a few hymns. Even children read the Bible praises, although they may not understand their meanings. They also pray for all the participants.
>
> After the service, we eat the dinner prepared by the host family. Then we have fellowship until 11 and sometimes 12. We talk about different aspects of this world, our children's education, and what has happened in the church, the Korean community, and Korea.

We also laugh a lot. Going to the same church and living in the same neighborhood are enough to make us feel close. Moreover, our regular meetings at home for worship service and fellowship for a long period of time have further strengthened our friendship networks. We all feel like brothers and sisters.

## Programs and Activities to Preserve Ethnic Culture

Korean churches also help Korean immigrants preserve their ethnic culture. The Shin Kwang Church helps its members retain their cultural traditions in several ways. First, it celebrates two major Korean cultural holidays: New Year's Day and Chooseok (Korean Thanksgiving, on August 15 by the lunar calendar). To celebrate New Year's Day, the church has two services, one on New Year's Eve and the other on the New Year's Day.[9] After the main service on the New Year's Day, members eat *ttockguk* (rice-cake soup), which is typically served in Korea on the day. Some women and girls come to church wearing *chima jogori* (Korean women's traditional dress). After lunch, the church observes the Korean custom of *sebae*. In one *sebae* ceremony I attended, ten children lined up and bowed deeply to ten elderly members sitting in a room while their parents watched them. In return, the elderly members gave candy to the children, although in Korea they give them money. All the children and adolescents from kindergarten to high school take turns participating in this *sebae* ceremony.

The Shin Kwang Church also holds special services on the March 1 Independence Commemoration Day and the August 15 Independence Day. Korean patriotism is featured in the senior pastor's sermon, with its reminiscing about the role of the earlier Korean Christians in the independence movement against the Japanese.[10] Many other Korean immigrant churches sing the March 1 and August 15 Independence songs, but as the senior pastor insisted, to "remain sacred," the Shin Kwang Church does not sing these "patriotic songs."

The senior pastor underscored the importance of the church in preserving Korean cultural traditions. As soon as the church moved to its new building in 1992, he established a school to teach children the Korean language and culture. The school provides three hours of classes between 9:30 and 12:30 on Saturdays, devoting two hours to teaching the Korean language and the remaining hour to an exhibition by experts of *taekwondo*, *samulnori* (Korean traditional music/dance), and other folk activities. The approximately forty students enrolled in the school pay $140 a semester. In two summer months, the school offers an expanded program that includes Korean dance, *taekwondo*, English, and math. Approximately eighty students—both church members and others—are enrolled in the summer program. The senior pastor insists that the Korean language be used for all instruction at the Korean school, but the younger education pastor, who is in

On the New Year's Day, children at the Shin Kwang Church of New
York make deep bows to elderly members to reproduce the Korean
*sebae* ceremony.

charge of the Korean school, disagrees, arguing that the school should focus on
teaching 1.5- and second-generation Korean children and adolescents Korean
culture and history and that these Americanized Koreans can learn better when
they are taught in English.

All but ten of the approximately 160 Korean (language) schools in the New
York / New Jersey area are attached to Korean churches.[11] A few of the churches
hold annual Korean essay or speech contests for second-generation Koreans in
the New York / New Jersey area, and in 2003, the Council of Korean Churches
of Greater New York, an umbrella organization of Korean churches in the area,
also began holding a Korean speech contest. Many other churches have their own
Korean writing or speech contests. Thus Korean churches in New York and other
Korean communities play a central role in providing Korean-language and ethnic
education to Korean children.

To teach adolescents Korean cultural traditions as well as religion, the Shin
Kwang Church has arranged for the youth group to attend once a month the
Sunday bilingual worship service with adults at 11 am. In its observance or celebration of Easter, Thanksgiving, and Christmas, the church also has arranged for
all children and adolescents to attend the services. A 47-year-old male member
who has attended the church for thirteen years reported that the arrangement
to have services with adults helped his "children learn Korean etiquette and be
proud of Korea." The senior pastor has also arranged bilingual Sunday school

services, contending that "Korean children get more God's blessings when they sing hymns in Korean than in English."[12] Accordingly, Sunday schools use Korean more often than English, listening to bilingual sermons and prayers and singing hymns in two languages, two verses in English and two in Korean. The Sunday school's bilingual worship services are necessary, too, because both native-born and immigrant children and adolescents attend, providing greater opportunities for the native-born children and adolescents to learn the Korean language, customs, and values from the immigrant children. As a bilingual 1.5-generation Sunday school teacher remarked, "Second-generation Korean children in my Sunday school class learn a lot about Korean customs and values from their immigrant friends."

Sunday school and even the daily kindergarten program also help teach Korean children and adolescents the Korean Confucian customs, which include children's bowing deeply to their parents and other adults when greeting them, using two hands when handing something to them, and not talking back to them. The senior and education pastors and most of the teachers involved in the educational programs are Korean immigrants who came to the United States after age 12. Thus they are not only fluent in Korean but also very familiar with Korean Confucian customs. Strongly supported by the senior pastor, they try to teach their students Korean etiquette, both inside and outside class. The church's kindergarten is open from 9 am to 4 pm five days a week. Three Korean teachers and a white American teacher teach approximately thirty Korean preschool children, mostly children of nonmembers, using both Korean and English.

Filial piety, children's respect for and obligations to their parents, constitutes the core of Korean Confucian values. On Korean Parents' Day on May 8, children in South Korea express their appreciation of their parents in a number of ways.[13] Like many other Korean churches in South Korea and the United States, the Shin Kwang Church observes Parents' Day on the second Sunday of May, when the Sunday school and youth group teachers have the children and adolescents make special cards for their parents. Members eighteen to twenty-nine years old pin carnations, prepared by the church, on middle-aged and elderly women (50 years and older) and give gifts to women seventy and older.

## Patriarchal Traditions and Gender Hierarchy

Korean immigrant churches not only help preserve the Korean language, holidays, and values such as filial piety but also enforce Confucian patriarchal traditions and the absence of women from the church leadership. A number of studies have pointed out that Korean immigrant churches are very sexist and patriarchal in their organization and interpretations of the Bible (Alumkal 1999; A.

Kim 1996; J. Kim 1996; Kim and Kim 2001; Min 1992, 2008). In particular, data show that very few women are pastors and elders in Korean immigrant churches, although women make up the vast majority of their members. For example, the results of the 1997–1999 Presbyterian Racial and Ethnic Panel Study conducted by the Presbyterian Church USA reveal that only 8 percent of Korean elders are women, compared with 44 percent of white elders (Kim and Kim 2001, 84). An analysis of the names of elders in the Korean immigrant churches in the New York / New Jersey area, listed in *The 2006 Korean Churches Directory of New York* also shows a similarly low proportion of women (Min 2008). The male dominance of Korean immigrant churches' elders is an important gender issue, especially because Korean elders have a high status and much power and authority, much more than elders in white American or other minority churches (Kim and Kim 2001, 84). Furthermore, elders in Korean churches usually hold their position until retirement, whereas those in non-Korean churches have term limits.

Some social scientists have attributed the near-absence of women pastors and elders in Korean immigrant churches and other sexist elements to Korean Confucian patriarchal traditions (A. Kim 1996; Kim and Kim 2001; Min 1992). For example, based on her interviews with Korean Christian immigrant women, Aira Kim, a Korean feminist minister, commented, "Most women accept women's inferior status and adjust to their Korean-Christian environment, which is ruled by age-old Confucian notions of gender hierarchy" (A. Kim 1996, 91). By contrast, a few researchers cite the Bible, and therefore Christianity itself, as its major source (Alumkal 1999; J. Kim 1996). In his study of a second-generation Korean congregation, Alumkal (1999) reports that most of his informants disapproved of women's ordination as ministers and that they justified this view with teachings of the Bible. He suggests that patriarchal gender values prevalent in Korean immigrant churches may be rooted more in evangelical subculture than in Korean cultural norms.[14]

Still other scholars have emphasized Korean immigrant men's loss of social status as a major reason for the gender hierarchy in Korean immigrant churches (Hurh and Kim 1990; Kim and Kim 2000). In this view, because most Korean immigrant men have lost status owing to the loss of their professional and managerial occupations held before their immigration, Korean immigrant churches have created many lay positions, such as elders and deacons, for them. Kim and Kim (2000, 65) argue that the male domination of elders is "not just a longstanding church practice in Korea but a practice that has been resolutely reinforced by Korean males to redress their experiences of social and occupational deprivation in the United States." Analyses of head pastors' names listed in *The 2006 Korean Churches Directory of New York* and *The 2006 Korean Churches Directory* in Korea show that women account for a substantially smaller proportion of head pastors in the Korean community in the New York / New Jersey area than in South Korea (Min 2008). This finding seems to support Kim's suggestion that Korean immigrant men oppose allowing women to serve as head pastors or elders.

All three factors, not just one, seem to have contributed to the exclusion of women from leadership role in Korean immigrant churches. To shed more light on gender hierarchy in Korean immigrant churches, we consider the gender dynamics at the Shin Kwang Church. It is affiliated with the Reformed Church in America (RCA), a conservative Presbyterian denomination, which long ago approved the ordination of women. Officially, therefore, the Shin Kwang Church can have women pastors and elders. Nonetheless, the senior pastor and all five associate or education pastors are men, with the only woman being the not-ordained evangelical pastor (*jondosa*). A woman who served as an associate pastor in the past has now retired. Because she was ordained to be a pastor in Korea and was a founding member of the church, she was permitted to serve as an associate pastor for the Shin Kwang Church. Still, all twelve of its elders are men, and all five exhorters are women. Whereas the elders have power and authority, the exhorters tend to caring tasks, such as visiting sick members and praying for the church (A. Kim 1996).[15] All ten functional committees have male chairmen and female assistant chairwomen. Although most of the Sunday school and youth ministry teachers are women, the Education Committee is led by a man.

When I asked Pastor Han why his church did not have a female pastor or elder, he replied that neither his American denomination nor his theological position prohibited women pastors and/or elders but that they simply had not found well-qualified women candidates for eldership and that the church would have one or more women elders in the future. I also asked an elder of the church why his church did not have a woman elder. The following response sheds light on why this and many other Korean immigrant churches affiliated with an American denomination do not have woman elders:

> All twelve elders of our church are men. Those old-timers who emigrated from Korea twenty or more years ago do not consider women qualified for elders because of Korean patriarchal traditions. Even women members in our church have never taken the absence of women elders as an issue. In my first Korean immigrant church in New York City, some women raised this gender issue. But male elders quickly rejected the idea.
>
> The *danghe* [the consistory], in which only the senior pastor and all elders participate, has to nominate candidates for elders. To become an elder, a nominee needs to get an approval by adult church members with two-thirds of votes. The *danghe* is not likely to nominate a woman for eldership soon, nor are two-thirds of church members likely to approve her nomination.

To confirm his statement that female members had not contested the absence of women elders, I asked a woman deacon at the Shin Kwang Church why her church did not have a single woman elder, even though the RCA allowed the church to have women elders. She replied, "I understand that according to the American denomination's [RCA's] regulations, only men are supposed to serve as elders, while women are supposed to serve as exhorters." Appointing men to serve as elders and women to serve as exhorters comes from Confucian patriarchal traditions. But the female deacon misunderstood this as an application of the U.S. denomination's rule. I also asked the retired woman pastor why her church did not have a woman elder. She responded that her church leaders sometimes follow the RCA's regulations and other times follow the Korean Presbyterian denomination's (Daehan Yesu Jangro Gyohe-Tonghap's) regulations, whichever best serves their purposes. She said that her church "was under pressure by the U.S. denominational hierarchy to ordain women elders." Her answer reveals that the church's failure to have a woman elder is due mainly to the male leadership's adherence to the regulations of the Presbyterian denomination in Korea concerning gender issues.

These comments indicate that Korean Confucian patriarchal traditions are mainly responsible for the Korean church's organization. But there is evidence that the church's conservative theological position, which includes a literal interpretation of the Bible, also is responsible for the gendered hierarchy in this and other Korean immigrant churches. I asked a woman member why the church's women leaders did not consider the absence of women elders to be an important issue. She answered that most other women members believe that according to the Bible, women are not supposed to serve as elders. I asked the senior pastor of another Korean Presbyterian church with only male elders whether female members of his church would support a woman elder. He said that the women in his church were not likely to accept the idea of women elders in the near future on theological grounds, even if he supported it. He then told me about an episode that occurred in a Korean Presbyterian church in Dallas where he served as an associate pastor about ten years earlier:

> It is an episode that occurred in Dallas about ten years ago. The Presbyterian church was affiliated with the PCUSA but had only a few male elders. So it was under pressure by the U.S. denomination to include women elders. All-male *danghe* once nominated only two men for eldership. But following the PCUSA's regulations, lay members from the floor were also able to nominate candidates for elders. When a woman nominated another woman for eldership, a third woman quickly stood up and strongly opposed the nomination, using a phrase from the Bible. I remember she read, "Women should be calm" from Corinthians 14:34. Everyone kept silent after her opposing statement. When members cast votes, the woman nominee got [only] a small number of votes.

# 5 Ethnographic Research on the Hindu Temple Society of North America

IN THIS CHAPTER we move to the Hindu Temple Society of North America for ethnographic information about Hindu temples' ethnicity functions. We found that members of the Shin Kwang Church preserve their ethnicity mainly through church-related close fellowship and active social networks. In contrast, the Hindu Temple Society does not contribute much to its devotees' fellowship. Instead, the temple contributes to Indian Hindu immigrants' ethnicity by reproducing Indian cultural traditions and enhancing ethnic identity through its architecture, rituals, and cultural activities.

## History, Location, and Structure

Ganesh Temple is so named because the name of the main deity housed there is Ganesha. Its full name is Sri Maha Vallabha Ganapati Devasthanam, but it is often referred to as the Hindu Temple Society of North America, the name of the nonprofit organization that manages the temple. For this temple, I use the terms Hindu Temple Society and Ganesh Temple interchangeably. It is the first Hindu temple established in the tristate area (New York, New Jersey, and Connecticut) and the largest Hindu temple in New York City. According to its public relations officer, there is now a physically larger Hindu temple in New Jersey, but Ganesh Temple has more devotees.

A group of Indian professionals and business owners organized the Hindu Temple Society of North America in 1970 while planning to construct the first Hindu temple in New York City. In the 1960s and the early 1970s, most Indian immigrants were professionals, especially medical professionals. They bought a defunct Russian Orthodox church and the adjacent lot in 1972, and to cover the cost of the building, they obtained a loan from a Manhattan branch of the State Bank of India, the largest bank in India. They consecrated the temple in 1977 on July 4. After the incorporation of the Hindu organization, it took seven years, which is not uncommon, to consecrate the temple because its construction was complicated, including bringing architects from India. In contrast, the Shin Kwang Church and other Korean churches usually start holding worship services in a rented location, such as a school gymnasium, a private home, or a white American church. After a few or several years of services, they organize as a nonprofit and construct their own church buildings.

The main building of the Ganesh Temple is at 45-57 Bowne Street, the southeastern part of Flushing where many Indian immigrants live. Flushing is the only neighborhood outside the West Coast where Asian Americans are the majority of the population. Chinese Americans are the largest Asian group there, with about 34,000 in 2000, followed by Korean Americans with approximately 20,000. About 9,400 Indian Americans lived in Flushing in 2000, making it the third largest Asian group there. These 9,400 Indians also are the largest Indian group in any part of the New York City area, as Indian immigrants are more widely scattered than either Chinese or Korean immigrants. Indian immigrants in Flushing are concentrated in southeastern Flushing, where the temple also is located. An Indian business district has grown up on Main Street (covering the six blocks between Franklyn Avenue and Dahlia Avenue), about six blocks away from the temple. In addition to the concentration of Indian immigrants in the area, Dr. Uma Mysorekar, the president of the temple, told me that the location was selected because of its convenience for transportation from all directions: Manhattan, Long Island, New Jersey, upstate New York, New Haven, and Boston.

The temple has continued to construct more buildings since it first opened in 1977, and as of 2005, it had five major complexes. The main building, which is designed like a temple in south India, has a huge worship room that contains more than twenty statues of deities and a few sages. Its basement is used for meetings, cultural activities, and fine arts classes. The community center is located to the right of the main worship building; it started construction in 1985 with the acquisition of fourteen properties and was completed it in 1997. The community center has two wedding halls (Lakshmi and Parvati) on the first floor, an auditorium with a seating capacity of seven hundred on the second floor, and a temple canteen / dining hall and a gift shop on the lower level. The third building, located to the left of the main worship building, has several classrooms for children. The building across the main worship hall, completed in 2003, has a senior center on the main floor and an auditorium in the lower level, called Saraswati Hall, which has a spacious stage ideal for cultural programs, lectures, and so forth. On its second floor are several apartments used as staff quarters. The temple also purchased seven houses in the area to be used as staff quarters.

The temple accommodates a range of devotees, most from southern Indian regional subcultures and speaking five different languages (Hindi, Telugu, Kannada, Tamil, and Malayalam). About 90 percent of the temple's devotees are Indian immigrants and their children, with Bangladeshi and Guyanese Indian Hindus making up the remaining 10 percent. A few white Americans come to worship services on the weekend. I talked with a white American woman who visited the temple from Long Island. She said that although she had been raised as a Catholic, she decided to visit the temple because she was impressed by her Indian Hindu immigrant neighbors' acceptance of all other religions. Depending on the region and/or sect, Hinduism has many faces in regard to deities worshipped, sacred texts, institutions, and cultural practices (Williams 1988, 39). I chose the Hindu Temple Society for my study mainly because its approach and organization are ecumenical, incorporating many different regions and sects. Although Sanskrit is used for worship services, English is used for communications among the devotees and for committee meetings. Some, usually older devotees, speak their own dialect with their family members and friends.

As of December 2005, the Hindu Temple had more than thirty employees, including nine priests, eight cooks, and several administrative office staff members. For the first two to three years, temple priests were invited from India by the temple leaders to conduct services at the temple. They were hired mainly for their ability to perform various Hindu rituals. Whereas the senior pastor has the dominant influence in the decisions and policies at the Shin Kwang Church of New York, the temple priests do not make or enforce policies. Instead, the eleven-member board of trustees makes important decisions and policies and is responsible for the temple society's assets. When a member retires, creating a vacancy in the membership, all members of the board elect a new member to fill it. The board members are not elected by the members of the temple, just as they usually are not in India. But the temple's administration is more democratic than that in India because in India most temple trustees are inherited positions based on family connections with the founders of the temple or are government-appointed trustees (Kurien 2007, 96). The board has at least four formal meetings a year at the temple, and according to Dr. Uma Mysorekar, the trustees communicate with one another as often as necessary over the phone or by e-mail.

The temple also has a twenty-one-member executive committee, which enforces the temple's policies. Other subcommittees perform particular tasks in close coordination with the executive committee. The subcommittees have more than one hundred members, and many belong to two or more committees. The priests do have some influence in the temple in that members of the executive committee use their knowledge and advice to enforce policies and organize religious rituals and cultural activities.

In regard to lay control, this Hindu temple is more similar to American Christian congregations than is the Shin Kwang Church of New York. My review of the webpages of the Hindu temples in the United States (prepared by the Council of Hindu Temples of North America) shows that for other Indian Hindu temples, either the board of trustees or the board of directors is the central decision-making organization. Researchers have pointed to the transformation of non-Christian immigrant religious institutions in the United States that follow the congregational form of American Protestant churches in emphasizing lay leadership (Warner 1994; Yang and Ebaugh 2001b). However, my informants at the temple said that Hindu temples in India, whether run by the government or private, are usually controlled by a board of trustees and that priests do not have much power. Thus Indian Hindu immigrant temples controlled by lay leaders, with the priests having no power, reflects the transplantation, rather than the transformation, of Hindu religious institutions from India. The governance of the temple, however, is less democratic than that of American churches in that its trustees are not elected by its members.

Dr. Uma Mysorekar has been serving on the board of trustees for several years and has been the president of the temple since 1994. A medical graduate of Bombay University, she originally immigrated to North Carolina in 1970 and then moved to New York City in 1974. Since she became president of the temple in 1994, she has been responsible for planning and carrying out the temple's various programs and its day-to-day operations, organizing various programs, and inviting visitors to the temple. Almost giving up her lucrative career as a medical doctor, she has worked eight to ten hours every day at the temple for two decades. The temple's public relations officer told me that she had donated more than $1 million to the temple. Dr. Mysorekar's devotion to the temple and contribution to cultural diversity in New York City through her involvement in the temple and other social organizations have been recognized by both Indian immigrants and local political leaders. In 2000, she was awarded a "token of esteem" by the City Lore's People's Hall of Fame for her contribution to beautifying the borough of Queens (Joseph 2006), and in 2001, she received the Governor's Award of Excellence for her outstanding achievement and community service to New York State.

Beginning in 1999, six Indian immigrants filed a series of complaints against the Hindu Temple Society of North America and its board of trustees. One of their demands was voting rights for "members." The 1970 bylaws, their lawyer found, stipulated that members of the temple have voting rights, but the trustees later changed the bylaws so that the board of trustees, headed by Dr. Mysorekar, could manage all the temple's affairs and vote on its own members (Worth 2003). The plaintiffs asked for the right to elect the board members, as well as to prevent the Temple Society from proceeding with the planned building expansion projects, and made several other allegations (see "Status Report on Current Litigation," December 2003 issue of *Ganesanjali*). In response to their demand for members' voting rights, the board of trustees argued,

In the early days, the organizers of the Temple Society resorted to collecting "membership fees" merely as a fund-raising tool. However, all devotees were allowed to enjoy the same privileges, regardless of their financial contribution to the Temple Society or "membership" status or participation in the activities of the Temple Society. Accordingly, the size of one's financial contribution to the Temple Society or a devotee's "membership" status by itself did not confer any additional privileges not otherwise available to any "non-contributing" or "non-member devotees. ("Status Report on Current Litigation," December 2003 issue of *Ganesanjali*)

The Appellate Division of the Supreme Court of the State of New York sided with the petitioners, ruling some of the bylaws adopted after 1970 were not valid and that members of the board must be elected by the temple's members. Justice Joseph Golia of the New York State Supreme Court appointed a referee to oversee the election, a move that the board unsuccessfully challenged (Worth 2004). In the court-ordered election, in which the majority of the more than eight thousand dues-paying members voted, all eleven incumbent candidates won, and no candidate representing the opposing (petitioners) group won a seat (Joseph 2006). Dr. Mysorekar has not changed her position that the current management of the temple, though not including the election of the temple's trustees by its members, serves the temple's best interests. She believes that a "homogenous" board of trustees is needed for the temple's effective operation and that a general election could destroy its homogeneity by bringing in trustees who may "have other motivations than religious faith." Kurien points out that many other Hindu temples in the United States, including the object of her own study, have had similar battles over leadership (2007, 96–97).

### Programs and Activities for Fellowship and Ethnic Networks

Compared with Korean churches, temples do not serve as places for fellowship and social networks. First, the temple does not consider its devotees "members," although it has a mailing list of about 20,000. Neither do Indian Hindus who go to the temple consider themselves its "members." All Hindu devotees at the temple with whom I spoke told me that they went to two or more temples. For example, a middle-aged Gujarat Indian who lives in the Bronx says that he goes to Queens every week to this temple but that he also goes to two other temples, depending on their programs and cultural functions on particular days.

Even a trustee of the temple reported that occasionally he also visits other temples for important cultural functions. Whereas the Shin Kwang Church refers to its members as *sungdo* (sacred friends), this Hindu temple calls its attendants *devotees*. The use of these two different terms suggests that the Korean church puts more emphasis on fellowship than does the Hindu temple. Immigrant Buddhist temples, as well as immigrant mosques (Abusharaf 1998), have membership.[1] Thus in regard to membership, Indian Hindu temples are less congregation oriented than even other non-Christian religious institutions.

As we have seen, most Indian Hindus do not go to temple regularly. As the public relations officer at the Hindu Temple said, "Many of them visit this temple daily, every week or more often, but most of them visit it monthly or a few times a year. Many Indians who live outside New York State send checks to ask us to perform regular services and pray for their families." The irregularity of their visits to the temple makes it difficult for the devotees to make friends with one another, which suggests that they stress religion and spirituality more than socializing. Moreover, the temple's style of worship does not give its devotees many opportunities for fellowship and social interaction.

The members of the Shin Kwang Church usually go to church on Sunday for the main service, and many go on Friday for a prayer meeting and/or on Wednesday for Bible study. In contrast, the temple is open from eight in the morning to nine in the evening seven days a week. Indian Hindus go to the temple at different times on different days, although most go on weekends because of convenience. Alone, in a family unit, or in a small group, they worship Lord Ganesha as the presiding deity and/or one or more of the other deities and sages housed in the temple. Several times a day, the priests regularly chant mantras to help small groups of devotees worship particular deities of their own choosing. Devotees sit cross-legged, kneel, or stand with their hands clasped together in front of their deities. Staff members told me that devotees are not supposed to wear shoes or socks in the main worship room, not only to show respect for deities but also for cleanliness. Devotees who worship deities symbolizing planets also spin the deities for several minutes. Many devotees worship the deities for several minutes alone or as a family unit with no help from priests. Because of the noncongregational nature of worship services, the temple does not facilitate its visitors' friendships, although it does organize special social and cultural programs.

Some Indian Hindu immigrants visit the temple frequently. I asked a 65-year-old Indian immigrant man from Tamil Nadu how often he went to the temple. In addition to going to the senior citizens' meeting held every Wednesday, he usually visited the temple three times a week with his wife. As he put it,

> Every Saturday morning I come to the temple with my wife and stay for three
> hours for service between 7:30 and 10:30. Thursday evening at 7, I visit the temple
> and have a half-hour service. Weekly on Sunday or another day when there is a
> lecture on music or another cultural function, I also go to the temple. I often bring
> my relatives visiting from India. If I lived closer, I would visit the temple more
> frequently.

This is a photo of Lord Ganesa, the presiding deity of Ganesh Temple. Lord Ganesa is the god who, according to the public relations officer, "removes any obstacle in whatever they want to do."

He told me that he had done this for the past thirty years since the temple was built.

Of course, all the trustees and various committee members also visit the temple frequently, spending much time on volunteer activities. I interviewed a south Indian immigrant man in his mid-sixties who was one of the founding members and had served as a trustee since 2000. Before retiring he visited the temple almost every day for about an hour. Since his retirement he has spent about four hours every day in the temple, devoting about half the time to praying and the other half to volunteer activities for the temple. As a member of the *puja* and publication committees, his activities include helping the priests organize *pujas* and writing and editing articles for the temple's monthly newsletter. An Indian woman who serves as a trustee and the vice president of the executive committee has worked full time as a cardiologist for nearly thirty years. She visits the temple every Saturday and Sunday for a few hours, but just before major religious festivals (eight such festivals a year) she spends far more time there, helping decorate the deities as a member of the decoration committee. She observed, "Devotees feel good, feel vibrations when gods and goddesses are properly decorated. All members of the decoration committee get busy with decorations of deities before major religious festival."

The occasions on which the devotees of the Ganesh Temple, as well as those of other Hindu temples, meet many relatives and friends are the life-cycle events usually held on weekends by particular host families. To celebrate the birth of a child, a parent's sixtieth birthday, weddings, or other life-cycle events, devotees have special *pujas* (rituals and prayers) performed in the basement of the temple or at the community center, inviting many—from thirty to one hundred—relatives and friends. Relatives and friends come from Long Island, upstate New York, and New Jersey, as well as from the New York City area. A *puja* ceremony performed by a priest may last one to two hours, after which the guests usually enjoy a *puja* party over lunch or dinner purchased from the temple's canteen by the host family, which takes another one or two hours. The major *puja* ceremonies performed in the temple also are followed by both Indian cultural and social functions. Indian Hindus perform *pujas* for smaller auspicious occasions at home more often than in temples, and Indian Hindu immigrants usually invite many relatives and friends to these domestic *puja* ceremonies, thereby expanding their friendship networks.

After a worship service at the temple, many devotees eat snacks or vegetarian food at the temple canteen or one of the two private vegetarian restaurants located next to the temple building. Some of them eat with their relatives or friends, who more often are visitors from another U.S. city or from India, rather than friends made at the temple. I spoke with an Indian computer programmer in his forties who had finished praying with two others around 12 pm one Saturday. I asked him whether meeting his friends or relatives was an important reason he went to the temple regularly, and he answered,

> I live in Manhattan and visit this temple with my wife usually once a month. I often come with a friend or relative visiting my home. My friend in Bombay is visiting New York City for two weeks. He is staying at my home this weekend. I have come with him because he wanted to visit the temple for peace of mind. We prayed for less than ten minutes here. Like my friend from India, getting peace of mind is the only reason I come to temple regularly. Making friends is not a good reason to come here.

After talking with me, he, along with his wife and friend, went to the temple's canteen to eat lunch. Even the trustee who spent four hours every day in the temple said that meeting his friends was not an important reason for his daily visits.

In addition, unlike the Korean church, the Hindu temple does not organize group activities comparable to the summer retreats or one-day athletic activities at a public park. The temple's group program that is most likely to contribute to ethnic friendship networks is its senior program, which started in 2002. Under the program, a group of fifteen to twenty senior Hindus regularly meet on Wednesdays and Thursdays between 10 am to 1 pm at the newly established senior citizens' center. I attended three of their Wednesday meetings. They started the program with yoga exercises and then studied Bhagavad Gita and other Hindu scriptures by listening to invited *swamis* (holy men). After the lecture, they ate a vegetarian lunch together. The participants in the senior program have taken field trips to multireligious and multicultural organizations in the tristate area and held daylong seminars on yoga, classical dance, and the Vedas (Hindu scriptures). They plan to extend these group activities to five days a week.

The majority of the participants in the senior program are women, five or six of whom told me that they engaged in volunteer activities for both the senior citizens' center and the temple, arranging flowers and helping visitors. Since these women meet together twice a week and participate in the temple's volunteer activities, they create strong friendship networks. But the number of participants in the senior citizen's program established in the largest Hindu temple in New York City is surprisingly small, and only five or six women have formed strong friendships.

In contrast, as we saw earlier, elderly members of the Shin Kwang Church form fellowship and ethnic networks through their frequent participation in the church and informal social interactions outside church. Moreover, several other Korean churches in New York City have established senior schools to provide elderly members with fellowship, cultural programs, and English lessons. Thus Korean immigrant churches help elderly Korean immigrants who do not speak English and are unfamiliar with American culture feel at home. But since Indian elderly immigrants usually do not have a language barrier, there may be less demand for elderly programs in the Indian community than in the Korean community. Nevertheless, Indian Hindu temples could be used more effectively to help elderly Indians adjust to American society. The small number of participants in the senior citizens' center at the Ganesh Temple once again suggests that the fellowship and social service functions of non-Judeo-Christian religious institutions are limited.

The findings regarding the lack of activities in the Hindu Temple that enhance devotees' fellowship and social interaction may be generalized to most Hindu temples in New York City, although the Swaminarayan Hindu temples organize religious and sociocultural activities similar to those of Christian churches. Swaminarayan Hinduism is a sectarian Hindu religion that originated in Gujarat in the early nineteenth century (Williams 1988, 152–85). The central organization in Gujarat maintains that there are one million followers of Swaminarayan Hinduism in India and abroad, along with 550 temples. Six of the twenty-five Hindu temples in the New York / New Jersey area are Swaminarayan, with five of them in New Jersey.[2] I visited a Swaminarayan temple in New York City twice on Sunday, to interview a staff member and observe the worship services and other social activities. The temple has formal worship services between 4:30 and 6:30, and about 600 of the 1,200 regular worshippers come to the Sunday worship service. The service starts with the devotees singing devotional songs and chanting mantras, and then two worshippers deliver sermons to the congregants in the Gujarat language. As in Christian churches, children, adolescents, and young adults who are not fluent in Gujarat have separate services in English and Gujarat. After the service, adults and children eat dinner together and enjoy talking with their friends and relatives.

## Preservation of Ethnic Culture and Identity

Even though the Hindu Temple does not contribute much to its devotees' fellowship and social interaction, it does help them retain their Indian cultural traditions and ethnic identity. We noted earlier that the Shin Kwang Church helps its members maintain Korean cultural traditions because they actively participate in church activities and practice Korean customs and etiquette there. In contrast, the temple helps Indian Hindu immigrants maintain their cultural traditions and ethnic identity because of the strong association between the Hindu religion and Indian culture.

Religious practices enabled white Catholics to retain their ethnic culture because their churches' architectural design was similar to that of the churches in their home countries (Conzen 1991; Dolan 1985; Ebaugh and Chafetz 2000, 386–90). The Hindu temple also contributes to the preservation of Indian culture and identity because its architecture, interior furnishings, and other visual representations reflect Indian culture. When the founder built the temple, he invited eight architects from southern India to make it resemble Tirupati Devasthanam, a large temple in the state of Andhra Pradesh. In addition, all the statues of deities were sent from southern India. The temple's architectural design reminds Indian immigrants of their home country. Some devotees told me, "I like to come to this temple regularly because here I feel like I am in little India." According to a staff member, Indian immigrants from the tristate area visit the temple on the weekend to see "Little India." Many middle-aged Indian immigrants and their families visit the temple from Philadelphia and even as far away as New Hampshire a few times a year to get this "feeling of being at home."[3]

The authentic architecture of the Hindu temple also sends to New Yorkers a strong message about the presence of the Indian community. In an article entitled "Stamp of India Heavier in City," published in June 1978, one year after the temple building was completed, a reporter for the *New York Times* wrote (Gupte 1978):

The Hindu temple always catches pedestrians and motorists by surprise. What is this architectural oddity, with its solid stone exteriors, pyramid-like dome and marble steps, doing in a neighborhood of plain single-family homes in Flushing, Queens? Nothing testifies more vividly to the arrival of a community of Indians in the metropolitan area than the Hindu Temple of New York at 45-57 Bowne Street, sponsored by the Hindu Temple Society. It is a community that has been growing rapidly since the liberalization of the immigration laws in the 1960s.

OPENHOUSE New York, a nonprofit organization, was founded in 2002 to promote awareness and appreciation of New York City's architecture, design, and cultural heritage. Each year since 2003, it has selected the Ganesh Temple as one of major sites for New Yorkers to visit for a citywide celebration of New York City's greatest architecture and design. On the 2005 OPENHOUSE New York weekend (October 10 and 11), many groups of visitors took tours to the temple. Many professors, teachers, and students from East Coast high schools and colleges also have visited the temple as part of their religious or cultural history courses or for research. OPENHOUSE's 2005 annual report lists thirty-two school groups visiting the temple that year, including the New York Theological Seminary, Baruch College, Columbia University, New York University, Cornell University, Temple University, and a Unitarian Universalist church.

By contrast, the physical characteristics of the Shin Kwang Church and other Korean immigrant churches virtually never reflect Korean culture. Most Korean immigrant churches rent space from or share church buildings with white American churches. Some small Korean congregations use private homes or commercial buildings (often the second floor) for their services. Other medium-size or large Korean congregations, like the Shin Kwang Church, have their own buildings, but they have a Western Gothic architectural style rather than a uniquely Korean style. Even the newer Christian churches in South Korea do not have a uniquely Korean design; instead, they have a Western rather than a Korean style.

Second, the temple helps Indian Hindus maintain their cultural traditions and ethnic identity by celebrating major Hindu festivals. The temple observes eight major Hindu holidays each year, many of which are also Indian national holidays, with various cultural activities, including Indian concerts and plays. Most Hindu devotees attend the temple several times a year on these holidays. Most of the women and many of the men wear traditional clothing (*saris* for women and *dhoti* for men). Its biggest cultural event is an annual parade on the last day of the Sri Ganesh Chaturthi festival period, which is ten days from Friday to the next Sunday in fall (September or October). To celebrate his birth, they carry a statue of Lord Ganesa in a beautifully decorated, 16-foot silver chariot and parade around the major streets in Flushing for a few hours. About three thousand Indian and

This is a photo of the temple's tower and the walkway to the main worship room, which houses more than 20 deities. More than 3,000 Hindus walk here every week to visit the worship room.

other South Asian Hindus, many driving in from Long Island, New Jersey, and upstate New York, went to the parade in 2001. Accompanying devotees, most of them barefooted and dressed in traditional Indian costumes, sang and danced.

The New York Chapter of the Association of Indians in America, a major Pan-Indian organization in the United States, began holding its Diwali fair at the South Street seaport in lower Manhattan in the early 1990s. The Diwali fair, a Hindu religious festival, has become the most important South Asian cultural event in the New York area, which not only South Asians of all religious backgrounds but also other Americans enjoy.[4] It features several Indian cultural programs, including dance, music, arts, and crafts (Khandelwal 2002, 60–62). In 2003, the Jackson Heights Merchants Association and the Hindu Temple Society of North America, along with several other Indian American organizations in the New York area, lobbied members of the New York City Council to suspend alternate-side parking regulations (for street cleaning and traffic flow) on Diwali (M. Joshi 2005, 2006). The New York City Council passed the proposal in October 2005 and, a year later, overrode a veto by Mayor Michael Bloomberg a year after it had passed the proposal to suspend the same regulations on lunar New Year's Day. Diwali and lunar New Year's Day are on the list of forty ethnic and religious holidays that the New York City government formally recognizes for the suspension of alternate-side parking regulations, reflecting the growing cultural impact of Asian immigrants in New York City.

Since 2003, the White House has hosted a Diwali celebration, with many Indian leaders participating. In October 2004, at the urging of the Hindu American Foundation, the Congressional Caucus on India and Indian America introduced House Resolution 816, recommending that the Citizens Stamp Advisory Committee issue a stamp commemorating Diwali (Haniffa 2004). Although the committee has considered the proposal, it has not adopted it. On July 12, 2007, Rajan Zed, the Hindu chaplain of the Indian Association of North Nevada, opened the U.S. Senate with a Hindu prayer, the first ever in American history, with protests by some Christian fundamentalists (Haniffa 2007). Now Diwali is becoming a secular holiday just as Rosh Hashanah and St. Patrick's Day have become holidays for Jewish and Irish Americans (Gans 1994). Like other non-Christian immigrant groups, Indian Hindus have encountered resistance by local city councils and residents in many cities when trying to build temples (Pais 2004). But because Hinduism symbolizes India's culture and heritage and because it is very different from Christianity, Indian Hindus have introduced their religious prayers, holidays, and other rituals to Americans as representing Indian traditions.

Third, the temple has helped preserved Indian traditions through various cultural activities, such as lectures, dance performances, and music concerts related to the Hindu religion and other Indian cultural traditions. In December 2002 I attended a lecture given at the temple's auditorium and attended by about two hundred people. The lecture, by a well-known Indian Hindu scholar, was entitled "The Face of Hinduism in America: Threats and Opportunity," in which he discussed the "pervasive biases against Indianness and Hinduism by U.S. higher educational institutions, high schools and the media" and suggested strategies to enhance the influence of Hinduism and Indian culture in the United States. After the lecture, the audience debated how to present Hinduism and Indian culture to Americans accurately and positively. My attendance helped me understand the extent to which Indian Hindu immigrants approach Hinduism mainly as an Indian religious and cultural heritage.

The temple also offers Veda classes, taught by the temple priests, twice a week, as well as a class on yoga and meditation on Sunday. Many white and black Americans, as well as South Asian Hindus, take both the Veda and yoga classes, which is another way the Hindu temple teaches Indian and South Asian cultural traditions to the American public.

Fourth, the temple helps preserve Indian cultural traditions by performing various rituals for Indian Hindu families. It built the community center to be used for various cultural and social activities not only by the temple but also by Indian immigrants. The wedding hall is used for wedding ceremonies, birthday parties, and many other life-cycle rituals for Hindu families, usually on weekends. The temple also performs a number of rituals, including weddings and funerals, at Hindu homes, hotels, and crematoria.[5] It charges a fixed fee for performing the rituals, which has become an important source of its revenues. A gift shop in the center's basement sells pictures of deities, idols, coins, Veda and prayer books, videotapes of Hindu religious epics, and Hindi music tapes. The temple is planning another program to promote Vedic studies, yoga, and senior and youth programs and has already bought buildings for them.

In September 2001, I attended the Hindu wedding ceremony of an Indian bride and a white American groom performed in the temple's wedding hall. I was impressed that not only the white groom but also his parents and relatives observed the Hindu-style wedding ceremony presided over by a Hindu priest, wearing traditional Hindu dress and accompanied by Indian music and dances. After the ceremony, all the white participants ate vegetarian food. I asked the groom's parents whether they had converted to Hinduism. They told me that they were Catholics but had followed the Hindu rules for their son's wedding because the bride's parents wanted a Hindu wedding. Only a few mixed Indian/white weddings are performed at Hindu temples.[6]

I have attended a few Christian wedding ceremonies performed in a Korean church for a Korean bride and a white groom. But the wedding ceremony was not very Korean other than the Korean food served at the reception. In fact, many non-Christian Korean immigrants and their children have a Christian wedding ceremony, either inside or outside a church, presided over by a pastor, with most guests saying prayers and singing hymns. The presence of many Korean Christians in the Korean community has to some extent Christianized Korean culture, including weddings, funerals, and other formal meetings. In contrast, even the wedding of an Indian Hindu bride and a white Christian groom followed the traditional Hindu wedding ceremony.

Finally, the temple encourages the preservation of Indian cultural traditions by offering various language and other cultural classes and programs to Hindu immigrants and the second generation. In 1998 it started a program called *ganesa patasala* (education center) that offers various classes on Saturday to children from kindergarten through high school. In 2002, these were Indian-language classes—Sanskrit, Hindi, and three other local languages—a Hindu religion class, and SAT and high school entrance exam preparation classes. Enrollees pay a nominal fee per year to attend the twelve sessions between 9 am and 2:30 pm, taught by parent volunteers. In 2007, some 1.5- and second-generation Indian high school students were teaching math to elementary students. In addition, the temple offers different levels of dance and music classes during the same time period on Saturday and Sunday. Several Indian dance teachers at the center often participate in intercultural programs, performing traditional Indian dance and music for New Yorkers.[7] The director of the school told me that these Indian language, religion, and dance classes had become increasingly popular since their beginning in 1998 but that the temple did not have room to accommodate all those interested. Consequently, the temple started constructing additional buildings in 2001 and completed them in 2004. One of them is being used as the education and art center, and the director of the children's learning programs told me that now the temple offers thirty language, music/dance, and religious classes for children on Saturday.

In 2002, on the second and fourth Saturdays each month, about seventy second-generation Hindus (8 to 24 years old) regularly attended the youth club meetings for religious education and cultural activities. To celebrate special Hindu religious and Indian national holidays, the youth club performs traditional Indian plays and organizes an Indian music festival for children. The *pujas* for children and adolescents who take the Saturday classes and join the Youth Club are separate from those for adults. For the children of Indian or South Asian Hindu immigrants, learning about worship services, Vedantic philosophy,[8] religious music/dance, and religious plays means learning about their ethnic traditions. Accordingly, Hindu parents take their children to the temple to teach them religious rituals and values. For the children of Korean Protestant immigrants, however, religious education and ethnic education are different, so Korean churches must decide whether they should concentrate on their children's religious or ethnic education.

As noted earlier, Hindu temples have advantages over Korean Protestant churches for children's ethnic education mainly because of Hinduism's strong association between religion and ethnicity. But because the Hindu worship is not congregational, temples offer less to children's ethnic and religious education than Korean churches do. The Hindu Temple Society of North America is one of only about twenty-five Hindu temples in the New York / New Jersey area and has the most devotees of any temple in the area. Nonetheless, only about one hundred children were enrolled in the language, religion, and dance classes in 2003. The seventy-member youth group that meets every other week for religious and cultural education also is too small to have much impact on Indian Hindu children's ethnic retention. In contrast, many Korean children were enrolled in the Shin Kwang Church's Korean school, and many other Korean churches offer similar Korean language and cultural education programs. In sum, only about 35 percent of Indian Hindu immigrants go to a religious institution weekly, compared with about 80 percent of Korean Protestant immigrants.

The Council of Hindu Temples of North America, to which the Ganesh Temple belongs, organized an essay contest for Indian adolescents and college students in the United States. It assigns three different topics, all pertaining to Hinduism and Indian cultural traditions, each year to middle school (750 words), high school (1,000 words), and college students (1,500 words). Prize-winning essays from the contest each year are published in *India Abroad*, a major Indian ethnic weekly, and in the newsletters of the member temples, including the Ganesh Temple's *Ganesanjali*. But this national essay contest may be the only one organized by Hindu temples in North America. In contrast, as pointed out in chapter 4, several Korean churches in the New York area have organized their own or community Korean-language contests, although Christianity has little connection with the Korean language. Many Korean immigrant churches have been able to organize these contests only because they have established effective educational programs.

## Patriarchal Traditions and Gender Hierarchy

It is extremely difficult to separate Korean Confucian culture from the theological position of each Korean church because both clerical and lay leaders in Korean churches try to justify patriarchal practices through biblical phrases. It is even more difficult to separate the effects of culture from those of religion on patriarchal practices in Hindu temples because Hinduism does not have one central scripture comparable to the Bible. Instead, it has several scriptures, including the Vedas and the Bhagavad Gita, each of which provides guidelines for Hindus' religious life. Moreover, since Hindu rituals have evolved by incorporating local cultural traditions in different Indian states, it may be impossible to disentangle the religious and cultural sources of their patriarchal practices,

When Indian Hindu immigrants, Hindu scholars, and Hindu organizations tried to correct texts relating to ancient Hinduism in Grade 6 history and social science textbooks in California in 2005, they did not agree on the changes (Hindu American Foundation 2006; Kurien 2007, 204–5; Mozumder 2006a, 2006b), particularly those pertaining to the caste system, the lower position of women, and other "defamatory references to ancient Hinduism." Since classical Hinduism is part of Indian culture, it may be impossible to determine to what extent women's lower status among Hindus was supported by the original sacred texts. During my interview, I reminded a vice president of the Ganesh Temple that Hindu scholars found phrases in Hindu scriptures that support the lower position of women. Her response was that

> in ancient times women had power under Hinduism. But while the Upanishad was
> being orally transmitted, men modified the scriptures to their benefit. They included
> social practices not supported by the ancient scriptures. But we can also find in
> Hindu scriptures many phrases that associate women with power, courage, and
> glory, probably more phrases than we can find in scriptures of any other religion.

In terms of leadership positions, the Ganesh Temple seems to be more gender egalitarian than the Shin Kwang Church. As we saw earlier, the *danghe* (the consistory), consisting of the senior pastor and twelve elders, makes all important decisions for the Korean church, and all elders are men. The senior pastor and all four other associate/education pastors are men, with almost all committees chaired by men. All five exhorters are women, but they play a nurturing role, such as visiting sick members and praying for the church, that does not involve power and status. As I have documented elsewhere (Min 2008), women are severely underrepresented in leadership positions in other Korean immigrant churches in New York City.

By contrast, as previously noted, as of December 2005, four of the eleven members of the temple's board of trustees were women, and half of the Executive Committee members (11 out of the 22) were women. Women were well represented in other subcommittees. As previously noted, Dr. Mysorekar, an Indian physician, has played the central role in the operation of the temple since 1994 when she became president of the temple. It is she who has introduced speakers to the audience for lectures given at the temple. It is also she who has generally accepted the visitors to the temple. She conceded that overall men are more actively involved in the operation of other Hindu temples, but she emphasized that because of their family obligations, many Indian women with leadership skills were reluctant to take the main responsibility for the operation of the temple. Remember that her dedication to the temple for thirty years has been possible partly because she has no child.

The woman president's central role in the operation of the temple for a long period of time seems to be an important factor that has contributed to women's great representation in leadership positions in the Ganesh Temple. Dr. Mysorekar's leadership is reflected in the fact that women comprise half the twenty-two members of the Executive Committee headed by her. Dr. Mysorekar said that women were serving as the presidents in a few other Hindu temples in the United States but that men serve as presidents in a predominant majority of Hindu temples. Under the influence of the male top leader men are likely to play a more active role in leadership positions in other temples.

I believe that the Ganesh Temple and other Hindu temples are more gender equal than the Shin Kwang Church of New York and other Korean immigrant churches. First, the Ganesh Temple does not have semiclergy male positions, such as eldership, that give their holders a great deal of power and authority. All the priests at the temple are men, but they only perform rituals and do not make important decisions or enforce policies. Moreover, in answering my question about why women do not serve as priests in Hindu temples, Dr. Mysorekar emphasized a practical, rather than a theological, reason:

> Hindu scriptures do not say anything that does not allow women to serve as priests. But traditionally only men became priests mainly because they were different from women in their functions and physical characteristics. The duty of Hindu priests is strenuous. Constant chanting in front of a fire requires a lot of energy and strength. In physical strength, women do not fit this job. Moreover, women have family obligations. However, this does not mean that men have more power than women. God made us equal, but God gave men and women different functions. Functions are differently delineated.

In her study of a large Buddhist temple in Los Angeles Suh (2004, 137) also pointed out that it is less patriarchal than most Korean immigrant churches because it has no positions comparable to the elders in Korean churches, which give power and authority to men. Hinduism, like Buddhism (see Suh 2004, 22), and unlike evangelical Christianity, does not hold—or at least does not emphasize—a theological position that justifies the subordination of women to men. Hindu scriptures, such as the Vedas, may include statements that degrade women. But neither the Ganesh temple nor other ecumenical Hindu temples in the United States seem to accept these sexist and other hierarchical elements as core Hindu values. Instead, they stress religious freedom, nonviolence, vegetarianism, and other positive universal values, as well as spirituality (Williams 1992).

Moreover, Hinduism supports gender equality to a greater extent than does the Korean version of evangelical Christianity, in that it has both female and male deities and saints. In Hinduism, "the Goddess is considered the embodiment of the strength of the male god and, as such, is described as Energy (Shakti)" (Michell 1988, 31). By contrast, the sexist anthropomorphic views of God, strengthened by the repeated reference to God the Father in the Bible, sermons, hymns, and prayers in Korean immigrant churches, perpetuate this patriarchal ideology by underscoring women's subordinate position in the family, church, and society. In her interviews with Korean Christian immigrant women, Ae Ra Kim (1996) found that many of them tried to resolve these conflicts resulting from their subordinate position by accepting the Christian religious belief that God made men superior to women.

Finally, the Ganesh Temple is less sexist and less patriarchal because it is not dependent on a Hindu religious hierarchy in India. As I explained in chapter 3, the organization of most Korean immigrant churches is based in Korea. Even those churches affiliated with American denominations, including the Shin Kwang Church, are strongly influenced by Korean Protestant denominations in regard to gender issues. By contrast, the Ganesh Temple and other Hindu temples in the United States, with the exception of sectarian temples like the Swaminarayan and Swadiyaya temples, are not dependent on any Hindu denominational hierarchy in India because Hinduism does not have a central organization.

The absence of the central hierarchical organization for Hinduism means that their temples can differ in their organizational structure, deities, rituals, and languages, which can also help Hindu temples in the United States moderate their organizational structure's caste and gender hierarchies. Prema Kurien, a sociologist of Indian ancestry, pointed out that Pan-Indian and Pan-Hindu organizations in the United States, led by upper-class male professionals, emphasize the "figure of the chaste, nurturing, and self-sacrificing Indian women" to present a model minority image of their culture and religion (Kurien 1999, 655). Thus Hindu immigrants "have institutionalized a more in-egalitarian and restrictive model of Indian womanhood than that prevalent in India" (Kurien 1999, 648). Other Indian American woman scholars have provided similar arguments (Bhattacharjee 1992; DasGupta and DasGupta 1996), but none used empirical data to examine whether and to what extent large temples in the United States are more or less patriarchal in organizational structure than those in India.

# 6 Participation in Religious Institutions, Family Rituals, and Identity

IN THIS CHAPTER, I supplement my ethnographic information about the relative importance of the fellowship or cultural retention function of Korean Protestant churches and Indian Hindu temples with interviews with Indian Hindu and Korean Protestant immigrants.[1] My interviews with fifty-six Korean Protestant immigrants and fifty-nine Indian Hindu immigrants provide information not only about their participation in religious institutions but also about their family rituals and the relationship between their religious and ethnic identities.

The advantage of interviews conducted outside a religious institution is that I could ask the informants about their views of the relationship between religion and child socialization, ethnic identity, and other related issues. Responding to the question of why they thought it important for their children to adopt their religion, Ganesh Prasad, a middle-aged Indian Hindu, owner of a clothing store, and mother of two children, offered the following comment:

> It is very important that my children maintain Hindu religion. It's their culture. It's who they are. It's a way for them to identify themselves. They have a right to know who their ancestors are and what they believed. It's also important to pass down religious beliefs and customs to future generations.

This suggests that her intention to teach her children religion is closely related to her desire to teach them their Indian ethnic heritage and identity. The response by Young-Sook Lee, a middle-aged Korean Protestant, owner of a furniture store, and mother of three children, was this:

> For my children to maintain their religious belief is as important as their lives. Their belief in God will always give them the security of mind and the courage to cope with difficulties in life. I had many hardships in my life. But my firm belief in God helped me overcome them without wavering in life. In the Bible we can find the best wisdom and the most important moral codes.

Her answer emphasizes the psychological and moral values of religious belief, such as security of mind and the courage to cope with adversity in life. Again, these comments largely represent the differences between Indian and Korean immigrant parents' views of the importance of religion to their children.

## Participation in Religious Institutions

Earlier I noted that Korean Protestant immigrants participate in religious institutions far more frequently than Indian Hindu immigrants do. My interviews revealed that Korean Protestant immigrants also spend more time on each visit to a religious institution than do Indian Hindus. Koreans usually spend two to five hours at the Sunday worship service and fellowship and an average of more than eight hours a week for the church more generally, including the time spent on volunteer activities. Seven of the fifty-six Korean respondents reported that they spent twenty or more hours each week on their church activities. According to the 1997–1999 Presbyterian Racial and Ethnic Panel Study, based on a national sample of Presbyterian churches belonging to the Presbyterian Church USA (Kim and Kim 2001, 83), Korean Presbyterians spent more time at and gave more money to their own church than did any other Presbyterian groups (black, white, and Latino), but they spent less time and gave less money for nonchurch community activities.

Most Hindu respondents reported that they spent time from half an hour to a few hours on each visit to the temple. The religious service usually takes less than a half hour, but they generally spend one to three hours at a lecture and/or other cultural activities. Far fewer Indian Hindus than Korean Protestants did volunteer work for their religious institution.

Both Indian Hindu and Korean Protestant immigrants usually go to their place of worship as a family, but my interviews revealed that the women in both groups went to their religious institution more frequently than the men did. For example, 35 percent of the female Hindu respondents, compared with 17 percent of the males, went to temple at least once a week. Forty-four percent of female Korean Protestant respondents, compared with 26 percent of males, attended church twice or more a week. In both groups, too, women spent more time at their religious institution for both religious and volunteer activities. Women generally have more free time than men do. Indeed, several Korean and Indian male respondents complained that their long hours of work did not allow them to attend church or temple as frequently as they wished to. The gender differential in the time spent at the religious institution is also due to the general tendency of women to be more religious than men, regardless of their ethnic and racial background (Ozorak 1996; Suziedelis and Potvin 1981).

Korean Protestant immigrants spend a great amount of time in church partly because they consider coethnic fellowship to be important. We asked them: "What are the reasons you attend a Korean church (a Hindu temple) regularly?" The majority of both Koreans (57%) and Hindus (66%) cited religious or psychological purposes, such as (in order of importance) "to worship God," "to glorify God," "to enhance my religious belief," "for peace of mind," and "to cope with personal difficulties." But there was a significant difference between the two groups in their emphasis on coethnic fellowship. Forty-two percent of the Koreans cited coethnic fellowship and other related factors, such as "to belong to a Korean group," "to maintain ethnic networks," "to enjoy a familylike atmosphere," and "to cope with alienation from American society," as their primary reasons, and another 20 percent cited these as the second most important reason.

The following response by Jin-Su Park, a Korean male retailer in his mid-forties, is typical:

> Although I live in a white neighborhood, I do not talk much with my neighbors. For six days, I serve black customers and get stressed. I need an outlet to express my feeling with fellow Koreans. That is a Korean church. When I talk and eat lunch with my friends in my church on Sunday, I feel at home and relaxed. A Korean church is a Korean community. I don't know how other Korean immigrants who don't go to a Korean church can survive in this country.

An overwhelming majority of the Korean respondents reported that after the Sunday service. they eat at the church, spending one to two hours talking with their friends. Husbands and wives often eat separately to be with their own same-sex friends, and the children eating with their peers, too. Fifteen of the fifty-six Korean respondents (27%), who were either Buddhists or atheists in South Korea, became Protestants in the United States, citing coethnic fellowship as the main reason for their decision. A 62-year-old Korean man who had come to the United States as a foreign student thirty-one years earlier explained: "I had no religion in Korea, but I started to attend a Korean church in New York City because there was no major Korean organization other than a few Korean churches at that time. To learn about the Korean community, I had to go to a Korean church."

By contrast, only two of the fifty-nine Indian Hindu respondents cited coethnic fellowship as the main reason for their going to a Hindu temple regularly, and nine of them listed it as the second most important reason. About half the Hindu respondents reported that they had a meal after the service, but they usually ate with their family members rather than with friends. Only nine Indian Hindu respondents indicated that they often ate Indian food after the service with their friends. This difference is partly due to their different styles of worship. On Sunday, Korean Protestant immigrants have services together, but separately from their children, with the two groups listening to sermons by the pastor or the Sunday school teacher. Indian Hindus, with the exception of those who go to Swaminaryan and Caribbean Hindu temples, usually go to worship at various times and on various days, either alone or as a family. For this reason, it is difficult for them to meet their friends unless they make arrangements in advance.

While Hindus do not consider fellowship an important reason for going to temple, they do emphasize the preservation of their ethnic culture and identity as a major reason. The majority (58%) of the Hindu respondents chose the retention of ethnic culture and identity for themselves and their children as the most or the second-most important reason for going to temple. For example, Jaya Patel, a 40-year-old Hindu woman, responded: "We are from India. Helping our children learn about their roots is the main reason for going to temple. Having them know about Hindu gods and goddesses." Another informant, Sandeep Gupta, a 35-year-old man with two children, put it this way: "I think the main reasons are for my own peace of mind and my children's development. We want our kids to know as much as possible about their religion and culture." Many respondents reported that they went to temple with their children a few or several times a year to celebrate religious holidays, to observe cultural activities, and/or to have rituals performed for their children and/or other family members.

We asked the Hindu respondents: "Do you think attending an Indian Hindu temple is helpful to maintaining Indian cultural traditions? In what ways?" Nearly all answered this question affirmatively. The following statement by Sanjay Ghosh, a male Hindu who had lived in the United States for twelve years, is typical:

> Yes, it definitely is. Temple reinforces the teachings of the holy book. It helps us to follow the customs and so on and to keep our faith, even though our society is different from India. It's a place where we feel that we belong, plus we get to associate with people of the same beliefs and culture at the temple.

A 46-year-old Hindu woman who works as a bank teller stated: "I think by going to temple, my Indian identity is made stronger. Hinduism and Indian culture are linked, so by going to temple I am reminded of my roots and I bring this home with me."

We asked the Hindu respondents with one or more children, "Do you think going to temple is helpful to teaching your children Indian cultural traditions? In what ways?" Again, all agreed that it was helpful. Chandrakant Patel, a biological researcher with one child, said, "Yes, it is. My daughter was born in the U.S. So taking her to temple is a good way of teaching her the rituals, customs, and beliefs of her people. She will learn how to make the proper sacrifices to the gods and how to perform their *pujas*."

Shankar Reddy, a middle-aged Indian male immigrant with two children, also believed his children's going to a Hindu temple would help preserve their culture: "Yes, they see what Indian values are when they hear the sermons. It's very important that they learn about our culture."

We asked Korean Protestants the same questions regarding the relationship between their belonging to a church and preserving their culture. The results show that the vast majority of Korean Protestants do not consider cultural retention as a major reason for their going to church. Only twelve of the fifty-six Korean respondents (21%) chose cultural preservation for themselves and/or their children as the most or the second-most important reason for their participation in a Korean church. But most of the respondents agreed that their going to a Korean church was helpful in maintaining Korean cultural traditions (75%) and teaching their children the Korean language and culture (89%). Many respondents, however, pointed out that cultural retention was the result of their regular attendance at a Korean church rather than its objective.

How did Korean Protestants think that attending a Korean church would help them preserve their Korean culture? Many respondents reported that they were too busy with their work to prepare food to celebrate traditional Korean holidays at home (New Year's Day and Korean Thanksgiving Day) but that they could celebrate the holidays with traditional Korean foods at their church. Some also pointed out that in the United States, without going to a Korean church they could never observe Korean national holidays. Several respondents indicated that their church helped them continue the Korean values of "group orientation and filial piety" over the American value of "individualism." Three respondents reported that their attending a Korean church rather than an American church helped them hold memorial services for their deceased parents with the main pastor and close church members invited to their homes.[2] These three cases indicate that a small proportion of Korean Protestant immigrants observe such memorial services for their deceased parents, the Protestant version of Korean ancestor worship service. Most Korean Protestant immigrants, especially evangelical Protestants, usually do not practice these memorial services, which they consider "idol worship."

The Korean Protestant respondents consider their church important especially for the intergenerational transmission of Korean culture. Many respondents indicated that they would not lose Korean cultural traditions no matter how long they lived in the United States but that they had difficulty teaching their children Korean cultural traditions at home alone. They felt that a Korean church, as a miniature Korean community, helped them teach their children the Korean language and culture. Several respondents reported that they went to a Korean church especially for their children's ethnic education. The following remarks by Sung-Min Kim, a 65-year-old Korean male immigrant who had lived in the United States for forty years, was typical:

> It is almost impossible for us to teach our children the Korean language and
> customs individually through instructions. The children can learn Korean cultural
> traditions effectively in a group setting. A Korean church is an ideal place they
> can learn Korean things naturally. Korean children can learn the Korean language

and history from the church's Korean program. They can also learn about Korean holidays and Korean etiquette in interaction with other Koreans, especially with Korean adults, there.

Many respondents emphasized that the church particularly helped their children learn the Korean custom of showing respect to their parents and other adults. Gil-Ja Choi, a 37-year-old Korean woman with two children, commented about how effectively a Korean church could teach children Korean etiquette:

> Korean etiquette places emphasis on children showing respect when talking with adults. American children say "you" when they talk to parents, just like when they talk to their friends. But Korean children should not say "you" to parents. They are supposed to say "Yes, father" or "Yes, mother." And they greet an adult by giving a deep bow instead of saying "hello." This kind of Korean etiquette I cannot teach at home. Children can learn it naturally in a Korean church from their friends and Sunday school teachers. We have asked Sunday school and Friday Bible study teachers to teach Korean etiquette as well as Christian values.

As noted earlier, Indian Hindu respondents consider going to a Hindu temple as facilitating their children's learning Indian culture because religious rituals and values are, to them, the central elements of Indian culture. By contrast, Korean Protestant immigrants consider their church as the best place to teach their children Korean, especially Confucian etiquette, rather than Christian norms. Christian values and rituals are not part of their children's ethnic education because Christianity contains few Korean cultural elements.

While Korean immigrants' affiliation with Korean churches has helped them preserve Korean cultural traditions, it also has contributed to the Christianization of Korean culture, an important point that has been overlooked in the literature. Since about 75 percent of Korean immigrants go to Korean Christian (Protestant or Catholic) churches, non-Christian Korean immigrants usually participate in their relatives' and/or friends' weddings and funerals presided over by pastors or Catholic priests. Even some non-Christian Koreans organize Christian weddings and funerals for themselves and their family members because Korean pastors are happy to preside over these rituals. When the Korean Association of New York or another Korean ethnic organizations hold formal meetings, they often begin by singing one or more hymns and end with a pastor's prayer. Although most Buddhist and other non-Christian Koreans do not like this Christianization of community meetings, it is virtually impossible to stop, since many leaders of Korean ethnic organizations are Christians.

In summer 2006, I attended a twenty-year anniversary banquet organized by a Korean ethnic organization in Flushing. The organizers invited a middle-aged Korean trumpeter to play at the beginning of the banquet. Even though the emcee announced that the trumpeter would play the "American and Korean national anthems," he started with a hymn and finished with the two anthems.[3] I thought that some of the guests might protest his unexpected playing of a hymn, but surprisingly many joined the trumpeter in singing the hymn.

## Domestic Religious Practices

Previous studies of the religious practices of immigrant/ethnic groups—both earlier white and current third-world immigrant/ethnic groups—are largely congregational. Accordingly, they did not gather any systematic information about how members of a particular group practice their religion at home. Data from interviews with Indian Hindu and Korean Protestant immigrants do, however, provide information about their religious practices at home. As expected, Indian Hindu immigrants were found to have a significant advantage over Korean Protestant immigrants in preserving their ethnic traditions through their religious practices at home.

The interviews reveal that Indian Hindus spend much time performing religious rituals at home, indeed, far more time than in the temple. More than any other immigrant group, Indian Hindus perform rituals at home. All but one of the Hindu respondents had a shrine at home, consisting of religious statues, pictures of gods/goddesses and saints, incense stickers, and/or lamps. One respondent reported that he had even built a miniature Hindu temple at home.

Results of the 2003 New Immigrant Survey, which was conducted by Massey and his associates, show that more Indian Hindu immigrants (72%) than any other religious immigrant group reported having a religious display at home, while Protestant immigrants showed the lowest rate (16%). Catholics, Eastern Orthodox, Buddhists, and Muslims stood between these two extremes in the percentage of home displays. Moreover, this survey likely underestimated the percentages of immigrants who had religious displays because many who did not have a display at home in the first year of their residence were likely to create one in the future.

All my Hindu informants indicated that they put up decorations signifying their Hindu religion and identity at home, such as pictures and statues of gods and goddesses. Some had Hindu symbols all over their houses. I asked a 39-year-old woman with two children:

> Q: What decorations do you put at home to signify your Hindu identity?
>
> R: Yeah, all over. I have a big statue of Lord Ganesha in my living room, so you can see it as soon as you enter. Then I have another one in my party room. Then I have a temple upstairs. And in my foyer I have a Lord Krishna statue. Then I have a little temple in my kitchen. Almost in every room I have something.

Gujarati Indian immigrants in their early sixties allowed me to visit their home to observe their *puja* ceremony on Saturday. They used both their living room and bedroom for the family rituals and posted two large pictures of gods in the living room. Visitors could see the pictures easily when entering the living room. In addition, they had five little trees in pots beside the windows, each of which symbolized a god or a goddess. And they used their bedroom as the main worship room, in one corner of which they had hung pictures of eight gods and goddesses with five metal idols attached to them.

All but four respondents prayed at least once per day, usually in the morning, often offering food, milk, flowers, and/or money, and many (36%) prayed twice or more each day. Many respondents performed other Hindu rituals at home as parts of their *puja*, such as reciting a few mantras, meditating, and reading scriptures from the holy book. All but three Hindu respondents reported that they fasted at least once a year, most fasting once a month or once a week. Rupam Prasad, a 52-year-old woman, stated: "Every Tuesday, my husband and I fast. We do not eat any solid food. We also do not consume any food with salt. In the morning we drink cups of orange juice and tea. After six in the evening, we eat bread and yogurt for dinner." The majority of the Hindu respondents reported that they never ate beef or pork at home and tried not to eat any meat products at least once (on a particular day) a week. Many said that it was difficult for them to remain strictly vegetarian in the United States, and Indian Hindu males reported that they had to compromise their vegetarian rule at their workplace.

All but one respondent said that they regularly listened to tapes of Hindi songs, usually every day, at home and/or at work. All stated that they celebrated Indian religious holidays, such as Diwali, Holi, and Hanuman Jayanti, at home, with Indian food prepared and relatives invited. Many celebrate one religious holiday almost every month, according to a 48-year-old Indian woman: "We have almost one Hindu holiday every month. We do a *puja* at home and go to the temple and sing *bhajans* [devotional songs]. We make food for offerings, it's called *prasad*. And everybody gets together to celebrate." By contrast, a small proportion (18%) reported that they celebrated non-Hindu Indian holidays at home or in the community, mostly taking part in the Indian Independence Day parade held in Manhattan. One Hindu respondent asserted: "Indian culture is so much based on Hinduism that there is no nonreligious Indian holiday." Her statement is factually wrong, but it reflects the perception of many Indian Hindus that Hindu rituals are the central elements of Indian culture.

The majority of Indian Hindu respondents named Diwali as the most important religious holiday on which they prepared special foods and lit candles to welcome Lord Ram. In September 2001, my wife and I were invited to visit an Indian Hindu home not far from our house to see how they celebrated the Diwali. We arrived there around nine in the evening, but the house was bright because of the many candles. The host and several visitors had just completed a *puja* and were eating vegetarian food while watching an Indian TV program on the celebration of Diwali in India. Our host showed my wife and me the family shrine, which contained several statues of gods and goddesses. In fact, he used an entire room as a family shrine. Our host offered us vegetarian food and explained the significance of Diwali for both Hindus and other Indians. The interviews indicate that when celebrating special days for their family members, they have religious rituals performed at the temple more often than at home. But more than two-thirds of the respondents reported that they invited a Hindu priest to their home at least once a year to perform a special ritual for their family members.

When Indian Hindus celebrate major religious holidays or perform important family life-cycle rituals at home, they usually invite relatives and friends, which is one of the ways that Indian Hindu immigrants maintain kin and friendship networks. In August 2005, an Indian friend invited me to his home to observe a *puja* in order to help me with my research on Hindu family rituals. He organized a *satynarayan puja*, a *puja* for a blessing to the family, to wish good luck for their two daughters who were leaving home in a few days, one going to India for a job after graduating from a college and the other starting a college in another city.

Seven families came to his home on Long Island, including his married daughter and two other relatives. My friend told me that only a few families were able to come to his home for the *puja* because it was a weekday but that more than a dozen families usually visit his home when he celebrates important Hindu holidays such as Diwali. His daughter and two other relatives brought vegetarian food. They had the *puja* in a room in the basement, used as a special room for a family shrine, presided over by a priest from a temple in Flushing. All the visitors, including my wife and me, participated in the worship service. The priest started the *puja* by chanting mantras in Sanskrit representing particular deities with the two daughters, in *saris*, sitting in front of the shrine. The daughters followed the priest in chanting while the incense burned. The priest chanted again while the daughters gave the food (apples, rice, milk, and grapes) and flowers to gods and goddesses. This took about thirty minutes. The priest then gave a sermon for more than thirty-five minutes, both talking to the daughters in Hindi and chanting in Sanskrit. The *puja* ended after the priest daubed the daughters' foreheads with water and they threw incense on the fire. All together, the *puja* took about one and a half hours. Afterward, they ate a late, vegetarian dinner, after which they, men and women sitting separately, talked until even later at night. My friend told me that he had had such a *puja* led by a *pundit* (priest) twice or so each year while his three daughters were children but that after they left home for marriage or college, he had one once every two years.

We asked the Korean Protestant informants how often and how long they read the Bible, prayed, and/or sang or listened to hymns at home. Seven of the Korean informants (13%) did not do any of this at home, but most did practice their religion at home. Thirty-six percent of the fifty-six respondents read the Bible almost every day, for about fifteen to thirty minutes. About 40 percent reported that besides praying before each meal, they prayed twice a day, usually when they got up in the morning and before they went to bed at night. About 35 percent sang hymns and/or gospel songs a few times a week or more at home. But many said that their long hours of work gave them little time to sing hymns at home, and others commented that it was difficult to sing hymns alone at home. Most, however, regularly listened to tapes of hymns or gospel songs, and/or Korean Christian radio programs at home, while driving, and/or at work.

Although most Korean Protestant immigrants remain very religious at home in regard to reading the Bible and praying regularly, they do not engage in religious practices directly or indirectly related to Korean cultural traditions. Korean Protestant immigrants benefit from their church to preserve their cultural traditions mainly because they practice Korean culture through the church's group services and other activities. But those who extensively practiced their religion at home practiced it alone rather than as a family. Individual religious practices do not help them maintain Korean cultural traditions. Non-Christian Korean immigrants, such as Buddhists and Confucians, who do not pray, read the Bible, and/or listen to tapes of hymns or gospel songs at home, were more likely to read and watch Korean media materials and listen to tapes of popular Korean songs. Thus they are likely to absorb more ethnic culture than Korean evangelical immigrants who extensively practice their religion at home.

The interviews showed that most Korean Christian immigrants celebrate or observe Easter at a church rather than at home and that they celebrated Christmas in a Korean church with many religious activities but few Korean cultural activities.[4] Even when celebrating traditional Korean holidays, most Korean Protestant immigrants do not do much at home, usually celebrating them in a church eating traditional Korean food and often playing traditional games with their church members. Moreover, Korean Protestants are not comparable to Indian Hindus in putting up religious decorations at home. Nine of the fifty-six Korean respondents reported that they had no religious decorations at home, and the others had one or more of the following items: a picture of Jesus Christ, one or two panels with biblical phrases (*sunggu*) in Korean calligraphy, and a cross (*sipjaga*). Although Korean Protestant immigrants put up fewer religious decorations at home than Indian Hindu immigrants do, because they are generally very religious they are more apt to have a religious display than other Protestant immigrants do. According to the results of the 2003 New Immigrant Survey, only about 16 percent of the new Protestant immigrant sample reported having a religious display at home.

A high correlation between participating in a religious institution and practicing religion at home was found for Korean Protestant respondents. The Korean Protestant respondents who went to church twice or more a week also performed more religious rituals at home, were more apt to read the Bible regularly, and prayed a few times a day, more often than did those who attended church less frequently. Some respondents who attended church only once a week did not practice religion at home at all; they seemed to go to church mainly for fellowship and cultural retention. However, there was no significant relationship between Hindu respondents' going to temple and practicing their religion at home.

We asked those Indian Hindu respondents with one or more children at school several questions about how they taught their children religious rituals and values at home. A few said they made their children pray, read the holy books, and regularly perform other religious rituals. But most confessed that it was difficult to make their children regularly perform religious rituals at home. Instead, as the following response by a 41-year-old deli owner with two children suggests, they hoped their children would learn by example by watching their parents at home: "When I do my daily prayers, sing *bhajans* [devotional songs], recite mantras, make offerings to the gods, etc., I expect them to learn and follow my footsteps. I cannot force them to practice rituals. I hope they can learn by themselves." Many respondents said that they tried to teach their small children religious values by reading a comic book of religious stories from the Ramayana, and others used videotapes of religious programs and/or tapes of Hindi songs.

A small proportion (20%) of Hindu respondents enforced the no-meat dietary rule at least once a week for their children, although Gujarati Hindus were much stricter in imposing the no-meat rule on their children.[5] About two-thirds of the Hindu respondents brought a priest to their home, usually once or twice a year, to perform life-cycle and/or family rituals for their children and other family members. A few respondents with teenaged children did not allow them to date or hang out at night with their friends. But the Indian Hindu respondents pointed out that they were much less successful than Indian Muslims in imposing the no-meat or no-dating rule on their children. Most Hindu respondents indicated that they wanted their children to learn how to observe Hindu religious holidays properly from their own observations of celebrations of the holidays at home. Finally, some respondents who visited India with their children reported that they took their children to the Golden Temple and other famous religious sites.

Kyung-Sik Shin, a Korean immigrant in his early fifties with a master's degree in political science, has two children, a 12-year-old son and a 9-year-old daughter.

I asked him how often and how he and his wife conducted services with their children at home. He made the following comment:

> Although my wife is more religious than I, due to her early morning work schedule, I usually guide a worship service with children in the morning. Around 7 am we have a twenty-minute service. We start the service reciting the Apostles Creed and then sing a hymn. After that I read a Bible verse for children using a bilingual Bible. Although my children encounter difficulty understanding the Korean version of the Bible, they can read the English translations on the right side of every page. Both of my children are familiar with the Bible because we have read it to them before going to bed for many years. Finally, we three take turns every day in offering a prayer. On Saturdays, my wife does not work outside, so all of us can have a service together.

When I asked him why he continued to hold a family worship service almost every morning despite the time pressure, he pointed out its practical benefits:

> I once read an article by a theological professor about the importance of having a regular family ritual as a means to maintaining a family bond. Due to their language barrier and cultural differences, Korean immigrants and their children have a great deal of difficulty maintaining a family bond. But a regular family service can be the most important family ritual through which we can sustain a strong bond with children. When they pray, my children often confess their misconducts committed on the previous day and also talk about how they feel about their parents.

Shin is one of only a few (less than 10%) Korean Protestant immigrants who regularly hold family worship services with their children at least once a week. Although Shin and his wife went to a very evangelical Korean immigrant church, he estimated that only about one out of ten members of his church with children in school held a family service at least once a week. Many Korean informants reported that they could not have a regular family service partly because they had little time together.[6] Many others attributed their inability to hold family services to the intergenerational language barrier. But most informants said that they had family services on special occasions, such as when celebrating family members' birthdays, when family members got sick, when their children came back from college, and/or at a time when they had special visitors at home. Some informants reported that they depended on the church's Sunday school and other prayer meetings for their children's regular services. Several believed that their children would automatically learn religious beliefs from their own religious practices at home. The following comment by Kwang-Ja Yoon, a furniture store owner in her early sixties, reflects this:

*Shinangsim* [religious belief] is not something parents can teach children. They can develop it by themselves from the family environment, from watching their parents live Christian lives. I have never forced my children to pray and read the Bible. But both of my children personally accepted God in their high school years and have followed the sincere Christian ways of life.

Although most Korean informants did not hold family services with their children, approximately two-thirds of them were found to have done one or more things at home to transmit the religion to their children. The most commonly cited was making their children pray before meals and before bed. Some informants reported that they tried to eat dinner with their children, especially in order to teach them how to say grace before meals. The second most frequently cited thing was regularly making their children read the Bible and/or write one or two paragraphs from the Bible. Some respondents reported that they regularly checked whether their children finished the Bible reading or writing assignments for Sunday school or Friday Bible study. One Korean woman admitted that she even gave money to her children as an incentive to read the Bible regularly. A few Korean women with kindergarten or elementary school children said that they regularly read a few verses from the Bible and tried to explain their meanings to their children.

### Identity and Related Issues

We asked our informants with one or more children whether they believed it was important that their children adopt their religion, and why. We also asked them whether they considered it more important for their children to be good Christians (or Hindus) or good students. Their responses provide further evidence for the strong association between religious inheritance and retention of ethnic culture for Hindus and the weak association for Korean Protestants.

Most of the Hindu informants believed that it was very important for their children to adopt their religion, but only 38 percent believed that it was more important for their children to be good Hindus than to be good students. Twenty-two percent put priority on being a good student, and the remainder (40%) thought that both were equally important. As for why they believed it important for their children to adopt their religion, 73 percent of the Hindu informants emphasized preserving their ethnic heritage and identity. As a Hindu informant, a 50-year-old bank teller with two teenaged children, commented, "For me it's very important that my children adopt the Hindu religion. Just to know who we are, what we are, and what our culture is." About 40 percent of the Hindu respondents cited "to find peace of mind" and other moral benefits, such as "to follow a code of conduct," "to show love to others" and "to learn how to stay honest" as the main or an important reason why their children should adopt their religion. Three informants emphasized that preserving Hinduism would protect their children from the American youth culture associated with drugs, drinking, and sex.

All the Korean Protestant informants agreed that it was very important for their children to maintain their religion. Responding to the question of whether it was more important for their children to be good Christians or good students, 76 percent said that their children's being good Christians was more important than their being good students, and only 19 percent put priority on being good students. Thus more Korean Protestants than Indian Hindus regard their children's religious life as more important than education. Young-Sook Lee is a middle-aged woman with three children, one a high school junior and the other two college students. After completing a master's degree in pipe organ, she has served as an organist for a Korean church in New Jersey for many years, while her husband has served as an elder for the same church. In answer to why they put priority on their children's being good Christians over being good students, she made the following comment:

> If my children preserve strong religious faith, it will guide their attitudes and behaviors throughout their lives. If they follow words of God, they will always be humble to other people and control their lives no matter what difficulties they encounter. But if they become good students without preserving strong religious faith, it will never guarantee their good personality. Their success in life will not be determined by their academic achievements alone.

We noted earlier that more than 70 percent of Hindu informants wanted their children to adopt their religion mainly or partly to preserve their ethnic heritage and identity. But none of the Korean informants cited their children's preservation of Korean cultural traditions and identity as the major reason why their children should adopt their Christian religion. Instead, 32 percent of the Korean informants gave purely religious reasons, such as "because they can go to Heaven," "because that is the only road to eternal life," "because God takes care of everything in this world, including our life," and "because with religious belief they can go to the road prepared by God." Also, more than one-third of the Korean informants—a higher proportion than Indian Hindu respondents—cited psychological ("for peace of mind"), moral ("because the religion can protect my children from juvenile delinquencies" and "because it purifies their minds"), and practical benefits ("because it helps them overcome difficulties in this world" and "because they can have strong confidence to achieve their goals with the help of God").

Responding to the question, "Do you think being a typical Hindu means being a typical Indian?" 31 percent of the Indian Hindu informants said yes.

When asked why they believed being a typical Hindu means being a typical Indian, many informants pointed to the strong association between Hinduism and Indian culture, as in this example: "Yes, very much. A typical Hindu meal is a vegetarian meal. It represents Indian cuisine. Most of Indian cultural holidays are Hindu holidays." Another informant reported: "Because most of Hindus live in India and Hinduism is practiced mostly in India." Those Hindu informants who said no pointed out that there were other religions in India.

No Korean Protestant informant, however, agreed that being a typical Christian means being a typical Korean, although two Korean informants found a strong link between "Korean values" emphasizing filial piety and respect for adults in the Bible, especially in the Ten Commandments. We also asked the Korean immigrant informants which of the two, being Christian or being Korean, was more important to their personal identity. Given the cultural homogeneity of Korean society and the relatively short history of Christianity in Korea, we expected that almost all Korean Protestant informants would choose being Korean as their primary identity. Surprisingly, however, about 38 percent of Korean Protestant informants said that their Christian background was more important to their identity than their Korean background. Although more informants considered their Korean background more important (52%) than their religious background, it is surprising that more than one-third chose their Christian background. Naturally, those respondents who cited their Christian background were more religious than the others.

Many Korean Protestant immigrants' adoption of Christian identity as their primary identity has implications for understanding their identity patterns because of the tensions between their religious and ethnic identities. We thus asked them why they considered their Christian background more significant than their ethnic background. Their responses make clear the tensions between their religious and ethnic identities. Typical is the answer by So-Young Park, a woman in her early forties who has read the entire Bible each year since 1997:

> My Christian faith is far more important than my Korean background. For those who believe in Jesus Christ, in what country we were born does not matter. That we were born in Korea does not mean that we become brothers and sisters automatically. I believe we can be real brothers and sisters when we all believe in Jesus Christ. We should make all efforts to Christianize our siblings. But the Bible says that if they continue to reject Christianity, we should be ready to give up our sibling ties for the sake of Christian faith.

Another respondent proclaimed: "My Christian identity supersedes my Korean ethnic identity. Why? Because we are all the same before God. Since God created human beings, racial and ethnic differences are superficial."

Many informants who put their Korean ethnic identity before their Christian identity were, not surprisingly, also liberal and/or nationalistic. Many also had converted to Christianity after migrating to the United States and thus had many non-Christian relatives. For example, Jung Re Min, a 46-year-old woman, explained:

> I was born and spent my first twenty-seven years in Korea as a non-Christian. I began to attend a Korean church seven years ago. My mother is a Buddhist and two of my brothers are atheists. My parents-in-law are Buddhists, too. My brothers and mother in Connecticut still practice ancestor worship. When I go there for the Confucian ritual, I have to follow my brothers in giving deep bows to my deceased ancestors. As a Christian I should not worship anyone else than God. But I feel like breaking ties with my family members if I do not follow their Confucian rituals. Since I have many close non-Christian family members, it is natural that I consider my Korean background more important for my life than my Christian background.

One male respondent in his late fifties emphasized his Korean ethnic identity over his Christian identity on the grounds that "white American Christians do not accept Korean Christian as their brothers and sisters because of their racism." One male respondent in his early forties with a master's degree asserted: "I cannot choose between my Korean and Christian identities because I am a Korean in physical characteristics, but Christian in my spirituality. The two are not separable. You should have asked me which part I feel more proud of."

In general, immigrants who are members of the majority religion in their countries of origin, such as Indian Hindus and Iranian Muslims, tend to identify with their national origin, and most members of minority religious groups in their home countries use their religion as the basis for their identity (Bozorgmehr 2000, 174). However, in answer to the same identity question, 36 percent of the Indian Hindu respondents chose their Indian national or South Asian background, 37 percent chose their Hindu religion, and 27 percent insisted that their "Indian and Hindu" identities were not separable. A large proportion of Indian Hindu informants seem to have emphasized the importance of their religion to their identity because of the strong impact of Hinduism on their cultural lives in the United States. But whether more Indian Hindu respondents chose national origin or religious identity is not important, because for them, their religious and ethnic identities are complementary. For most Indian Hindus, their religion is the most significant component of their Indian heritage, and thus their Hindu background enhances their Indian identity. In this connection, it is important to reiterate that 27 percent of Indian Hindu respondents insisted that they could not choose the one over the other because the two were inseparable.

We also asked the Korean respondents whether they would prefer their child to marry a non-Christian Korean or a non-Korean Christian. Most preferred a Korean Christian, but when forced to choose between the two in a hypothetical situation, 46 percent of the respondents preferred a non-Christian Korean and 39 percent chose a non-Korean Christian. Another 13 percent asserted that neither the Korean nor the Christian background mattered if their child loved the partner and if he or she had a good personality. One respondent declined to choose either, insisting that the Korean and Christian backgrounds could not be compromised. It was surprising that so many of the informants preferred a non-Korean Christian to a non-Christian Korean as their child's marital partner and also that many were ready to accept whatever partner their child chose, regardless of his or her religious and ethnic background.

In her case study of a Korean English (second-generation) congregation, Chai (1998, 309) pointed out that many second-generation Korean Christians questioned their parents' religious faith when the latter emphasized a Korean over a Christian background for their children's marital partners. My data suggest that a larger proportion of Korean Protestant parents than we expected were ready to accept their children's choice of a non-Korean Christian partner over a non-Christian Korean partner. Naturally, the respondents' choice of Christian identity was closely correlated with their preference for a non-Korean Christian marital partner for their child. In fact, 25 percent of the informants considered themselves primarily as a Christian and also preferred a non-Korean Christian marital partner for their child.

When asked why they would consider a non-Korean Christian better as their child's marital partner, many respondents said that sharing universalistic Christian values was more important to a successful marital adjustment than sharing Korean ethnic values. For example, Sang Hyun Park, a 41-year-old man with two children, explained this stress on universalistic Christian values:

> I have no difficulty in choosing non-Korean Christian marital partners for my children over non-Christian Koreans. If they share core Christian values, they can overcome marital problems deriving from ethnic and racial differences. When my wife had a lot of difficulties in the first stage of her adjustment to American society, a white pastor helped her like an adopted parent. A white pastor was able to help an Asian woman mainly because he was a sincere Christian. Just like that pastor, we as good Christians should not draw lines based on ethnic and racial differences.

Another respondent, a 52-year-old woman, gave a similar reason: "When my daughter marries a non-Korean Christian partner, their ethnic and racial differences will not matter because both are the children of God."

The informants who preferred a non-Christian Korean to a non-Korean Christian noted that the non-Christian Korean partner could be converted to Christianity but that the non-Korean partner's physical differences could not be changed. But many of the informants who preferred a non-Korean Christian pointed to the difficulty in making a non-Christian Korean a Christian. For example, So-Jung Lee, a woman in her mid-forties with two children, observed:

> I have kept emphasizing to my son and daughter that the most important crite-
> rion for selecting their marital partners should be whether the partners are sincere
> Christians or not. I have told them again and again if they marry non-Christian
> partners, they are more likely to stop their religion than to convert their partners
> to Christianity. Based on my own experiences, I can say it is extremely difficult to
> convert anyone to Christianity. My husband was not a Christian when I married
> him. It took me ten years to convert him to Christianity. I cannot find suitable
> words to describe the struggles I went through for ten years to make him convert
> to Christianity.

Another woman informant confirmed the validity of this comment: "Neither one's parents nor one's partner can influence a person to become a Christian. He or she can become a Christian only when he or she accepts God spiritually. And we don't know when that will happen."

A significant proportion of Korean Protestant informants emphasized universalistic Christian values over ethnic values in choosing their Christian identity, as opposed to ethnic identity, and choosing non-Korean Christians as their children's marital partners over non-Christian Korean partners. Korean Protestant immigrants see tensions between universalistic Christian values and Korean ethnic values because they practice a Christian religion not indigenous to Korea. But an important reason why a significant proportion of Korean Protestant immigrants prefer universalistic Christian values to Korean ethnic values is their strong evangelical background. Most Korean Protestant churches are evangelical in their institutional arrangements and congregational culture, although they also contain enough Korean cultural elements.

# 7 Younger Generations' Preservation of Ethnicity through Participation in Religious Institutions

I do not think the church should offer anything cultural. The church should offer programs that bring people to worship. If you offer programs on culture, you are limiting the people who can come. You are looking for people with the same background. That's not what church should be about. I don't go to a Korean church right now. We are Korean, but we are not there because we're Korean but because we are Christian.

—Jason Kim, 25-year-old second-generation Korean Protestant

I don't find Hindu *bhajans* [Hindu devotional songs] or temple practices to be very peaceful. Luckily, I've read the Bhagavad Gita and I know that loud cymbals, fluorescent colors, and superstition are not essential to Hinduism. Therefore, I still consider myself to be Hindu, mainly because of my spiritual beliefs in humility, detachment from results, meditation, and attempting to live a less materialistic lifestyle.

—Anjali Prasad, a second-generation Indian Hindu woman

WE HAVE EXAMINED how Korean Protestant and Indian Hindu immigrants use their religion to maintain their ethnic heritage and cultural traditions: Indian Hindu immigrants take their children to the temple partly or mainly to teach them ethnic traditions, and Korean Protestant immigrants consider their children's participation in the Korean church helpful to preserving Korean cultural traditions. To determine the extent to which each group has achieved the intended goal of transmitting its ethnicity through religion, we need to study second-generation Korean Protestants and Indian Hindus. This chapter looks at how second-generation Korean Protestants and Indian Hindus have retained their ethnicity by participating in a religious institution.

The chapter's opening observation by Jason Kim, a graduate student at the time of the interview, is typical of younger-generation Korean Protestant informants' views about the need to include Korean cultural traditions in Korean English-language congregations. By contrast, younger-generation Indian Hindu informants were found to go to temple substantially less frequently than their immigrant parents. One of the main reasons for their unwillingness was their

TABLE 7.1

Choice of 1.5 and 2d-Generation Koreans of Previous and
Current Religions and Current Affiliations with Religious Congregations

| | Religion during Childhood | Current Religion | Affiliation with Religious Congregation |
|---|---|---|---|
| Protestantism | 118 (58%) | 109 (54%) | 72 (36%) |
| Catholicism | 37 (19%) | 23 (11%) | 11 (5%) |
| Buddhism | 4 (2%) | 4 (2%) | 1 (0.5%) |
| Other religions | 2 (1%) | 2 (1%) | 0 (0%) |
| No religion or no affiliation | 40 (20%) | 64 (32%) | 118 (58%) |
| Total | 201 (100%) | 201 (100%) | 202 (100%) |

Source: Telephone survey conducted in 1998 by Dae Young Kim of 1.5- and 2d-generation
young adults (23 to 35 years old) in randomly selected households with 20 prominent
Korean surnames in the New York / New Jersey metropolitan area.

rejection of the rituals practiced there that they considered too excessive, superstitious, and even materialistic. The criticism by a second-generation Indian woman that opened this chapter is typical of this rejection.

## Younger-Generation Korean Protestants' Participation in Church during Childhood and Ethnic Retention

As noted in chapter 1, three sets of data pertain to 1.5- and second-generation Koreans' religious practices: (1) a survey of 1.5- and second-generation Korean young adults, (2) a survey of thirty-five Korean English-language congregations, and (3) personal interviews with sixty-six 1.5- and second-generation Korean young adults. The first and third data sets provide information about younger-generation Koreans' religious practices.

As shown in table 7.1, in a random-sampling survey based on prominent Korean surnames, 58 percent of the 1.5 and second-generation Korean respondents chose Protestantism and 19 percent chose Catholicism as their childhood religion, whereas 20 percent reported that they had no religion. That such a large proportion of the respondents chose Protestantism or Catholicism as their childhood religion should not be surprising, since as children they usually attended Korean churches accompanied by their parents. The proportions of the respondents who chose Protestantism and Catholicism as their childhood religion are similar to those of Korean immigrant respondents who chose these two Christian religions in my survey of Korean immigrants in New York City and in other survey studies (Hurh and Kim 1990; Park et al. 1990).

Korean immigrant churches emphasize their members' regular participation in congregation, with about 90 percent of Korean Protestant immigrants attending church every week and about 35 percent going twice or more each week (see table 3.5). Because as children, most 1.5- and second-generation Korean Protestants attended a Korean immigrant church with their parents, their attendance during childhood is likely to have been very frequent as well. We asked younger-generation Korean Protestants about their parents' and their own attendance at a Korean church during their childhood. The results revealed that their parents were generally very active in their church. Of course, not all their parents were very religious; some of their fathers were Buddhists or Catholics; and their fathers were generally less religious than their mothers. We noted this gender difference earlier with regard to religious affiliation. Nevertheless, both parents, or at least their mothers, of the vast majority of the 1.5- and second-generation informants were very active at church and in religious rituals at home. The fathers of three of the younger-generation informants served as pastors for Korean immigrant churches, and two other informants had other family members (either their uncle or grandparent) who were pastors.

In regard to the frequency of their attendance at church during childhood and adolescence, 74 percent reported that they attended every week, and 22 percent went twice or more often each week. Only three informants did not attend church regularly during their childhood because their parents did not attend church. They went to church during childhood slightly less frequently than their immigrant parents did and less frequently than they currently do as young adults. But their attendance during childhood was much higher than that of white American Protestants (as noted previously, only 28 percent of white Presbyterians attend the Sunday worship service every week).

Many informants may have attended church during their childhood and adolescence because their parents took them. But their regular attendance at the Sunday worship service as children or adolescents significantly affected their religious values and retention of ethnic traditions. As we saw earlier, the vast majority of Korean Protestant immigrant informants agreed that their attendance at a Korean church helped them teach their children the Korean language and culture, although they, unlike the Indian Hindu informants, did not consider it their main reason for joining an ethnic religious organization. Our interviews with younger-generation Korean young adults confirmed the view that their immigrant parents' wishes for or expectation of the positive function of a Korean immigrant church for their children's retention of Korean culture were fulfilled.

Our interviews with younger-generation Korean Protestants asked the following questions: "Do you think being active in a Korean church during your childhood/adolescence helped you maintain Korean cultural traditions and identity? If so, how?" About 62 percent of the sixty-three informants (remember that three of them became Christians in college) said "definitely helped" or "greatly helped." Another one-fourth reported that it helped "a little" or "somewhat," and only nine replied that it was not helpful. Responding to the next question of how it helped, they listed learning the Korean language, practicing Korean customs, eating Korean food, and celebrating Korean cultural holidays. This is exemplified by the response by Nadia Han, a 30-year-old second-generation woman who was in graduate school at the time of the interview: "Yes, I learned the language, customs, Korean holidays, learned respect and bowing to older people. People were speaking Korean, I only saw Korean people at church." A 26-year-old second-generation Korean woman even mentioned playing Korean games in weekly district meetings: "Yes, for language in communicating with my parents, eating Korean food together. For Christmas performances we would have Korean influences in the dramas. We would have district meetings every week at people's homes and we always played Korean games."

About half the informants stated that they had attended a Korean (language) school in their church, usually for a semester or less. Although many 1.5-generation informants did not need to attend a Korean school because they already were fluent in Korean, the majority of those not fluent seem to have attended it. They learned not only the Korean language but also Korean culture, history, and even *taekwondo*.[1] Regardless of whether they attended a Korean-language school, they all learned the Korean language through their interaction with immigrant students and adult members at church. For example, Julie Park, an informant in her late twenties who had graduated from law school, commented: "Yes, there were a lot of FOBs [fresh off the boat] or people who just came to America in our church and they all spoke Korean really well. While hanging out with them, I picked up a lot of Korean idioms and maintained the Korean language."

Most Korean immigrants attended Sunday school and/or the youth ministry, which were conducted in both Korean and English or predominantly English. But members of small churches had to attend the regular immigrant service, and so they had to improve their Korean-language skills enough to understand the pastor's sermons and prayers

We noted that some Korean immigrant informants considered the group setting of a church and group pressure more conducive to teaching their children the Korean language and culture than their private homes. Several younger-generation informants confirmed this. For example, a 28-year-old woman who came from Korea at age 9 and who lived with her parents-in-law explained how her Korean church helped her preserve Korean cultural traditions:

> Yes. Because, without Korean people around me, I don't think I would've made any effort to really understand Korean society. It's because of peer pressure. A couple of the people at church, they were far more Koreanized, or they didn't speak much English. So I forced myself to speak in Korean to them or try to understand their culture to fit in or attend church comfortably.

Many younger-generation Korean Protestants are well aware that their parents' decision to take them to a Korean church was partly influenced by this cultural benefit to themselves. In their answer to why their parents took them to a Korean church during their childhood/adolescence, about 30 percent pointed out that exposing themselves to Korean culture, such as going to a Korean-language class, was one of the main reasons. As a second-generation informant, Jessica Kim, who was enrolled in a MBA program, observed,

> They [parents] wanted me to get more affiliated with Korean culture and the people around me. This is because I didn't grow up with many Koreans. So they thought it would be a good experience for me. At the church most people spoke Korean. So I had to learn more Korean. Also, my parents were glad to have me attend Hangul [Korean-language] school at church.

Most of the nine younger-generation informants who did not believe their church attendance helped them learn Korean traditions reported that since their parents tried to teach them the Korean language and culture at home, they did not need to learn them at church. The following response by a 27-year-old woman who came to the United States at age 3 reflects this point: "My parents emphasized being Korean at home. They always spoke Korean at home. When I spoke in English, they did not answer. Therefore, I did not need to attend a Korean language school in the church." This suggests that those younger-generation Koreans who did not get enough ethnic education at home during their childhood learned about Korean culture mainly at church. These findings support the view (see Bankston and Zhou 1995) that participation in an ethnic church helped second-generation children and adolescents learn the ethnic language and culture.

### Younger-Generation Indian Hindus' Participation in Temple during Childhood and Ethnic Retention

The 2005 survey of Indian immigrants in New York City based on a random sampling of prominent Indian surnames showed that approximately 35 percent of Indian Hindu immigrants went to temple once or more a week. Our interviews with 1.5- and second-generation Indian Hindus reveal that their parents went to temple with similar frequency. When asked about the frequency of their parents' attendance during their childhood, exactly one-third (33%) of them affirmed that their parents went at least once a week, with 22 percent attending only a few times or less a year. The others (45%) attended from once every two months to once every two weeks. The second-generation informants reported that their parents usually took them to temple on religious holidays or whenever there were cultural functions, such as performances of traditional Indian songs and dances.

An overwhelming majority of younger-generation Hindu informants (46/54 = 85%) reported that they went to temple during their childhood whenever their parents went. The others said that they did not go as often as their parents did or refused to go during their high school years. Thus their frequency of going to temple during their childhood was slightly lower than their parents', with 25 percent of them going every week. Their attendance at religious institutions was much lower than that of younger-generation Korean Protestants. Most Indian informants said that their parents took them to different temples on a few important Hindu religious holidays, such as for cultural functions and/or on family birthdays and anniversaries.

Even the irregular attendance of Indian Hindu immigrants helped them preserve their ethnic cultural traditions and identity, mainly because the architecture of the temple buildings and the religious rituals and other cultural activities symbolize Indian culture and heritage. Indian Hindu immigrants take their children to Hindu temples mainly or partly to help them retain Indian cultural traditions and identity. About two-thirds (66%) of fifty younger-generation Indian Hindu informants strongly agreed that their attendance during childhood definitely helped them retain their Indian culture and heritage, with another one-fourth partly agreeing. Only seven informants did not think it was helpful. These seven went to temple only a few times a year, and some, only every few years, because in the 1970s most temples were too far away from their parents' homes. To compensate, their parents constructed a family shrine at home. For example, a 32-year-old Indian man observed:

> I don't think it really meant anything. For me it all started at home. We had a
> temple in our house because at that time in New Jersey all the temples were
> very far away. We probably only went once every few years. For me, it all started
> at home. My surroundings at home really affected how I felt about culture. My
> parents made sure to show us and teach us about Hinduism and that's what made
> a difference.

Second-generation Korean Protestant informants emphasized their interactions with other church friends and adult members and the Korean-language program as helping them learn the Korean language and Korean etiquette. Accordingly, they had to go to church regularly and frequently. But attendance at temple likewise helped second-generation Indian Hindus preserve Indian cultural traditions and identity mainly because of the strong association between Hinduism and Indian traditions. They felt and experienced being Indian by watching adults bow to deities and perform other religious rituals and by eating vegetarian food at the temple. But they did not have to go to temple every week. Consider the following response by Indira Gupta, a 23-year-old female medical student who attended the temple only five or six times a year during her childhood: "It has helped me by at least making me feel some sort of bond with those of Indian descent and has definitely helped me develop my own sense of faith in god, and respect for some of the cultural traditions and practices associated with Hinduism."

Another Indian informant, a 27-year-old woman who worked as an administrative assistant, emphasized that visiting a Hindu temple helped her maintain her Indian identity, especially because Hinduism was her ethnic minority religion in a predominantly Christian world:

> I definitely think that it has, for many different reasons. Obviously my parents wanted to make sure that my identity included my Indian heritage during childhood. As I said before, they wanted to make sure that I knew what it meant to be Indian and to be a Hindu, especially because the society we live in is dominated by Christianity. Going to temple helped me be part of a society that was separate from the people I grew up with. It gave me a chance to explore my cultural roots.

Many Hindu informants pointed out that they reluctantly and mechanically followed their parents to temples and watched the rituals without understanding their true meanings. For example, when asked whether he had a problem understanding Hindu rituals in temples during his childhood, Vijay Patel, a second-generation Indian informant, said:

> Oh yeah, most definitely. Growing up you see all these different idols, but you have no true understanding of what the religion's about. So it's sort of a circus thing. You know you're just sort of praying to these statues, and as a kid I see lots of colors, bright interesting things, all these Indian people in the same place together. But it doesn't make a whole lot of sense. You are just sort of doing things because you are seeing other people doing them.

Nevertheless, he admitted that his "reluctant participation" in temples and boring observations of temple rituals in his early years gradually influenced his ethnic identity in later years:

> Yeah, I think so. Whether or not I was fighting against it [being forced to go to temple], I did learn a lot about my culture and my religion and about what different practices are . . . at sort of a basic level, but that sort of spurred me to read more, and to learn more as I grew older. So, you know, in high school I would start reading a lot more of the texts in a translated form on my own to sort of understand, you know, who I am, where do I come from, the issues you deal with as a second-generation Indian Hindu.

But some other informants did not agree that involuntary attendance at temple without knowing the meanings of rituals helped them preserve their Indian cultural traditions and identity. Suman Patel, a 20-year-old Indian woman who lived with her parents at the time of the interview, said that she had attended temple once every two weeks against her will during her childhood but that as a young adult she attended temple on her own much less frequently than before. When asked whether her more or less "involuntary participation" during her childhood had a positive effect on her ethnic preservation, she said no:

> No, not at all. I think the way my parents set up, and a lot of Indian parents did, they just threw things at you and didn't explain them. So going to temple was like a chore. It did not motivate me to find Indian roots.
>
> Being around a lot of Indians growing up, going to other cultural events, and having family in India and their perceptions of us being Americanized made me take certain initiatives [in learning Indian cultural traditions]. My father's being active in the Indian community also helped, but [the temple], not really at all.

Sixty-six percent of Korean informants attended a Korean-language program at their church during their childhood and/or adolescence, although many did so only briefly. By contrast, only eleven of the fifty-four Indian Hindu informants (20%) took a course in a dance ($n = 4$), Veda ($n = 4$) or Indian language ($n = 3$) offered by a temple. Most informants reported that they learned a Hindi and/ or another Indian language from their parents at home. The noncongregational nature of worship services at Hindu temples gives Hindu immigrants a disadvantage, compared with Korean Protestant immigrants, in teaching their children their home language through a religious institution. But many second-generation Hindu informants also indicated that since they spoke Hindi and/or another Indian language at home with their parents, they did not need to go to temple mainly for language education. Indian immigrant parents teach their children their native language at home. According to an analysis of the 2001–2006 American Community Survey, 59 percent of native-born Indian Americans immigrating after 1965 and married to other Indian Americans reported that they spoke their native language at home, compared with 48 percent of their Korean American counterparts (Min and C. Kim 2009).

The noncongregational nature of the Hindu worship services also places Hindu children at a disadvantage in forging coethnic friendship ties through participation in group activities. Because of their frequent church attendance and involvement in various church programs, Korean Christian children maintain strong friendship networks with coethnic members. In learning about ethnic cultural traditions, however, Indian Hindu children seem to benefit from their religious institutions as much as Korean children do. Moreover, Indian Hindu children have an advantage over Korean Christian children in confirming their Indian ethnic identity through their attendance at temple.

## Younger-Generation Korean Protestants' Retention of Childhood Religion and Frequency of Church Participation

Korean religious leaders, including second-generation Koreans, use the term *silent exodus* to indicate the drastic drop in second-generation Korean adults' attendance at ethnic churches (Cha 1994; Chai 1998, 2001a; H. Lee 1996). But no one provided concrete evidence to show the huge declines in ethnic church attendance by 1.5- and second-generation Koreans until Kim and I provided it in our 2005 article (Min and D. Kim 2005).

In his 1998 survey of 1.5- and second-generation Korean young adults (23 to 35 years old) in the New York / New Jersey area based on the Korean surname sampling technique, Dae Young Kim included four questions on religion: (1) the respondent's religion during childhood/adolescence, (2) his or her religion at the time of the interview, (3) the type of church with which he or she was affiliated, and (4) the frequency of his or her attendance at church (see Min and D. Kim 2005). Kim's was the only major survey study of 1.5- and second-generation Koreans in the United States whose results provide fairly accurate information about younger-generation Koreans' retention of Christianity and the frequency of their church attendance.[2]

Fifty-eight percent of younger-generation Korean American respondents cited Protestantism as their childhood religion, while 19 percent cited Catholicism. Only 20 percent reported that they had no religious affiliation during childhood. Responding to a question about their current religion, 54 percent chose Protestantism, 11 percent chose Catholicism, and 32 percent chose no religion. Some respondents who had attended a church during childhood but who were not attending at the time of the interview chose either Protestantism or Catholicism as their current religion. As we have seen, evangelical Korean Protestant immigrants usually consider regularly attending church as essential to their Christian life (Kim and Kim 2001, 86). Thus the responses to the question about their church affiliation seem to reflect the preservation of their childhood religion more accurately than do their responses to the question about their current religion. Thirty-six percent of the respondents were affiliated with a Protestant church, and only 5 percent were affiliated with a Catholic church. The proportion of respondents who attended a Protestant church dropped from 58 percent during childhood to 36 percent at the time of the interview, and those who attended a Catholic church decreased from 19 to 5 percent. Far more second-generation Protestants (more than 60%) than their Catholic counterparts (only about one-fourth) retained their childhood religion.

Given that Korean Protestant immigrant churches are theologically more conservative than Korean Catholic churches, this finding is not surprising. Korean

Protestant immigrants are adamant about their children retaining their religion, whereas Korean Catholic immigrants are more flexible.

Almost all these young Korean Protestant informants retained their childhood or adolescent religion, with a few converting to Protestantism after high school (only three of the seventy-two Protestant informants converted to Protestantism during college or after). This high retention rate, however, does not warrant the speculation that 90 percent of Korean Americans no longer attend church after college. Moreover, it is important to remember that the respondents to the survey were young adults 23 to 35 years old and most of them were not married. Some of these young respondents who did not attend church at the time of the interview are likely to go back to church when they get married and/or have a child.

Sixty-eight percent of the seventy-two Protestant respondents were affiliated with a Korean congregation, and the rest joined either a white or a multiethnic congregation. Twenty-four percent of all younger-generation Korean informants were affiliated with a Korean church (68% × 36%). Although Korean Protestant immigrants consider their church's various social and cultural functions extremely important, younger-generation Korean Americans are likely to attend church mainly for religious purposes and to consider social purposes less important (Chai 1998, 309). Nevertheless, many second-generation Korean Protestants attend an ethnic church, which is possible because of Korean immigrant churches' many English-language Korean congregations.

The survey data do not reveal whether those who go to a Korean church attend an English-language or an immigrant congregation. The personal interview results show that 62 percent (41/66) attend an English-language congregation and 18 percent ($n = 12$) attend a Korean-language congregation established primarily for Korean immigrants. All but one of the twelve informants who attended an immigrant congregation were 1.5-generation Koreans fluent in Korean. They felt more comfortable with an immigrant congregation than with an English-language congregation mainly because they had grown up in it from childhood. Because they were bilingual, most of them served as teachers for the immigrant church's youth groups or Sunday school. Another eleven informants (17%) reported that they attended a multiracial congregation, with only two informants going to a predominantly white congregation. Most of these eleven informants belonged to the Redeemer Presbyterian Church, a Manhattan-based multiracial church that many Korean and Chinese Christians attend. An associate pastor at that church told me that Asian Americans accounted for nearly half its members between 2002 and 2004, when our interviews were conducted. The fact that only two of the sixty-six informants belonged to a predominantly white American congregation suggests that younger-generation Korean American Protestants strongly prefer a Korean American or a multiethnic church.

**TABLE 7.2**

*Frequency of 1.5- and 2d-Generation Korean Protestants'*
*Participation in a Religious Congregation*

|  | Total | Protestants | Catholics |
| --- | --- | --- | --- |
| Once a year or more but less than once a month | 10 (12%) | 5 (7%) | 5 (45%) |
| Once a month or more but less than once a week | 11 (13%) | 8 (11%) | 1 (9%) |
| Once a week or more | 61 (74%) | 57 (82%) | 5 (45%) |
| Total | 82 (100%) | 70[a] (100%) | 11 (100%) |

Source: Telephone survey conducted in 1998 by Dae Young Kim of 1.5-
and 2d-generation young adults (23 to 35 years old) in randomly selected
households with 20 prominent Korean surnames in the New York /
New Jersey metropolitan area.

Note: [a]Two Protestant respondents who were affiliated with a church
did not respond to the question regarding frequency of participation.

About 90 percent of Korean Protestant immigrants go to church once a week
or more often, much more often than non–Korean Protestants (Kim and Kim
2001, 82). Table 7.2 shows that 82 percent of 1.5- and second-generation Korean
respondents affiliated with a Protestant church go at least once a week, a little less
frequently than Korean immigrants. But our personal interviews with younger-
generation Korean informants reveal a higher attendance rate. Eighty-eight percent of the sixty-six informants (58/66) reported that they went to church at least
once a week, with nearly half of them going twice or more. These findings suggest that those who have preserved their childhood religion are as active in their
church as Korean Protestant immigrants are.

My telephone interviews with thirty-five of about forty Korean English-language congregations in New York included a question about the number of weekly
meetings held inside or outside each congregation. The findings were consistent
with the findings from my personal interviews. All English-language congregations had at least one extra meeting, in addition to the Sunday's main service, for
Bible study, prayer, discipleship, and/or social activities. Most congregations were
found to have two or more extra meetings a week, usually on Wednesday, Friday,
and/or Saturday. Nearly half (46%) the respondents reported that their congregations held "small group" meetings regularly for Bible study and fellowship at
a private home, in the church, or at a restaurant. A few more respondents said
their congregations would start "small-group" meetings when they had enough
members. The frequency with which the congregations hold small-group meetings ranged from weekly to monthly. "Small-group meetings" for Korean English-

language congregations resemble the "district service" or "cell ministry" for Korean immigrant churches (Kwon, Ebaugh, and Hagan 1997; Min 1992). Although not included in the questionnaire, several respondents were asked whether the extra weekly meetings in their congregations could be attributed to the influence of Korean immigrant churches. They said that both Korean immigrant and American evangelical churches had influenced Korean English-language congregations in holding two or more additional meetings per week. Korean English-language congregations thus have been strongly influenced by the congregation-oriented approach of Korean immigrant churches.

Second-generation Korean Catholic respondents had a much lower rate of religious retention from childhood to adulthood than did their Protestant counterparts. Table 7.2 shows that even those Catholic respondents who went to church did so much less frequently than the Protestant respondents. Only 45 percent of younger-generation Korean Catholics went to the Sunday worship service each week, compared with 82 percent of their Protestant counterparts. Because Korean Catholic immigrant churches are more liberal than Korean Presbyterian churches, they seem to transmit a more liberal theology to the second generation, in addition to having greater difficulty in transmitting their religion.

## The Subculture of Korean English-Language Congregations
### Strong Evangelical Orientations

Younger-generation Koreans' exceptionally frequent church attendance is closely related to their strong evangelical orientation. Earlier studies, mostly congregational case studies, found that second-generation Korean Protestants and their Korean English-language congregations were heavily evangelical (Alumkal 1999, 2001, 2003; Busto 1996; Chai 1998, 2001a; R. Kim 2003, 2004, 2006; S. Park 2001). A survey of Korean English-language congregations also supported their heavily evangelical orientation. I asked each pastor whether his or her congregation had a mainline or evangelical orientation. Of the thirty-five congregations surveyed, twenty-nine (83%) were evangelical, and only six were mainline. One of these six congregations is really an immigrant congregation where parents attended services with their high-school children. Thus only five English-language congregations for young Korean adults were found to have a mainline orientation.

The specific orientation of a second-generation Korean congregation, whether mainline or evangelical, seems to be determined partly by the pastor's theological philosophy. The pastors of the five mainline congregations were trained at liberal to moderate theological seminaries (such as New York Theological Seminary and Princeton Theological Seminary), whereas those of the evangelical congregations were mostly trained or being trained at conservative theological seminaries or Christian schools (such as Westminster, Gordon-Conwell Seminary, and Biblical Seminary). Most Korean theology students go to conservative theological schools, such as Fuller, Westminster, Trinity, Gordon-Conwell, and Talbot theological seminaries.

No doubt, theologically conservative clergy leaders tend to lead second-generation Korean churches in an evangelical direction. But the conservative theological position of younger-generation Korean pastors cannot be considered the only major reason for the heavily evangelical orientation of second-generation Korean congregations. The fact that most younger-generation Korean theology students have chosen conservative theological seminaries indicates that they were theologically conservative even before they started their professional training. Like second-generation Korean clergy leaders, members of second-generation Korean congregations are generally conservative. Two pastors of second-generation Korean churches included in the survey commented that they had to follow the evangelical orientations to meet their members' spiritual needs, even though they themselves were more comfortable with a mainline approach.

Three other factors contributed to the heavily evangelical orientation of 1.5- and second-generation Korean Christians. As must be clear by now, Korean Protestant immigrants are usually very religious. They seem to be generally successful in transmitting their strong Christian values to their children, and most younger-generation Korean evangelical Christians grew up in very religious families. But I also found four English-language congregations that were evangelical, even though the immigrant congregations belonged to mainline denominations. This indicates the strong effect of the American evangelical movement on second-generation Korean congregations.

Korean immigrant pastors often deplore the deterioration in the United States of moral standards, which were initially established by the Puritans, and maintain that instead, Korean immigrant churches are the true bearers of the Puritan heritage (Chong 1998; R. Kim 2003; Min 1992). Several years ago, I asked an associate pastor at a Korean immigrant church in Queens what he thought about the almost complete elimination of the Korean language and culture from his church's English-language congregation. He stated:

> Whether the second-generation church uses the Korean language for worship
> services and celebrates Korean holidays or not is a superficial thing. A far more
> important thing is whether it has carried over the Korean traditions of Christianity. Korean Christians pray fervently, have frequent prayer meetings, and work
> hard and compete effectively in missionary activities. When we talk about special
> characteristics of Korean Protestantism, we should emphasize these spiritual
> foundations rather than Korean cultural rituals. Second-generation Korean Christians have learned these characteristics from immigrant churches. . . . We Koreans
> have the mission for evangelizing the world. They can use these strengths of

Korean Christianity and their fluency in English effectively for global evangelism. And the elimination of Korean cultural rituals from second-generation Korean churches will be a strength, rather than a weakness, for global evangelism.

Younger-generation Korean Protestants are generally critical of Korean immigrant churches' overemphasis on Korean culture. Yet most of them also regard the conservative/evangelical orientations of Korean immigrant churches as a very positive element. For example, in a telephone survey, many pastors of Korean English-language congregations considered "being church oriented" and "being fervent Christians" as unique aspects of Korean Protestantism and wanted to maintain these Korean traditions of Christianity. As a 1.5-generation Korean pastor noted, "Korean people have developed a different style of Christianity. Korean Christians are fervent, church centered, and strongly committed to Christian life. They spend a lot of time for the church. We, younger-generation Koreans, should preserve these unique elements of Korean Christianity." Many second-generation evangelicals have embraced Koreans' sense of destiny for global evangelism. In her study of Korean American evangelical college students, So-Young Park (2004, 187) reported:

> Second-generation evangelicals also maintain a sense of their unique destiny. At the Pan-KSC Unity '97 the speakers claimed that God had chosen Korean Americans for the special purpose of evangelizing the world. God had brought them to the United States to learn English and get American citizenship so that they could go more easily to any other country. The second generation, one speaker said, was like the Apostle Paul who used his Roman citizenship to protect himself and open the door to further travel.

In addition, the evangelical movement on college campuses has had a strong effect on the evangelization of younger-generation Korean Christians. Michelle Shin, a second-generation Korean woman informant who was very religious and was attending a theological seminary, commented: "Before I went to college, I did not accept Christ in my mind. I simply went to church every week because my parents took me there. But I began to accept Christ individually when I attended college." This informant's confession and similar comments by other 1.5- and second-generation Korean Christians demonstrates the significant effects of campus ministry on the evangelization of younger-generation Korean Christians.[3] The number of Korean American college students has gradually increased since the early 1970s when parachurch organizations, such as Campus Crusade for Christ, InterVarsity Christian Fellowship, and the Navigators, began to have an effect on the evangelical movement on college campuses (Busto 1996). Korean Christian students in many major private colleges and public universities now join an ethnic fellowship (Korean Christian Fellowship) or a Korean chapter of one of the parachurch organizations.

Both the style of ministry by Korean pastors, mostly *chondosa*, in Korean Christian fellowships on college campuses and the new situation of Korean Christian students seem to have evangelizing effects. Whether it is an independent, ethnic fellowship or a Korean chapter of a parachurch organization, a mission-minded 1.5- or second-generation Korean pastor who is fluent in English usually ministers the Korean congregation on the college campus. His or her ministry can have more positive effects on the religious growth of younger-generation Korean Christian college students because he or she is more mission minded and can better understand the students than can the pastors of youth groups in Korean immigrant congregations, the majority of whom were born and raised in Korea.

Moreover, Korean Christian college students' loneliness on campuses away from their parents and their reflection on their identity as young adults can lead them to become born-again Christians. While most younger-generation Korean Protestants may have accepted their Christian background as an ascribed status before college, they came to accept it as their chosen identity while in college. A 1.5-generation Korean pastor who served as the education pastor for the Shin Kwang Church said that he had ministered a Korean Christian fellowship at a university in Illinois while he was attending Trinity Theological Seminary. When I asked him how campus ministry turned many younger-generation Koreans into born-again Christians, he e-mailed me the following:

> There are many reasons why 1.5- and second-generation Korean Christians have become more evangelical during their college years. One of the reasons is that leaders in these campus ministries, either seminary students or ordained ministers, are evangelical in their religious faith. Non-evangelicals are not as committed to reach out to the "lost" or to strengthen the faith of believers. Another reason is that for the first time, they are on their own, finding each other that share similar experiences as 1.5 or second generation. Many times, small groups and the congregational meetings provide the place for network and fellowship. They are in place and time of searching: searching for identity, searching for answers, and searching for the meaning. Often they find their identity in Christ.

In her study of younger-generation Muslim college students, Peek (2005) also pointed out that the transition from high school to college is the turning point during which young Muslims experience a major change in their Muslim characteristics from an ascribed status to a chosen identity. Interestingly, she also found that both young Muslim students' search for personal identity and their contact with more Muslim friends on college campuses through their participation in Muslim student associations enhanced their consciousness of their Muslim identity. Younger-generation Korean and other Asian Christian college students are more likely to be attracted to a strong religious identity than younger-generation Muslim students are because of the decades-long existence of well-developed evangelical campus ministries.

## Lack of Korean Culture in Second-Generation Korean Congregations

Korean English-language congregations in Korean immigrant churches in New York City usually are financially dependent on the immigrant church but hold separate worship services and other sociocultural activities. They usually join the immigrant congregations two or three times a year on important religious holidays, such as Easter and Thanksgiving. But as second-generation Korean researchers have pointed out (Chai 1998, 2001a; S. Park 2001; see also Alumkal 2003), the worship styles of Korean English-language congregations are entirely different from those of Korean immigrant congregations. Korean immigrant congregations sing traditional hymns accompanied by piano and organ. By contrast, Korean English-language evangelical congregations sing contemporary gospel songs projected through overhead speakers, accompanied by guitar, drum, base, and/or keyboard. They also use praise songs and other materials produced by white American evangelical organizations, such as PASSION, Calvary Church, and Vineyard Christian Fellowship.

In addition, Korean immigrant congregations emphasize formality and a collective experience, especially for the Sunday worship service, so almost all the participants dress up, with the men wearing neckties. They communicate with God largely through the medium of the pastor's sermons, although many communicate also through individual prayer and the Bible. By contrast, English-language Korean congregations have an informal style of worship and emphasize each individual member's spiritual connection with God. Most attendees, even at the Sunday worship service, dress more casually for singing and clapping their hands to the praise songs. Many of the pastors of Korean English-language congregations that we interviewed said that for an evangelical Christian, worship is the personal encounter with and celebration of God. Therefore, spirituality and emotional engagement are more important than formality and collectivity, and consequently, many of the respondents were very critical of the Korean immigrant congregations' emphasis on participation in the congregation and group activities.

Russel Jeung's study in San Francisco (2002, 2005) revealed that Pan-Asian evangelical congregations identify primarily with the broader American evangelical subculture and thus pay little attention to ethnic and Asian cultural heritage, whereas mainline congregations try to integrate Asian cultural resources with Christian rituals. The major findings of my survey of second-generation Korean congregations strongly support his conclusion. I asked thirty-five pastors about the ethnic and cultural components of their congregations. Only one mainline English-language congregation, at which parents and their children, along with some white Americans, held services together, was found to provide bilingual services. This congregation, in an immigrant church in a white, upper-middle-class neighborhood in Westchester, held bilingual services, mainly because the immigrant parents, highly educated and fluent in English, wanted their children to learn Korean cultural traditions. None of the other English-language congregations used the Korean language in any of the three components of worship services (sermons, praise songs, and prayers). Because all but three of the pastors interviewed were Korean (the exceptions were two white American and one Asian Indian), this finding is surprising. In the early twentieth century, other non–Korean Protestant ethnic groups were better able to teach their native language to the second generation than Korean immigrants. For example, Mullins (1987) analyzed how Japanese American churches in Canada had changed from the Japanese-language service for immigrants, through the bilingual-bicultural service for the second generation, to the English–language service for the third generation.

The pastors also were asked how many times they had mentioned Korea and the Korean American community in their sermons during the past year. To my surprise, 40 percent reported that they had never mentioned Korea, and 20 percent said they had never made reference to the Korean community. These findings are in sharp contrast with pastors in Korean immigrant congregations who almost always mention Korea and/or the Korean immigrant community in their sermons. All Korean immigrant congregations in my 1988/1989 survey study observed two major Korean cultural holidays (New Year's Day and Korean Thanksgiving Day) and two national holidays (March First Independence Movement Day and August 15 Independence Day) (Min 1992). By contrast, only four Korean English-language congregations celebrated and/or observed one of the four Korean holidays. In another five congregations, the pastors referred in their sermons to two or three Korean holidays but did not celebrate them. The four Korean English-language congregations celebrated Korean holidays largely because many members of each congregation had parents who attended the immigrant congregation in the same church. When these English-language congregations become separated from immigrant congregations, they are unlikely to celebrate or observe Korean cultural or national holidays.

Most other Christian immigrant groups in the United States, including Irish Catholics and Greek Orthodox, have been far more successful than Korean Protestant immigrants in transmitting their cultural or national holidays to their descendants (Ebaugh and Chaffetz 2000; Waters 1990). They have been successful mainly because their Christian religions, with a long history in their homelands, already had absorbed their folk cultures, including holidays, weddings, and funerals. By contrast, Korean immigrant Protestant churches cannot transmit their cultural holidays to second-generation churches because Korean

Protestantism, with its short history in Korea, has not incorporated Korean folk culture. Moreover, the leaders of Korean English-language congregations have intentionally minimized Korean cultural components in their worship services and other sociocultural activities so as to make their congregations consistent with their evangelical orientation.

As expected, the Korean English-language congregations led by immigrant pastors included more ethnic components in their worship services and other sociocultural activities than did those churches led by second-generation Korean or non-Korean pastors. But the reason that Korean English-language congregations do not use the Korean language and other Korean cultural traditions in their services is not that their leaders are not fluent in Korean and are not familiar with Korean customs. In fact, not only Korean immigrant and 1.5-generation but also some second-generation pastors were hired partly because they were fluent in Korean. Instead, the pastors of Korean English-language congregations avoid using the Korean language for worship services and Korean cultural activities mainly because they and their congregations are heavily evangelical. Five of the six mainline congregations put more emphasis on Korean cultural components in worship services and other sociocultural activities and had more services together with immigrant congregations.

The pastors of Korean English-language congregations were asked the following questions: "How important is it for a second-generation Korean church to preserve Korean cultural traditions? Why?" Only seven of the respondents (20%) considered it very important for a second-generation Korean American congregation to preserve Korean cultural traditions, five of them being pastors of mainline congregations. In regard to why they considered it important to emphasize ethnic elements, Man-Sik Choi, a 57-year-old Korean immigrant pastor who was serving in a mainline congregation, commented:

> I think it is important. We are all brothers and sisters under God. But we as Koreans have unique cultural traditions and a sense of affinity because we share blood. We can use our heritage and culture to strengthen our faith. I often pray for South Korea. When giving sermons I always make reference to Korean cultural holidays and Mother's Day.

About one-third of the respondents reported that it was somewhat important for second-generation Korean American congregations to preserve Korean cultural traditions. But they also emphasized that the priority should be religious faith rather than Korean culture. Some respondents pointed to the difficulty of striking a balance between religious faith and ethnic culture. The remaining 46 percent expressed the view that second-generation Korean American congregations should not play a role in preserving Korean culture. They emphasized that instead, the priority should be on spreading the gospel and "universal Christian values" and not on retaining ethnic culture. For example, a 1.5-generation Korean American pastor of a Korean- English-language congregation in a full gospel church remarked:

> When you minister a congregation, the first priority is the gospel. It is not good to emphasize a particular culture. Maintaining a Korean culture is not an agenda in service. They can get it elsewhere. There is no agenda other than the gospel. Individually, I have a strong Korean attachment. I often watch Korean soccer games at home. But I cannot make that Korean cultural thing an agenda in my congregation.

Peter Han, another 1.5-generation Korean American pastor who is fluent in Korean, made a similar comment:

> It is important we Korean Americans maintain Korean cultural traditions. I am very ethnic. I teach my children the Korean language and customs at home. But I try to separate the spiritual community from the family. It is the job of the family to teach Korean traditions. But our spiritual community should focus on the gospel. No particular culture should be emphasized and no politics should be involved in a congregation.

All but four Korean English-language congregations in my study have a small number of non-Korean members. Most respondents tried to justify their effort to minimize Korean cultural components in their congregations by indicating the presence of a few or several non-Korean members. One female pastor asserted that the presence of even one non-Korean member justifies not using the Korean language in worship services. Some of the pastors were very critical of Korean immigrant churches' "overemphasis on Confucian cultural components," which they viewed as "un-Christian." Responding to my question of whether they believed Korean immigrant churches put too much emphasis on Korean culture, Eddy Jung, a second-generation pastor, said: "Definitely, I agree. They put Korean culture ahead of biblical teachings. Korean cultural things get in the way of doing Christianity. Sexism, ageism, and overemphasis on going to good colleges are incongruent with Christian values. They also prevent outreaching non-Korean members and thus churches' growth." Previous studies also have indicated that second-generation Korean Protestants view Korean immigrant churches' overemphasis on Korean culture, such as educational success, as un-Christian (Alumkal 2003, 113; Chai 1998, 312; Ecklund 2005, 2006, 47).

As we have seen, gender hierarchy and other patriarchal elements are common in Korean immigrant churches. Because the majority of the surveyed pastors are critical of Korean Confucian cultural elements in Korean immigrant congregations, their English-language congregations also are likely to be more gender egalitarian than immigrant congregations. As expected, the survey revealed that in regard to representation on functional committees, women seem to do much better in English-language congregations than in immigrant congregations. When asked how well women are represented in leadership positions in their congregation, many respondents said: "Women are very active," "Women are more active in my congregation than in the immigrant congregation," "Half and half," and "Eighty percent are women." However, all but four respondents stated their theological position that women should not be allowed to serve as pastors or elders. Although four of the thirty-five surveyed Korean English-language congregations were led by woman pastors, even one of the women pastors agreed that men were more effective pastors than women.

The respondents attributed the underrepresentation of women in leadership positions in Korean immigrant congregations to Korean "Confucian patriarchy." But they pointed to the "biblical patriarchy" to justify the principle of no women pastors and elders. The following comment by a second-generation respondent who served one of the largest Korean English-language congregations in New York City best summarizes their effort to separate "Confucian patriarchy" from "biblical patriarchy," and functional committee leaders from clergy leadership positions:

> Unlike Korean immigrant congregations, we do not endorse the position that men are better than women. Most of functional committee leaders in our congregation are women. But according to the Bible, men and women have different roles. Most of our members accept the biblical position that women should not serve as elders or pastors. Most women members do not feel comfortable with a woman serving as a pastor. But it does not mean that men and women have different levels of power and status. We do not accept Korean Confucian patriarchy.

Another respondent remarked, "I support more male leadership in the congregation. But I do this not because of Korean cultural traditions but because of my biblical theory. That is how God made men and women. They have different roles."

This discussion helps us locate the sources of gender hierarchy and patriarchal practices in both Korean immigrant and Korean English-language congregations. Although some researchers have attributed gender hierarchy in Korean immigrant churches to Korean Confucian cultural traditions and others have focused on the Bible as the main source, I believe that both factors—Korean cultural traditions and evangelical Christianity—are responsible for the highly gendered structure of Korean immigrant churches and other patriarchal practices there. Korean English-language congregations have moderated gender hierarchy by discarding "Confucian patriarchy," but they still maintain some level of hierarchy by embracing evangelical Christianity. Despite my effort to associate second-generation Korean congregations only with biblical patriarchy, other researchers have argued that both Korean cultural traditions and evangelical theology are responsible for the gendered structure of second-generation Korean congregations (Alumkal 2003, 162; Ecklund 2006, 106–7).

To examine the cultural retention function of their congregations, I asked the sixty-six younger-generation informants, "Do you think attending a Korean Christian church is helpful in maintaining Korean cultural traditions? In what ways?" All twelve respondents who attended a Korean immigrant congregation reported that their participation in a Korean church was extremely helpful in preserving Korean cultural traditions. The majority of 1.5 and second-generation Korean Protestant informants (62%) reported that their participation in an immigrant church during childhood had positive effects on their ethnic retention. But only one-third of the forty-two participants in an English-language congregation agreed. When asked how the church helped, Jason Kim, a 1.5-generation Korean who worked as an information technologist, commented:

> Yes, we're predominantly Korean. Yet most of them don't speak Korean at all.. But there is a small group of people whose main language is Korean. Since I do speak Korean, I want to associate with them. They tell me what's going on, an update on Korea. For example, new untraditional ways of thinking in Korea.

But the majority of the participants in Korean English-language congregations do not view their church attendance as helping them preserve Korean cultural traditions. Many offered comments reflecting their strong opinions about how their English-language congregations deemphasize Korean culture. Responding to my question of how much his participation in a Korean congregation helped him preserve Korean cultural traditions, In-Chul Kim, a 29-year-old male informant, replied:

> No. I remember the pastor said after service we should not try to go to just Korean restaurants because the few people in our church who are not Korean feel like that they have to assimilate to Korean, sort of, food and stuff. The identity of the church, the vision is not a Korean American church. In practice, it is, but in vision it is not.

Kim said that his church, which had several Chinese members, celebrated Good Friday, Christmas, Passion Week, and Lent, but none of traditional Korean cultural holidays. A 25-year-old female member who attended another second-generation Korean church also pointed to the presence of non-Korean members in her church as justifying the absence of Korean culture:

> Not necessarily. I think the direction of the EM is that we're very aware of our community. Because we have a lot of Chinese members we don't upgrade one above the other. I've identified myself as more of a Christian than Korean. I've gone to white churches and I was comfortable. My identity as a Christian is more central.

I asked the informants a related question: "How important do you think it is for a second-generation Korean church to maintain cultural traditions through various programs?" Again, only about one-third of the forty-two informants who attended a second-generation Korean church responded that it was very or moderately important, with the majority strongly disagreeing. The 25-year-old male informant opening this chapter did not want his church to incorporate Korean cultural traditions because they would interfere with evangelism. Likewise, Jonathan Roh, a 27-year-old second-generation Korean pastor who wanted to turn his second-generation Korean church into a multiethnic church, opposed the idea of a Korean ethnic church because it would create divisions:

> We go to church only for religious purposes. That's what is all about church.
> Nationalism is the most detrimental thing to Christianity. All this Korean stuff, it
> shouldn't be mixed with Christianity. Because it causes division and exclusivity, and
> because it makes people confused about the Law of God and the law of culture.

I noted earlier that the majority of the informants felt comfortable attending a Korean church and that many enjoyed their friendships with Korean church members. But their "feeling comfortable attending a Korean church" does not necessarily mean including Korean cultural traditions. In answer to the question of whether attending a second-generation Korean church was helpful in maintaining Korean cultural traditions, a 1.5-generation Korean woman said, "For me, no, but for other people, maybe. But for me, church is not Korean just because it is a Korean church. I just go there because it's comfortable. But the Korean culture is not that important to me."

Korean English-language congregations provide a space for comfort and ethnic networks for second-generation Koreans, but most of the congregations do not help their members preserve Korean cultural traditions because both the leaders and their members consider them mainly as faith communities rather than as Korean communities.

## Recreated Korean Culture and a Korean Christian Subethnic Boundary

We have seen that second-generation Korean Protestant congregations are heavily evangelical and have eliminated many Korean cultural traditions. By underscoring the loss of Korean cultural traditions in second-generation Korean churches, I do not mean to suggest that members of these churches do not share ethnic commonalities (new cultural components) that bind them together. Since this is not one of my study's main objectives, I did not ask my informants about the Korean Christian subculture prevalent in Korean English-language congregations. But two earlier studies shed light on the subculture of Korean English-language evangelical congregations.

In his study of heavily Chinese and Japanese American Pan-Asian congregations, Jeung (2005) claimed that mainline Pan-Asian congregations have incorporated Asian cultural traditions, including language, food, and cultural holidays, in services and other congregational activities but that evangelical Pan-Asian churches have deemphasized them. Yet he pointed out that members of Pan-Asian evangelical congregations also are bounded by their common family upbringing, especially by their individual "therapeutic needs" deriving from their parents' overemphasis on education and success during childhood, and by their common professional lifestyles. Second-generation Korean American adults also suffer from a similar psychological problem deriving from their parents' excessive stress on achievement.

In her study of Korean Christian fellowships on college campuses, Rebecca Kim (2006, 79–80) also emphasized "pressures to excel in school and career" as the most common familial experiences binding members of Korean Christian fellowships together. Partly because they share these family experiences associated with their parents' zeal for children's education, second-generation Asian Americans prefer to attend an ethnic or Pan-Asian congregation. Thus Jeung and Kim provide an alternative interpretation of the subculture prevalent in second-generation Asian or Korean evangelical Christian congregations, one not linked to cultural heritage. Rebecca Kim (2006) indicated that her interpretation of second-generation Korean Christians' creation of Korean subculture within a Korean ethnic congregation, like the emergent theory of ethnicity developed by Yancy, Juliani, and Erikson (1976), does not consider ethnic heritage as a main source of ethnicity. But she also criticizes Yancy and his colleagues' emergent theory of ethnicity for focusing on only structural factors without considering the personal social interactions among members of an ethnic group (R. Kim 2006, 143–44).

When asked why they decided to attend the current church, the majority of the participants in a Korean English-language congregation (62% of the 44 informants) replied that because of their family members' and/or Korean friends' affiliations with the church, they had to go there, too. In fact, a significant proportion of them came back to their childhood church, which they had stopped attending during college. Many informants also indicated that they felt more comfortable attending a Korean church than a white American or multiethnic church because of the members' similar background. To explain most second-generation Korean Christians' preference of attending a Korean church, Rebecca Kim uses the term *homophily*, the tendency of people to like people similar to themselves (R. Kim 2006, 78–81).

After the Sunday's main service, many of them meet their parents who attended the immigrant service in the same church. Most of the congregations that the informants attended had services with the immigrant congregations a few times each year on important holidays. Many of the informants were Sunday school teachers for the immigrant churches. Of course, they had Korean friends in the same English congregation, and all the congregations arranged to have a few or several picnics, retreats, and other social activities together each year. We asked the informants how many of their five best friends were attending the same congregation. Nearly 70 percent of the Korean informants who attended a Korean second-generation or immigrant congregation had at least one of their five best friends in the same congregation, with 40 percent having two. These findings suggest that their participation in an English-language Korean church contributes to the preservation of ethnicity by enhancing their family ties and coethnic friendships. Most second-generation Koreans have difficulty maintaining close friendship ties with non-Christian Koreans owing to their different values (S. Park 2001). But they definitely preferred Korean Christian friends to non-Korean Christian friends.

As Rebecca Kim (2006) pointed out, both the racial categorization in the United States and their actual experiences with racial discrimination have created racial boundaries between Korean/Asian American and white evangelical Christians. I included the following question in my interviews with younger-generation Korean Protestant informants: "Do you think you have been discriminated against because of your Korean/Asian background? Give examples." Seventy-nine percent of the informants (51/65) reported one or more cases of discrimination. Many said they encountered subtle forms of prejudiced and/or stereotypical racial slurs and name callings, such as "Chinaman," "Chink," "ching-chong ching-chong," "dog eaters," "gook," and "Go back to your country," mostly by school peers. Others complained about their teachers asking them whether they understood English.[4] Still others pointed out that they received poor service or even rude treatment from restaurants and fast-food stores because of their Asian or Korean appearance. Four said that they encountered racial discrimination at their workplace. These experiences with racial prejudice and discrimination, along with no common family experiences with white evangelical Christians, seem to lead second-generation Korean Christians to choose a Korean or at least a Pan-Asian/multiracial congregation.

Younger-generation Korean informants also were asked whether they had been discriminated against because of their Christian religious background. Only seven informants (11%) reported that they experienced discrimination because of their Christian background, compared with 79 percent of them who experienced discrimination because of their Korean/Asian background. Five of the seven informants had encountered prejudice or discrimination in the classroom or school. According to their reports, liberal professors or students were biased against them in class discussions because of their antiabortion position and belief in creationism. One informant claimed that he was not admitted to a medical school because he tried to defend his antiabortion position in the admission interview. Only one informant claimed that his job application was rejected because the manager did not like his "too socially conservative religious values." Alumkal (2003, 86–87) pointed out that the second-generation Chinese and Korean evangelical Christians in his study perceived themselves as marginalized religious minority members. But these findings suggest that only a small proportion of my informants experienced prejudice and/or discrimination because of their religious background.

### Younger-Generation Indian Hindus' Reduction in Temple Participation but Positive Effects on Ethnicity

One of the reasons that I used only one data set for the examination of second-generation Hindus' participation in religious institutions is that there is no separate Hindu temple for second-generation Indian Hindu adults. As I mentioned earlier, Swaminarayan temples have congregational worship services on Sunday similar to Christian churches. The Swaminarayan temple in New York City that I visited had a Sunday worship service for Indian immigrants in Gujarat and another service for 1.5- and second-generation Indians in English. But Swaminarayan Hinduism is a Gujarat-based sectarian religion with relatively few adherents. With the exception of special holidays, other major Hindu temples do not have separate worship services for younger-generation Indian Hindus.

We noted that younger-generation Korean Protestant adults do not attend Korean immigrant congregations mainly because they do not speak Korean. Indian Hindu immigrants, however, do not need to create a separate temple for the second generation because they can communicate with them in English in the same temple. Indian immigrants' fluency in English has enabled even second-generation Indian Christians to attend services with Indian immigrants in the same church.

Another and an even more important factor is that Indian regional and national cultural traditions are so much a part of Hindu rituals that American-born Indians would have great difficulty performing Hindu rituals in separate temples (Kurien 2007). In fact, Hindu priests are brought from India to lead religious rituals in Sanskrit in Hindu temples. Thus even most Indian Hindu immigrant professionals are not familiar with various rituals. By contrast, younger-generation Korean pastors who were trained in American theological seminaries can lead English-language congregations for second-generation Christians using materials mainly prepared by American evangelical organizations.

About 25 percent of younger-generation Indian Hindu informants attend temple once a week or more during their childhood, a slightly lower rate than that of their immigrant parents. The number of younger-generation Indian Hindus attending temple falls sharply between their childhood and their young adulthood. Only seven of the fifty-five Indian Hindu informants (13%) visited the temple every week at the time of the interview, and 62 percent went not at all or only a few times a year. The rest went to temple somewhere between these two extremes. In addition, three informants were involved in the Swadhyaya movement, occasionally participating in its religious rituals, donating money and/or doing volunteer work. One regularly gave money to the Hindu American Foundation, a powerful Hindu advocacy organization.

While their living arrangement (whether they lived with parents or independently) did not affect the church attendance rate of Korean Protestant informants, it did influence that of Indian informants. Of those living independently, only two of the thirty-three Indian informants attended temple every week and 84 percent of them went never or only a few times a year. Indian informants not living with their parents usually attended temple a few times a year, often involuntarily, when they visited their parents. Even those informants who lived with their parents also went to temple much less often than they had when they were children. The rejection of second-generation Indian Hindu adults to go to temple created tension in some families. When asked how often he went to temple, Jita Ram, a 29-year-old second-generation Hindu male informant, said: "Very rarely. I go when my mom gets upset that kids don't do anything religious so we get guilted into going."

About 40 percent of second-generation Koreans who attended Protestant churches during their childhood were not affiliated with a church at the time of the 1998 survey study. The second-generation former Christians who were not affiliated with congregations at the time of the interview were not included in the sample of Korean Christian informants. But we selected any Indian Hindus, regardless of their religious level or frequency of temple attendance, because Indian Hindus always are Hindu unless they change to another religion. The Korean–Hindu differential in frequency of attendance is partly caused by this selection difference.

But even if we consider this selection difference, the two second-generation religious groups differ significantly in their participation in organized religion. This finding suggests that Indian Hindu immigrants have difficulty transmitting Hinduism as an organized religion to their descendants. Nonetheless, 80 percent of Indian Hindu informants accept Hinduism in one form or another, although they do not go to temple regularly. Thus the great differential in participation in religious institutions between second-generation Korean Protestants and their

Indian Hindu counterparts is due mainly to their differences in worship style and theology. Protestants, especially evangelical Protestants, emphasize regular attendance as the central aspect of Christian life. But Indian Hindu immigrants do not consider attendance as essential to Hindu religious practices, as almost all of them practice Hinduism at home.

Based on results of personal interviews, I found three factors that contribute to the great intergenerational reduction in younger-generation Indian Hindus' temple attendance. First, Americanized second-generation Hindus do not attend temple regularly because they are not familiar with complicated Hindu rituals performed in Sanskrit by priests from India. Several informants pointed out that they did not feel comfortable in the temple because they did not understand the meanings of rituals. Vijay Patel, a young physician who lived with his parents, confessed that he attended temple once or twice a year involuntarily with his parents on major Hindu holidays. He often argued with his parents about his concern that many of the new Hindu temples might have to close in thirty years or so unless they trained Hindu priests in the United States and changed the language used from Sanskrit into English:

> I often had this philosophical argument with my parents because if you've noticed, the number of temples has proliferated multifold in this country and what's going to happen thirty years from now. Who's going to be going to all these temples and maintaining them? I really don't know. . . . What I really think we ought to start examining now is changing to the vernacular, using English a lot more in temples as the medium with which we do everything so that it's applicable to new generations. You know they don't use Latin for everything now in Christian churches, you know at some point you have to adapt if you want to survive. But I don't see Indian temples doing that at all.[5]

Like Indian Hindu immigrants, Korean Buddhist immigrants have difficulty transmitting their organized religion to their children because their worship styles and rituals are very traditional from the Christian point of view (Suh 2004, 68–69). In fact, children of Korean Buddhist immigrants often attend Korean churches. Likewise, second-generation Asian Americans may have more difficulty accepting Hinduism because it has more rituals than Buddhism does.

Second, and more important, as younger-generation Indian Hindus grow older and take courses on religion in college, they increasingly question the rationality of many Hindu rituals.[6] Many of them accept the spiritual and tolerant components of Hinduism as positive but consider praying to particular deities for blessings by giving milk, flowers, and other gifts to "idols" as superstitious. The interview with Vijay Patel reflects this concern. When asked if he thought going to the temple helped him maintain his Indian cultural traditions, he responded,

I mean, I think at some spiritual level I believe very strongly in everything, but there's so much ritual involved at the temple that I don't buy into . . . like I don't believe I need to feed the idol milk and give these offerings. That is just ritual, and it's more for uneducated masses who don't understand how to have a relationship with god, I guess.

Not only Vijay Patel, but several other informants expressed their rejection of rituals practiced in temples that they considered too excessive, superstitious, and even materialistic. Many informants read Hindu scriptures and found the contents of temple practices deviating from them. A second-generation Indian woman and lawyer, Sunita Gandhi, also expressed similar concerns about temples: "My relationship to my religion is more sort of a spiritual connection, as opposed to things based on particular gods and goddesses. For me, a temple is more about a home for particular gods and goddesses. I never had a good association with it."

In his study of two Theravada Buddhist temples in the United States, Numrich showed that Asian immigrant and American convert Buddhists in the same temple roof follow separate agendas (Numrich 1996, chap. 4). Compared with Asian immigrant Buddhists who are very ritualistic, American convert Buddhists "tend to be philosophical and meditative rather than ritualist" (Numrich 1996, 64). In her comparative study, Cadge (2005, 109–10) also pointed out that highly educated white American convert Buddhists at a meditation center in Boston focus on reducing their suffering and attaining freedom and liberation in this world and reject the supernatural ideas about the power of meditation and monks that members of a Thai immigrant Buddhist temple in Philadelphia consider important. Thus, converted American Buddhists have transformed Asian Theravada Buddhism by rejecting the rituals and ceremonies associated with belief in supernatural power that are observed in Asian countries. Cadge claims that white Theravada Buddhists consider their focus on meditation more consistent with the Buddha's original teachings and ideas than the rituals and ceremonies associated with Asian Theravada Buddhist traditions. In a strikingly similar way, many Americanized and highly educated second-generation Indian Hindu adults reject traditional rituals—more often practiced in Hindu temples than in Buddhist temples—that their parents accept as both culturally and religiously meaningful. It is interesting that in the opening of this chapter, Anjali Prasad also refers to a Hindu scripture to emphasize the legitimacy of her version of spiritual Hinduism, as opposed to the ritual-oriented practices common in Hindu immigrant temples.

Third, younger-generation Indian Hindus attend temple much less often than their parents because of their more liberal and more secular worldview. I believe that Hinduism's emphasis on religious pluralism and tolerance of other religions and values has also contributed to their liberal and secular worldview. Many informants expressed their concern about the political and proselytizing aspects of any organized religion but considered Hinduism more positive than other organized religions in regard to its openness and nonproselytizing style. One informant, who said he hated all organized religions, appreciated his father's not forcing him into Hinduism: "The fact that my parents didn't jam anything down my throat helped my view along. I might have rejected it if they had. They kept their aspect of the culture/religion but nonproselytizing and nonforceful. I give them credit for having it in the background, but not forcing it."

Rupam Sinha, another second-generation Hindu informant who married a white Christian, said she had gone to temple only about three times over the past five years. But she knew how different going to temple was from going to church, because she had gone once every few months during her childhood. She described the main difference:

> I don't go in there and sit and pray, but I may actually sit and try to clear my head
> for a while and meditate in that atmosphere. So that's the unique thing about
> temple and that's a little bit different from churches or other places of worship. If
> you just walked into church on a Saturday afternoon and there's no service going
> on, you can get the same thing. But if you go to church on a Sunday, you're going
> for a sermon by a minister and there are Bible readings and everything, and it's
> a much more active process of preaching and indoctrination. And that's where I
> think, with children, we need to draw the line.

Nonetheless, Sinha identified herself as an agnostic, denying her Hindu identity, because of her awareness of the negative political and social aspects of Hinduism and other organized religions that conflicted with her liberal worldview.

> I have grown to self-identify as agnostic. If somebody asked me, "What is your
> religion?" I would say I was raised Hindu, but I will not say I am Hindu. Because
> even though I might believe in some of the philosophical foundations of Hindu-
> ism, and I really do, any religion, and that's what Hinduism is, starts to embody
> a whole host of other things, its political and its social, starting from the status of
> different castes, women, status of different religions, and that's when things start
> to get a little dicey. So I would in my own mind have a spiritual and or philosophi-
> cal orientation that may be like Hinduism, even more like Buddhism, but not buy
> into it.

Sunita Gandhi even claimed that Hindu temples "promote the right-wing propaganda by politicizing religion."

We asked Indian informants what their important reasons were for going to temple regularly or occasionally. Most informants listed "for peace of mind," "to find roots," "to take part in family *pujas*," and "to belong to the community." The most commonly cited were religious purposes related to spirituality, peace of mind, meditation, and so forth. For example, Dinesh Patel, a Gujarati-born Hindu who came to New York City at the age of 11, asserted: "I go for religious purposes and knowledge. This then gives me peace of mind. The more I learn about the religion, the more I feel at one with myself and enlightened about the ways of life."

Second-generation Hindu informants tend to place more importance on the spiritual than on the cultural component of Hinduism. Kumar Rao, a 55-year-old second-generation Indian man who worked for a media and entertainment financing company, grew up in New York City in the 1950s and 1960s when there was no Hindu temple there. At the time of the interview, he said he went to temple several times a year. Responding to the question about going to temple, he commented: "I go to meditate and for peace of mind. Lots of people go to temples for social purposes, but I don't do this. Basically I go to temples to take *darshan* [seeing], be quiet and meditate."

The next most widely cited reasons are cultural retention and maintaining roots. Indian Hindu immigrants emphasize cultural retention and Indian heritage as important reasons for taking their children to the temple. Some second-generation Hindus tried to connect the cultural purposes of going to temple with their parents' teaching the importance of preserving their Indian roots. Sekhar Chowdhary, a second-generation Hindu woman in her late twenties who worked as an administrative assistant, reported that she attended temple almost every week, although she lived independently. She credited her parents for her learning about the importance of retaining cultural traditions by going to temple regularly.

> Well, I think it is very important to be close to your roots. That is the way that my parents always taught me. Going to temple provides me with a way to stay close to my culture. It gives me a sense of pride in my culture because I'm always learning more about who we are as a people and why we do the things that we do traditionally. That's just the way my parents have always taught me, to be proud and to learn as much as I can about the culture.

Regardless of the frequency of attendance, most Indian Hindu informants also answered affirmatively to whether they thought "attending Hindu temples was helpful in maintaining Indian cultural traditions and identity."

Benazir Ghosh is a second-generation Indian medical doctor who lives with his wife, independently from his parents. He had attended the temple about once a month during his childhood. But he worships more often at home and goes to temple once or twice a year "purely for religious purposes" to have "extra *pujas*." Nevertheless, he conceded that going to temple was helpful in maintaining Indian cultural heritage: "I think so, because a lot of Indian culture is based upon our religious beliefs, so for me at least, going to temple has been sort of reinforcing the fact that I'm a Hindu and why I believe what I believe—it's sort of a reminder. I think it provides me a visual reminder of Hindu tradition."

The most important way to measure the extent to which the children of Korean Protestant immigrants have retained their childhood religion as adults is to look at their church affiliation rate. About 60 percent of the younger-generation Koreans who attended church during their childhood are currently affiliated with a church. Those younger-generation Korean Protestants who have retained their childhood religion are very active in their congregation, as active as highly congregation-oriented Korean Protestant immigrants are. By contrast, younger-generation Indian Hindus attend temple less frequently than Indian Hindu immigrants do and much less frequently than younger-generation Korean Protestants do.

Despite the different frequencies of attendance, younger-generation Korean Protestants may not have a significant advantage over Indian Hindus in the positive effect of religious institutions on ethnic preservation. Younger-generation Korean children's participation in immigrant churches helped them learn the Korean language and culture. But their participation in Korean English-language congregations as young adults was not helpful in preserving Korean cultural traditions, because in order to emphasize Christian universalistic values, English-language evangelical congregations have eliminated much of Korean culture. They contain ethnic elements in that they facilitate Korean ethnic fellowship and kin ties, as well as a reconstructed form of Korean culture. By contrast, even the irregular attendance of younger-generation Indian Hindus reinforces their Indian heritage and identity.

# 8 Younger Generations' Preservation of Ethnicity through Domestic Religious Practices

ALTHOUGH MOST YOUNGER-GENERATION Korean Protestants actively participate in Korean English-language congregations, these congregations have eliminated much of Korean culture from worship services and other sociocultural activities. By contrast, although second-generation Indian Hindus do not go to temple often, their occasional visits still help them retain their Indian cultural heritage and identity. This chapter examines the extent to which younger-generation Indian Hindus and Korean Protestants continue their domestic and other noninstitutional religious practices and their effect on their ethnic retention.

## Indian Hindus' Childhood Religious Practices and Their Effect

To assess the level of intergenerational transmission of religious practices at home, we asked the fifty-five 1.5- and second-generation Hindus questions about their parents' religious practices at home during their childhood and adolescence and then about their own practices. Indian Hindu immigrants perform religious rituals more often at home than at a temple. The responses of 1.5- and second-generation Hindu informants yielded similar findings about their parents' religious practices.

All but one of the informants reported that their parents had a family shrine or a *puja* room. Ninety-one percent said that their parents prayed every day, with the majority praying twice or more each day. Only two informants said that their parents never prayed. Generally their mothers prayed at home more frequently than their fathers, although some informants indicated that the opposite was the case. A few informants noted that their parents spent a lot of time every day praying, as the following comment by Bharat Jain, a 32-year-old Indian physician, shows:

> At home, every morning when my parents wake up, the first thing in the morning they will do some quick prayers, very quick, but then Dad will sort of go into another room and he'll just do yoga and prayer for like forty-five minutes to an hour every morning, and then he will just have his day. And then my mom will sort of make sure he's taken care of, make sure all the housework is initially done

early in the morning, breakfast is taken care of, then she'll come upstairs and do prayers quietly on her own for an hour. Oh actually, they established a second little sort of *puja* corner in their bedroom as well, so that's where she does her prayers in the morning.

The informants' responses to several questions indicate that their parents' daily praying often was accompanied and/or was followed by chanting mantras, meditation/yoga, and/or reading Vedas (scriptures).

Most of the informants said that they saw their parents praying every day but that they did not join them. Instead, they were asked to participate only in special *pujas* given on religious holidays and for celebrations of family life cycle or joyous events. For example, when asked how closely she was involved in her parents' religious practices at home while growing up, Samita Sinha answered, "I participated in *puja* on important days, yes, and even on those days I would stay away from all the seriousness going on in the *puja* area until it was clear that I was absolutely being called upon . . . for *aarti* [ceremonial fires], to perform a part of the *puja*, etc."

But seven informants reported that their intensively religious parents made them pray with them almost every day. For example, Kanu Roy, a 31-year-old Indian man who came to the United States at age 9, said that his parents prayed at least once and often twice a day. When he was asked whether he prayed with his parents, he said,

> Yeah, we used to. . . . Until I got to high school, we used to pray every night with my mom. It would be my mom, my sister and I. But we stopped that in high school. And then through high school, every Saturday and Sunday my sister and I would join my parents. During weekdays, they would get up too early in the morning and we would have to rush to school. But on Saturday and Sunday we would join them in the morning.

Mahendra Patel, a 39-year-old college professor, mentioned that his parents, from Gujarat, were very religious, and his mother prayed twice a day at sunrise and sunset. He described his mother's attempt to teach him how to practice *puja*: "My mom asked me to pray together every day. She showed me Indian TV shows about religious rituals. I practiced praying during sunrise. Without chanting mantras, I kept silent, but I got more familiar with praying."

We asked our Indian Hindu informants how many Hindu religious holidays their parents had celebrated at home during their childhood. More than one-third of the informants (38%) reported that their parents celebrated all the major Hindu holidays, almost one every month, accompanied by vegetarian dishes. Another 42 percent said that when they were children, their families observed three to seven holidays each year. The most commonly celebrated Hindu holiday is Diwali, followed by Holi, Navratri, Raki, and Krishina. Only four informants said that their parents did not celebrate any Hindu holidays at home. Two of them indicated that their parents did not do any thing at home because they were not religious. But the other two informants emphasized that although their parents were very religious at home, they always celebrated religious holidays at a temples or in relatives' homes. Their responses demonstrate the different ways in which Indian Hindus practice their religion. Some Hindu immigrants celebrate several Hindu holidays a year at home, with many relatives invited and many vegetarian dishes, but they may do this more for the holidays' cultural and social aspects than for their religious aspects. A few did not celebrate any religious holidays at home but observed some outside, as a group.

All but eight informants reported that their parents invited a Hindu priest to perform religious rituals (major *puja* ceremonies) for family members at least once during their childhood or adolescence. About 27 percent said that their parents invited a priest at least once a year, and 67 percent, once every few or five years. Their parents invited priests to their home to perform important life-cycle events, such as birthdays, weddings, deaths and engagements, and/or for celebrations of important family events, such as purchasing a new house or a new car, starting a business, finding a new job, or starting college. Some of the eight informants who reported not inviting a priest during their childhood said that their parents had rituals performed in temples. Forty-six percent of the informants reported that at least one of or both their parents were vegetarians. Many other second-generation informants reported that their parents, especially mothers, ate only vegetarian food at least during religious holidays and/or particular day(s) of week (usually Tuesday and/or Thursday). Even if their parents ate meat, most of them tried not to eat it at home.

We asked the informants how much they thought their observations of and participation in their parents' religious practices at home during their childhood or adolescence helped them preserve Hindu religious and Indian ethnic traditions. We asked them to answer this question by comparing the impact of family rituals with that of their temple attendance. The majority of informants agreed that their observations and participation in family *pujas* had a greater impact than did their temple attendance. Neil Singh, a 32-year-old physician, said that he did not participate in family *pujas* frequently, although his parents were very religious at home. But he indicated that his parents' active religious practices had significantly affected him:

> I think the fact that my family was ultrareligious in the household probably played a larger role for me in preserving my cultural identity. I could see my parents, who are obviously role models in any child's life, constantly showing a reverence for religion and God that somehow over time seeped into my own consciousness. If we had merely visited temples once in a while, I don't think I would probably have as strong a sense of religious identity as I do now.

Vicky Bhattacharya, a 33-year-old Indian business woman, reported that she participated in family *pujas* often during her childhood and attended evening prayers with her mother and sister. Regarding the impact on her of family *pujas*, she responded: "I definitely think the home stuff had a much greater influence on my identity and preserving traditions than going to temple. We didn't spend that much time at temples. I would say that the home stuff was close to 100 percent responsible for what I do today."

A few informants commented that their experiences with family rituals in their early years had a greater effect than did their attendance at temple because family rituals are more personal and social and involve more regional cultural traditions. Hindu immigrants' celebrations of religious holidays at home contribute to social interactions among kin members and friends in a way similar to that of Korean immigrant churches. Like most other Indian Hindu informants, Rachel Pais occasionally participated in family *pujas* given on important religious holidays and for family life-cycle events. But she agreed that home rituals had a greater impact:

> I do believe that in some ways, doing things at home had a greater impact than going to temple, because going to temple was less social, family oriented, and personal. We went to temple to pay our respects occasionally or on certain holidays. Whatever was done at home was also in accordance with, I guess, the way my parents had done things growing up and also a part of our regional Indian culture, and that has mattered me more. For instance, I associate certain foods with our *pujas* and holidays. This is because they were at home the way they traditionally were where my parents came from. So those *pujas* or holidays were more personal for me.

### Korean Protestants' Childhood Religious Practices and Their Effect

Korean immigrant informants practiced religion extensively at home, regularly reading the Bible, praying every day, singing hymns and gospel songs, and listening to sermon tapes, gospel songs, and Korean Christian radio programs. Our interviews with younger-generation Korean Protestants show that their parents were as active in domestic religious practices during their childhood as the Korean Protestant immigrant informants were. For example, only six of the sixty-six younger-generation informants reported that their parents never performed any religious rituals at home, including three whose parents were not Christians during their childhood.

About 31 percent of the sixty-six informants reported that their parents read the Bible every day. Another four informants' parents read the Bible at least once a week, while ten informants' parents (15%) never read the Bible at home. Forty-five percent of the informants said that their parents prayed at least once every day, in addition to saying grace before every meal. Forty-two percent of their parents regularly listened to gospel songs, tapes of sermons, and/or the Korean Christian radio station. In almost half the cases, these practices involved only their mothers. Their fathers practiced religion at home much less intensively, owing to their long hours of work outside the home and less religiosity.

Only six informants told us that their parents had family worship services with them once a week or more. Five others remembered that they had had worship services together perhaps "now and then" or "monthly." Because Korean Protestant immigrants do not speak English well, they tend to practice religion at home entirely in Korean, using a Korean-language Bible. The language barrier and the time pressure are the main factors making it difficult for Korean immigrants to hold family worship services regularly. By contrast, Indian Hindu immigrants have difficulty making their children join *pujas*, not because they cannot speak English well, but because the worship services are conducted in Sanskrit.

Each month the Shin Kwang Church holds a small-group district meeting, combining short worship services with social activities at night at a different district member's home. In these small-group meetings, the children and their parents read the Bible and sing hymns in Korean, which helped the children learn the Korean language and customs. But only a few of these meetings include children, because of the language difficulty and time pressure for school work.

The majority of younger-generation Indian Hindu informants thought their parents' religious rituals at home affected their retention of Indian cultural traditions and identity more than their temple attendance did. I did not ask the younger-generation Korean informants about this. But since Korean immigrants' Christian religious practices at home tend to focus on reading the Bible and praying, they presumably do not affect their children's retention of Korean cultural traditions and identity. When Korean immigrant parents and their children hold worship services in Korean, their children benefit, learning Korean as well as strengthening their religious faith. But only a few younger-generation Korean informants said that they had regular family worship services. Most Korean Protestant immigrant parents depend on their church's Sunday school or youth activities for religious education, whereas Indian Hindu immigrants usually teach their children Hinduism through family rituals.

Indian Hindu immigrants' performance of rituals at home, particularly for religious holidays, help their children retain their ethnic culture. Korean Protestant immigrants celebrate Easter, Christmas, and Thanksgiving at church more often than at home. Many Korean Christian immigrants fast before Easter, although this is not a uniquely Korean ethnic tradition. Korean Protestant immigrants also celebrate two major Korean cultural holidays, New Year's Day and

Chuseok (Korean Thanksgiving Day), mainly at church, accompanied by traditional Korean food, and many women wear traditional dress.

On the two Korean cultural holidays, many Korean Christian immigrants and their relatives and friends eat *ddeukguk* (a soup made of beef or chicken broth and rice cakes) and *songpyon* (rice cakes shaped like half moons). Non-Christian Korean immigrants celebrate the two Korean cultural holidays more than Korean Christian immigrants do, as many of them also worship their ancestors then. A few younger-generation Korean informants reported that to keep their homes sacred, their parents did not celebrate any Korean cultural holidays but did celebrate all Christian religious holidays.

### Indian Hindus' Religious Practices as Young Adults and Their Effect

We asked our Hindu informants about their religious practices at home. Except for one, all the second-generation informants' parents had a family shrine for regular *puja*, and of the thirty-six second-generation informants who did not live with their parents, 75 percent had a family shrine. In addition, two graduate student informants who had recently moved to a dormitory said that they would set up a shrine for *puja* soon. Two of those who had a family shrine constructed a tiny temple in a separate room, but most had a small shrine on a shelf, along with statues and pictures of deities. Several of the informants who did not live with their parents had a child attending school. When other informants are old enough to have school-age children, many of them are likely to have a family shrine.

The fact that most second-generation Hindus not living with their parents have a family shrine with statues and pictures of Hindu deities indicates that they accept the basic elements of Hinduism and may pray regularly. But as we found, their temple attendance is exceptionally low. This finding suggests that second-generation Hindus have generally preserved their Hindu religious traditions mainly through their practices of family rituals and other noninstitutional religious practices.

Compared with 91 percent of their parents, only 35 percent of our informants prayed every day, revealing a significant intergenerational reduction in the proportion of Indian Hindus who pray every day. Most second-generation informants pray a few times a week and/or on religious holidays and when they have personal problems. Eleven informants reported that they never prayed at home. One of them, Paresh Roy, kept Hindu icons and the Bhagavad Gita at home, reading it often, although he did not perform any other religious rituals at home. Responding to how important Hinduism was to his personal identity, he said: "It is somewhat important. Because it shapes how I look at the world philosophically in dealing with death, disappointment and other types of misery. It provides tools to deal with the 'predicament of life.'" We regard him as a rational spiritual Hindu because he uses Hinduism to reduce suffering. Accordingly, only ten of the fifty-five informants (18%) were not religious.

Only one of the twenty-seven independent resident informants who had a family shrine never prayed, which suggests that when second-generation Hindus have a family shrine, they must be religious. But some second-generation Hindus who do not have a family shrine do pray regularly. For example, Rani Ambany did not have a family shrine in her Manhattan studio, but she prayed about three times a week, usually in the morning. She said: "My mom told me I do not need a shrine to pray. She said it is in my mind and heart. I can pray at home without a shrine. When I purchase my own house, I will create a family shrine."

We asked how many times a year and what religious holidays the younger-generation Indian Hindus celebrated. Of course, those informants who lived with their parents celebrated more religious holidays than did those living independently. Fifty-three percent of the thirty-six independently living informants reported that they celebrated one or more religious holidays at their own homes, usually Diwali and another holiday. Their celebrations of Hindu holidays at home included performing *puja*, cooking vegetarian food, and having friends over, but on a much smaller scale than their immigrant parents did. Another six informants said that they visited their parents' homes a few times a year to celebrate religious holidays.

The other eleven informants said that they never performed *puja* at home to celebrate any Hindu religious holiday. A few of them pointed out that it was difficult for them to perform religious rituals in an apartment. But they still celebrated Diwali by going to the South Street Seaport Diwali fireworks, going to a college Diwali event, or lighting candles with their friends. Two of them who were spiritual Hindus did not perform Hindu holiday rituals at home because they did not like them. One of them, Neil Kotari, said: "I don't do a lot of rituals. I find other Hindus practice them excessively, like in Catholicism. I reject the priestship and what they have imposed. But I believe in basic tenets of Hindu religion, dharma, karma, etc." The other three nonreligious informants, whose worldviews were extremely secular and liberal, did not regard themselves even as cultural Hindus but accepted the cultural benefits of Hinduism, especially for their children.

We asked what decorations they displayed at home to signify their Hindu background. All fifty-nine Indian Hindu immigrant informants reported that they put up such decorations at home. By contrast, only 51 percent of the thirty-six informants who did not live with their parents said that they had religious displays, reflecting a significant intergenerational difference. But because many second-generation Indian informants lived in apartments or school dorms, it was difficult to put up religious decorations. When they get married and have their own homes, more second-generation Indian Hindus are likely to decorate their homes with religious symbols.

Forty-six percent of our informants said that either one of or both their parents were vegetarians. Fourteen informants (25%) considered themselves full (eating no meat at all) or partial (not eating red meat) vegetarians. The majority seemed to practice vegetarianism as a part of Hindu religious traditions, and nine were very religious, praying regularly. I interviewed Neera Patel, one of the informants, a 27-year-old woman who worked for the U.S. government, while she was visiting her parents in Queens. She explained why she refused to eat meat and fish: "Hindu rules require people to be respectful of animals as well as of other people. In our religion, action determines our future. By eating animals, we accumulate karma." She was very religious, praying every morning for ten minutes before going to work.

Interestingly, three of the fourteen vegetarian informants were among those nine informants who never prayed at home. One of them, Khyati Ghosh, a woman lawyer, apparently learned her vegetarianism from her parents who, she maintained, were not religious. Like her parents, she did not follow other Hindu religious rituals, including regular praying, but accepted vegetarianism as the central value of Hinduism. When I asked her why she did not pray regularly and perform other Hindu rituals, she responded: "According to the Brahmin tradition, not eating animals comprises the central component of Hindu rules. Because of my vegetarianism, I could be considered a good Hindu despite my secular values. But I only moderately identify myself as an Indian Hindu."

Despite her failure to practice other Hindu rituals, Ghosh attributed her vegetarianism to Hinduism and moderately identified as a Hindu, probably because her parents had taught her that vegetarianism was a more important value of Hinduism than other Hindu religious rituals.[1] Khyati was married to a second-generation Indian Jain who was committed to vegetarianism. Jainism emphasizes nonviolence and vegetarianism more than Hinduism does. No doubt, the two shared their commitment to vegetarianism. Another vegetarian informant, who was not religious, asserted that she "stopped [eating] all meat six years ago for health and environmental concerns."

Second-generation Indian Hindu young adults practice religion at home and in noninstitutional settings less often than their immigrant parents do, but they are more religious than the existing literature suggests. For example, Fenton (1992, 263) pointed out that about one-third of Indian American students enrolled in his undergraduate course on Hindu philosophy at Emory University could be identified as cultural Hindus who accepted only the cultural, and not the religious, components of Hinduism. Our data indicate that substantially more younger-generation Indian Hindus accept the spiritual components of Hinduism (45/55 = 82%) than his undergraduate student sample may suggest and that a much smaller proportion of the informants can be described as cultural Hindus.

Our interviews showed that 1.5- and second-generation Indian Hindus accept three forms of Hinduism: (1) spiritual Hinduism, (2) cultural Hinduism, and (3) philosophical Hinduism (values and worldviews). Most of the informants accept all three forms. But some informants consider the spiritual aspect of Hinduism more important than the others, and others consider the cultural or the philosophical aspect more important. Four secular informants accepted only the cultural aspect of Hinduism without accepting its spiritual component or at least recognizing the usefulness of Hinduism as a tool for transmitting Indian cultural values to their children.[2] A few secular informants focused on only universally acceptable Hindu values, such as vegetarianism (no animal slaughter), tolerance, humility, and compassion. Because Hinduism is very flexible in regard to particular deities, theology, and rules for rituals, with no one central scripture, second-generation Hindu Americans have embraced different aspects of Hinduism that they find useful for living in the United States.

Some secular Indian immigrants mainly accepted Hinduism as a cultural construct or a philosophy emphasizing nonviolence and other humanitarian values. These cultural and philosophical Hindus made up a significant proportion of younger-generation Hindus, which I consider a noteworthy transformation of Hinduism by younger-generation Hindus. Regardless of whether they identified as Hindus, more and more second- and third-generation Indian Americans are likely to use the cultural aspects of Hinduism in the future. According to results of the 2001 American Jewish Identity Survey, only 51 percent of Jewish Americans accepted Judaism as a religion (Mayer, Kosmin, and Keysar 2003, 17), but Jewish religious holidays, especially Rosh Hashanah and Yom Kipper, and other religious rituals, such as bar mitzvahs and bat mitzvahs, have become important traditions that help secular Jews to identify as Jewish. Similarly, secular second- and third-generation Indian Americans are likely to use Hindu religious rituals to preserve Indian values.

Younger-generation Hindus' other important transformation of Hinduism is their greater emphasis on the rational aspects of Hindu religious practices, such as meditation and reading scriptures to find peace of mind and reduce stress without needing to believe in a supernatural power. An important reason that Indian Hindu immigrants perform Hindu religious rituals is to obtain "blessings," to enable their wishes to come true, by means of the supernatural power they believe that the various gods and goddesses possess. Likewise, many well-educated, converted white American Buddhists accept Buddhism mainly as a rational meditation technique to reduce stress without believing in the supernatural powers associated with various forms of Buddhism practiced in Asian countries. Chen's study shows that even well-educated Taiwanese Buddhist immigrants reject the supernatural elements of Buddhism as the product of Chinese culture and emphasize its rational and educational elements involving meditation and dharma as representing "pure Buddhism" (Chen 2008, 100–108). Highly educated second-generation Indians who are not accustomed to Asian supernatural beliefs understandably focus on the rational elements of Hindu.

The younger-generation Hindu informants' focus on the spiritual components of Hinduism and not on religious rituals and on the rational aspect of spirituality and not on supernatural beliefs has been strongly influenced by their taking Hinduism and other religion courses in college and at temple and reading Hindu scriptures translated into English. Although my questionnaire did not ask about their study of Hinduism, fifteen informants referred to these courses.[3] These courses and their reading of original scriptures seem to have led them to adopt more of Hinduism's rational spiritual and philosophical components.

A 23-year-old graduate dental student made a remark showing the influence of academic courses: "I took a class on Hinduism in college. It gave me a more objective view to the religion outside of my parents. They [parents] taught me what to do, but did not explain why." Krishna Mozumder, a married, 31-year-old, 1.5-generation Hindu, does not perform Hindu religious rituals much at home but still identifies himself as a Hindu. He suggested that his study of Indian culture through a college course helped him define Hinduism broadly so that he did not have to do much to be a good Hindu:

> The other thing is, I mean, my interpretation of Hinduism is a very broad one, and this comes a little from having studied it. I'm nowhere near a scholar on it, I took one semester, it wasn't even on Hinduism, it was, like, on Indian culture.
>
> But a lot of texts . . . every culture, and the origins of it are all in religion somehow. My interpretation of it is very broad, and I, just like you know, as a part of that group, don't feel like I have to do a lot to be a good Hindu. And that may not be the case for other religions where it seems like you have to do a lot more.

Their assimilation to American society and their learning of Hindu philosophy in college courses have influenced many second-generation Indian Hindus to reject first-generation Hindus' ritual-oriented religious practices and to embrace the more abstract meditational and philosophical form of Hinduism. This form of Hinduism is rooted in Neo-Hinduism, which originated in India. Neo-Hinduism, or modern Hinduism, developed in reaction to Hindu reformers' encounter with Christianity in the eighteenth and nineteenth centuries and emphasizes universally acceptable unifying elements of Hinduism rather than localized diverse religious rituals (King 1989). Fenton, who taught comparative religion at Emory University, related the abstract and philosophical form of Hinduism embraced by the majority of Hindu college students to their internalization of basic Neo-Hindu ideas (Fenton 1992, 264).

> Hindu religion for the second immigrant generation is more general and abstract than the first generation because they have not lived in India.
>
> In fact, college students' religiosity bears resemblance to Western Enlightenment morality, and their spirituality tends to be neither very specific nor very deep. They have internalized basic Neo-Hindu ideas and this orientation constitutes the basic stance from which they participate in classroom discussions. Many students who have no interest in religious organization, *puja*, or meditation are nevertheless attracted to a view of the world rooted in contemporary interpretations of the Vedanta systems of theology and Bhagavad Gita.

Although at the time of the interview, most of the informants observed an abstract form of Hinduism with no Hindu rituals, many of them may perform more Hindu rituals as they grow older. Only twenty of the fifty-five Indian Hindu informants were married at the time of the interview, and fewer than half the married informants had one or more children. Because of their unstable housing situation (living in an apartment), many independently living younger-generation Indian Hindu informants could not perform religious rituals in their own homes even if they wanted to. Moreover, having no children, many may not have felt they needed to. But when they marry and have their own children, more younger-generation Indian Hindus are likely to perform religious rituals and to go to temple in order to give their children an Indian religious and cultural foundation.

Some of the informants recognized the importance of Hindu religious rituals to their children's ethnic socialization. For example, Rachel Pais, a 22-year-old college graduate, reported: "I usually saw my father pray after showering in the morning. But he is not religious. It is simply his habit." She told me that to cope with many problems during her college years, she often prayed at the Friday Hindu prayer session at Columbia University. She emphasized that she "took Hinduism more as a spiritual thing, a meditation technique." But when I met her two years later, she conceded that looking back, her parents' performances of rituals on major Hindu holidays during her childhood, with relatives and friends invited, helped her retain Hindu religious and Indian cultural traditions. Moreover, she noted, "To teach my children the Indian heritage I may have to teach them Hindu rituals. On Diwali, what else can I do for my children other than performing the *puja* ceremony?"

## Korean Protestants' Domestic Religious Practices as Young Adults and Their Effect

Younger-generation Indian Hindus not only perform fewer religious rituals at home but also have transformed Hinduism by observing its spiritual, rational, and humanistic elements more than its rituals. More significantly, we found that whatever elements of Hinduism younger-generation Indian Hindus accepted, they contribute to their Indian heritage and identity because of the inseparable linkages between Hinduism and Indian cultural and philosophical traditions. Younger-generation Korean Protestant informants are slightly more likely to carry out religious practices at home than their parents, but their domestic religious practices, which are separate from their ethnic cultural traditions and history, do not help them preserve their Korean identity and culture.

The parents of the younger-generation Korean Protestant informants practiced their religion fairly actively at home during their childhood. For example, only six of the sixty-six informants (including three whose parents did not attend church during their childhood) reported that their parents did not observe any religious practices (reading the Bible, praying, and singing/listening to hymns or gospel songs).

Thirty-four percent of the informants responded that they read the Bible every day, compared with 31 percent of their parents who did during the informants' childhood. Another 28 percent said that they read the Bible a few times or at least once a week. The fact that more than 60 percent of the informants read the Bible at home at least once a week demonstrates that younger-generation Korean Protestants are very religious. Only six informants said they never read the Bible at home, compared with ten whose parents never did during their childhood. Sixty-nine percent of the informants prayed at least once daily, usually before bed, in addition to saying grace before meals, compared with only 45 percent who said their parents prayed daily during their childhood and/or adolescence. Most of the informants (52%) sang, listened to or read praise songs, sermons and/or Christian books, with 21 percent doing this every day. Whereas Korean Protestant immigrants usually listen to tapes of Korean-language sermons, often recorded by their own church pastors, and Korean Christian programs, younger-generation Korean Christians listen to Christian music and sermons on American Christian TV and radio.

Twenty percent of the informants fasted "once in a while" or "irregularly," especially during Lent. Twenty-two percent also said that they "meditated," "reflected," or had "quiet time" (QT) regularly or occasionally "to reflect on the God's words." In regard to Christian holidays they celebrated at home, all the informants cited Easter and Christmas, and a few included Good Friday and Lent. Many informants emphasized that they celebrated each day in their churches and prayed and meditated at home every day. A few pointed to the inadequacy of the term *celebrate*, as it did not reflect the meditative aspect of their religious practices at home.

Only six of the twenty-nine informants not living with their parents did something at home on one or two Korean cultural holidays. More younger-generation non-Christian Korean adults than their Christian counterparts were likely to celebrate Korean cultural holidays at home, although we do not have hard data on this issue.

Seven of the twenty-nine informants (24%) not living with their parents had no religious display at home. Nine of the fifty-six Korean immigrant Protestant informants (16%) did not put up any religious decorations at home, and only about half the younger-generation Indian Hindu informants, compared with all Hindu immigrant informants, had religious displays at home. Because most of the younger-generation Korean Protestant informants not living at home were unmarried and lived in apartments, the fact that one-fourth had no religious display at home is not surprising. Pictures of Jesus, plaques with Bible verses, and crosses were the most common religious articles, usually found in their bedrooms, kitchens, and/or cars.

Many younger-generation Indian Hindus used religious articles at home to show both their Hindu and Indian identity. Conversely, younger-generation Korean Christians used Christian symbols to represent their Christian, not their Korean, identity. Younger-generation Indian Hindus perform far fewer religious rituals than their parents did. But whether they perform simplified *pujas* at their home or participated in *pujas* at their parents' home, the *pujas* reinforced their Indian ethnic identity.

Other non-Protestant Christian groups, such as Greek Orthodox and Mexican Catholics, have transplanted and consolidated their religious rituals, which are best represented in their celebrations of religious holidays, including the preparation of ethnic foods. In this way, their domestic religious practices reflect their ethnic traditions, albeit less than younger-generation Indian Hindus' domestic religious practices do. By contrast, younger-generation Korean evangelical Protestants' Bible-based religious practices have few or no ethnic elements and so contribute little to their retention of ethnic traditions.

# 9 The Importance of Religion to Younger Generations' Identity, Socialization, and Social Relations

Yes, because that's how I think, or just who I am and what I am. After meeting Jesus, I never thought of myself having a nationality. My Christian religion supersedes everything. I . . . oftentimes hear things like this. . . . Three months ago, the U.S. military in Korea ran over two young Korean girls. I was angry for whatever happened not because I'm Korean.[1] I was angry because I was a Christian. I would have been angry for whoever got killed that way, not just for Koreans. So people might think I'm unpatriotic. That's the way I think.

—David Jung, a 1.5-generation Korean Protestant information technologist

Hinduism is important for my identity. I consider myself primarily as an Indian American. But my Hindu values and rituals strengthen my Indian identity.

—Neera Patel, a 27-year-old second-generation Indian Hindu woman

KOREAN PROTESTANTS' AND Indian Hindus' significantly different levels of religious faith are reflected in their personal identity, child socialization, friendships, networks, and selection of marital partners. In this chapter, I emphasize the differential levels of what Donald Smith (1970, 175) called "dogmatic authority," "the degree of conviction that one's religion has the absolute value," as the central reason for the difference in younger-generation Korean Protestants and Indian Hindus in the importance of religion for ethnic identity, child socialization, and social relations. Like other evangelical Christians, younger-generation Korean evangelical Christians accept three or four principles from the Bible as absolute truths. By contrast, Indian Hindus accept Hinduism as their worldview in varying degrees that they consider useful in reducing stress, enhancing their ethnic heritage, and/or strengthening their moral values. Many younger-generation Hindu informants have their own definitions of what a good Hindu is. This basic theological difference is important to understanding the differences between younger-generation Korean Protestants and Indian Hindus.

## The Importance of Religion to Personal Identity

Several studies pointed out that second-generation Korean Protestants regard being Christian as their primary identity and being Korean as their secondary identity (Alumkal 2003, 111–12; Chai 1998; R. Kim 2006; S. Park 2001, 2004). My interview data support this generalization. We asked younger-generation Koreans: "How important is Christian religion to your personal identity? Is it more important than your Korean national background, your Asian American background, and your gender status? Why?" Table 9.1 shows that 74 percent of sixty-six younger-generation Korean informants considered being Christian as their primary identity, while only 18 percent chose being Korean as their primary identity. Three informants said both their Christian and Korean ethnic backgrounds were equally important to their identity, and another two informants emphasized their gender status as their primary identity. Thirty-eight percent of Korean Protestant immigrant informants considered being Christian as their primary identity, and 52 percent considered being Korean as their main identity. Despite their high level of religiosity, a majority of Korean Protestant immigrants regarded being Korean as their primary identity because of their strong Korean ethnic attachment. In the past, religion has never served as a marker of subethnic division in Korea. But for second-generation Korean Christians, who have much less ethnic attachment than Korean Protestant immigrants do, their Christianity itself constitutes the core of their identity, the so-called religious global citizens identity that transcends racial and national boundaries (Levitt 2007, 86).

The fact that about three-fourths of younger-generation Korean Protestant informants chose being Christian as their primary identity indicates their strong commitment to the Christian faith. The informants' explanations of why they considered their Christian background the core of their identity reflect their strong commitment to their religion. Responding to the question of how important Christian religion was to his or her personal identity, Cynthia Lee, a 27-year-old special education graduate student, asserted: "Very important. My Christian identity is primary. Because that's where my faith stands. I firmly believe in my faith more than I believe in my ethnic group or gender. I would die for my faith, but I would not die for anything else." In the epigraph at the beginning of this chapter, David Jung, a 1.5-generation information technologist, emphasized the primacy of his Christian identity to the extent that after meeting Jesus, he never thought of himself as even having a national background.

Because evangelical Christianity has no close ties to Korean culture, many second-generation Koreans' Christian and Korean identities conflict. Despite the tensions, based on her ethnographic research on two Korean English-language evangelical congregations, Chong (1998) claims that Korean churches reinforce

**TABLE 9.1**

*Korean Protestants' Choice of Religion or National Background as Their Primary Identity, by Generation*

| | Generation | |
|---|---|---|
| Primary Identity[a] | Immigrant | 1.5 and 2d |
| Being Christian | 38% | 74% |
| Being Korean | 52% | 18% |
| Both equally important | 10% | 8% |
| Total | 100% $(n = 55)$ | 100% $(n = 66\%)$ |

Source: Personal interviews with 55 Korean Protestant immigrants and 66 1.5- and 2d-generation Korean Protestants.

Note: [a]How important is Christian religion to your personal identity? Is it more important than your Korean national background, Asian American background, or gender status?

second-generation Koreans' ethnic identities and boundaries because evangelical Christianity and Korean Confucian culture share many conservative values. Pastors of Korean immigrant churches emphasize that Korean Confucian values, such as filial piety, respect for adults, and no premarital sex, are more similar to conservative Christian values than to postindustrial American values (see also S. Park 2004). But second-generation Korean evangelical churches also stress universal Christian values and try to minimize Korean cultural components. In addition, second-generation Korean Christians try to separate their Christian from their ethnic identities.

To determine how closely younger-generation Korean Christians connect their Christian to their ethnic identity, we asked our informants, "Do you think your practice of Christian religion signifies your Korean identity?" Several informants (13/62 = 21%) pointed out similarities between Korean Christianity and Korean nationality. One was the prevalence of Christians among Korean immigrants and an overabundance of Korean churches in the Korean community. In answer to a similar question, "Do you think a typical Korean means a typical Christian?" only two Korean Protestant immigrant informants saw a significant association between Protestantism and Korean nationality, probably because Protestants are a minority population (only about 20%) in South Korea. But several younger-generation Korean informants found a strong association between Christianity and Korean nationality based on the prevalence of Korean American Christians.

Some informants cited the unique aspects of Korean Christians' religious practices, such as praying fervently and loudly, going to church a few or several days a week, and not drinking. Gil Soo Lee, a 27-year-old 1.5-generation Korean, was a member of a Korean-language congregation for young men and women:

> Yes, somewhat overlapping. If you're both a Korean and you're a Christian, the way Koreans practice Christianity is different from other nationalities. For example, if you're a Korean Christian, you're not encouraged to drink or do "bad things." But for other cultures, I think it's allowed. And for Korean Christians we go to Wednesday, Friday, Saturday, Sunday services. We spend many hours at church. Other nationalities are different in the number of hours invested throughout the week.

Only two informants, like Chong (1998), emphasized the "compatibilities" between Christian and Korean conservative values, although their examples were not convincing, as illustrated in the following comment by Angie Byun, a 40-year-old corporate lawyer:

> Yes. First, the Korean population as a whole is Christian. Second, I think traditional Korean values are very compatible with Christian beliefs. For example, doing good deeds. Korean stories like *Hyungboo & Nolboo*[2] are about how good overcomes evil. This is similar to Christian lessons. Also, Koreans have believed in supernatural higher being. This is compatible to Christian culture, too.

But the vast majority of the informants (78%) saw no linkages between Christianity and Korean traditions. According to Edward Jun, a 29-year-old engineer, "No. I put my Korean identity and religious identity totally separate from each other. Sure there are many Korean Christians, but not all Christians are Koreans. They are completely separate categories in my mind."

Julie Choi, an English teacher, criticized Korean immigrant Protestants for mixing religion and Korean traditions:

> No. I don't like to put religion and tradition together. Because that's what first-generation Koreans do all the time. When they're disciplining a child they don't do it biblically; they do it traditionally. I think sometimes it just gets mixed up. It's not right. Religion and tradition are separate.

Another informant pointed out that Christianity was imported from the West and was not indigenous to Korea: "No, it's absolutely unrelated. Korean traditions are based on Confucian values. Being Christian, some would say, is a Western concept that was brought in. Christianity was initially imported, and is not native to Korea."

According to the social constructionist perspective, people usually recognize multiple identities without conflict and use a particular identity in a particular situation and another one in another situation (Cornell and Hartman 1998; Frankenberg 1993; Lyman and Douglass 1973; Nagel 1994). Thus a second-generation Korean Christian may be able to have strong Korean and Christian identities and emphasize one or the other in his or her interactions with a non-Christian

Korean group or a Christian group. In reality, though, most people cannot hold two unrelated identities equally strongly. As Stryker found (1980), there is a hierarchy in identity salience; that is, one identity may be far more important than the others. According to his social structural version of symbolic interactionism, high-ranking identities are more likely to be invoked in different situations, and "as organizers of lower-ranking identities, they will be relatively stable through time" (Stryker 1980, 131). The stronger one identity becomes, the weaker the other identities will be. Most second-generation evangelical Christians favor their Christian identity over their Korean ethnic identity. Since they do not see any significant connection between Korean culture and Christian values, they strongly reject Korean cultural components found in Korean immigrant churches as "un-Christian." Thus we can surmise that Korean and Christian identities maintain a "zero-sum game or relation"; that is, as one gains, the other loses.

We asked younger-generation Indian Hindus similar questions about the relationship between their religion and ethnic identity: "How important is Hindu religion to your personal identity? Is it more important than your Indian national background, your South Asian background, or your gender status?" I content-analyzed their qualitative responses into the following three categories: very important, somewhat important, and not important or not at all important. Thirty-nine percent of the fifty-five informants considered Hindu religion very important for their identity, and 43 percent considered it somewhat important. The remaining 18 percent ($n = 10$) said it was not important or not at all important to their personal identity. These ten informants did not subscribe to any religion but still accepted Hinduism as their Indian cultural heritage or as a philosophy with important humanitarian values. But five of them did not identify themselves as Hindu. When asked to indicate their religion, only these ten younger-generation Indians chose the no-religion category. These figures indicate that Hinduism still is important to a majority of second-generation Indians' identity, although most younger-generation Indian Hindus are not very religious. Because Hindu religious boundaries are loose, both Indian Hindu immigrants and their children are able to continue being Hindu without being very religious. Thus it is not surprising that Hindu adults were the most likely of all religious groups to retain their childhood religion, according to the 2007 U.S. Religious Landscape Survey (Pew Forum on Religion and Public Life 2008, 30).

Another important issue is whether the informants consider Hindu religion more or less important to their identity than their Indian national background, gender status, or South Asian background. According to table 9.2, only 18 percent ($n = 10$) regarded being Hindu as their primary identity and their Indian national origin or, in a few cases, their gender status as their secondary identity. Most of these ten informants practiced their religion very actively at home, although most did not go to temple regularly. Pravin Reddy, a 27-year-old native-born Indian biologist, reported that he prayed at home twice a day and attended temple every other week. He commented on the importance of Hinduism for his identity:

> Religion identifies who you are. You could be born in any country, any time, any place, but religion helps you get in touch with your inside. It tells you that this is where you come from and this is where you are going. Any religion can help you understand that this is what you are and this is how you're supposed to live your life, and it can teach you the right path to walk down. Religion is definitely what I consider to be the most important.

For the majority of the informants (55%), however, their Indian ethnic background was their primary identity, and for 20 percent, their Hindu and Indian backgrounds were inseparable and thus equally important to their identity. Two informants gave their South Asian identity as their primary identity. The response by Mahenda Khator shows why the Indian national background may be more important than the Hindu religion. This 28-year-old married Indian who did not live with his parents remarked:

> I would say it's important but maybe not as important as the Indian background. Both of my parents were born in India, so that means a lot to me. People in India can have very different religious faiths but still have the same values. Those values are what I use in everyday life.

But many informants who chose being Indian or Indian American as their primary identity pointed out that their Hindu religious practices enhanced their Indian ethnic identity. For example, as shown in the beginning of this chapter, Neera Patel commented, "Hinduism is important for my identity. I consider myself primarily as an Indian American. But my Hindu values and rituals strengthen my Indian identity." Another informant said, "I am an Indian American, and being Hindu means a lot for my Indian American identity."

Personal identity is determined not only by one's primordial ties to the group to which one belongs, but also by how one is perceived by the larger society, especially in the United States in regard to race. Although only seven of sixty-six younger-generation Korean Protestant informants had experienced prejudice and discrimination because of their Christian background, a majority had encountered subtle forms of prejudice and racial slurs because of their physical differences. I suggested that their experiences with racial prejudice and discrimination led them to attend Korean English-language congregations or multiethnic congregations and to avoid predominantly white American congregations.

A number of studies have indicated that because of their physical appearance, geographical origin, and non-Christian religion, Indian and other South Asian Americans encountered more racial discrimination and physical violence than did other Asian American groups (Dhingra 2007, 99; Lessinger 1995, 135–36;

TABLE 9.2

*Indian Hindus' Choice of Religion, National Background, or
Regional Background as Their Primary Identity by Generation*

| Primary Identity[a] | Immigrant | 1.5 and 2d |
|---|---|---|
| Being Hindu | 37% | 18% |
| Being Indian (Indian regional) | 36% | 56% |
| Two inseparable | 27% | 22% |
| South Asian | 0% | 4% |
| Total | 100% ($n = 59$) | 100% ($n = 55$) |

Source: Personal interviews with 59 Indian Hindu immigrants and 55 1.5-
and 2d-generation Indian Hindus.

Note: [a]How important is the Hindu religion to your personal identity? Is
it more important than your Indian national (regional) background, South
Asian background, or gender status?

Sheth 1995, 181–83). We asked younger-generation Indian Hindu informants the
same two questions regarding their experiences with prejudice and discrimination based on their religious background and Indian/Asian background. Thirty-
five percent of the fifty-five Indian informants had experienced prejudice because
of their Hindu religious background, but most had encountered a subtle form,
related to being called names like "monkey," "idol worshippers," and "pagans" in
school. Many informants said that as young adults they tried to keep their Hindu
religion secret at their workplace. But about 60 percent of Indian informants
reported that they also experienced prejudice and discrimination because of their
physical differences. Some of them were subjected to racial slurs like "niggers" and
"sand-niggers." But others experienced more blatant forms of racism. For example,
Vijay Gupta, a 29-year-old American-born Indian musician and artist, recalled
his experiences with racism:

> Racially, all the time . . . I mean I grew up in Oklahoma. I got beat up as a kid . . .
> umm I got the normal teasing. I was the only Indian kid in school, and I got called
> names. When I went to restaurants in Oklahoma and North Carolina, I was
> denied service. Post-9/11 I had a bunch of Caucasian kids call me "terrorist loving
> nigger fuck."

These informants' many experiences with racism and tenuous commitment to
Hinduism contributed to their strong Indian ethnic identity and weak religious
identity.

Table 9.2 shows that 37 percent of Indian immigrant informants identified
first as a Hindu, and 27 percent felt that their Hindu and Indian national backgrounds were inseparable and thus equally important to their identity. Thirty-six

percent regarded their national or regional identity as the primary identity. But fewer (18%) younger-generation Indian Hindu informants cited the Hindu religion as their primary identity,[3] and more (56%) regarded their Indian national origin as their primary identity. This intergenerational shift in personal identity was inevitable, since the importance of religion to younger-generation Indian Hindus had substantially declined. Interestingly, exactly the opposite happened to Korean Protestants. Most Korean Protestant immigrants, who came from a culturally homogeneous country, where religion was not a subethnic identity, cited being Korean as their primary identity. But most second-generation Korean evangelical Christians, who have a strong religious faith but have lost many of their ethnic cultural traditions, cited being Christian as their primary identity and being Korean as their secondary identity.

This finding of the opposite directions of the intergenerational shift in the importance of religion versus national origin as the primary identity for Indian Hindus and Korean Protestants is sociologically important. Even more sociologically important to this book's main thesis is that religion and ethnicity maintain a complementary relation for Indian Hindus (see also Joshi 2006, 48) but a zero-sum relation for Korean Protestants. The opposite effects of religion on ethnicity for the two groups have become clearer for the younger generations. As younger-generation Koreans' religious identity has become stronger, their ethnic identity has become weaker, because Korean Christianity has not incorporated Korean folk cultural traditions. By contrast, Hinduism has incorporated Indian folk culture and an Indian philosophical outlook in its long history of development on the Indian subcontinent. Most Indian Hindu immigrant informants consider Hindu religious rituals and Indian cultural traditions closely linked, and therefore they try to teach their children Hindu rituals as part of their Indian cultural heritage (see also Joshi 2006, 48).

To examine the informants' perceptions of linkages between the Hindu religion and Indian cultural and spiritual traditions, we asked them, "Do you think your practice of Hindu religion signifies your Indian identity?" Their qualitative responses were content-analyzed in the following three categories: definitely yes, yes, and no. The definitely-yes category of responses included: "Hinduism and Indian things are hard to separate"; "The two are very similar"; "Yes, they are the same"; "Synonymous"; "Hand in hand"; and "I don't find the differences." Thirty percent of the informants ($n = 53$) said definitely yes; 62 percent gave a moderately affirmative answer; and only four informants answered negatively. This means that more than 90 percent of younger-generation Indian Hindu informants agreed that Hindu rituals and philosophy were strongly or moderately linked to Indian cultural and philosophical traditions.

Isha Sen, a 26-year-old, 1.5-generation, Indian computer specialist, actively practiced her Hindu religion, by both going to temple and performing family rituals. In answer to the question about the interrelation of Hinduism and Indian traditions, she remarked:

> Definitely, definitely. I think everybody knows that India is a very religious country and we have mostly Hindus there, so that connection is always there, you know. I know people here have their own beliefs, but it can't compare to all of the things we do in India. We have strong beliefs in Gods, and so many festivals, so many stories, and so many languages. People all celebrate festivals differently, so when I practice Hindu religious things, it's definitely part of my Indian identity.

Rany Ambany said that because Hindu rituals are inseparable from Indian cultural traditions, they reinforce her ethnic identity: "Yes. So many Hindu religious rituals are cultural. We cannot separate the two. But that is the beauty of Hinduism. I practice Hindu rituals because it reinforces my identity, makes me believe who I am."

Those informants who moderately agreed on the connection between the Hindu religion and the Indian identity also pointed out that there are other religions in India and other Indian cultural components, such as language, mythologies, and movies. "Cultural Hindus," especially, emphasized the multicultural nature of Indian society and celebrated Hindu holidays as well as Sikh and Muslim holidays.

## The Importance of Religion for Child Socialization

We asked all our Korean Protestant informants, "Which do you think is more important for your child, being a good student or being a good Christian?" For those who did not have a child, this was a hypothetical question. But many unmarried informants did not answer the question, so we got only forty answers. An overwhelming majority (88%) of these forty said their child becoming a good Christian was more important than being a good student, with only three informants, who were not religious, choosing the good-student answer. Two informants had difficulty choosing between the two, indicating that both were equally important. Seventy-six percent of Korean Protestant immigrant informants favored their child being a good Christian over being a good student. More younger-generation Korean Christians than their immigrant counterparts chose the good-Christian answer, because they were slightly more religious and because Korean Christian immigrants put more emphasis on their children's educational success than do younger-generation Christians.[4]

Many informants explained why they chose the good-Christian answer, with one group stressing the reward of salvation as the main reason for their choice of being a good Christian. Angela Park, a 28-year-old lawyer, still attended her father's Korean immigrant church a few times a week: "Good Christian. Eventually your soul is more important than this world. We're all going to die one day and go to an eternal life." Mike Han, a 31-year-old part-time premed student, also referred to "eternal life" as the most important benefit of a good Christian life:

> Good Christian. Recently I've come to the conclusion that the path I was taking in life was wrong. Also, especially when I lost my permanent job, I've realized my number one priority of making millions and retiring early was pointless. After meditation, I've realized that life should be about leaving a mark, no matter how small it is. Life is short. The eternal perspective is more important. Part of it is choosing to live as a Christian.

The other group of informants underscored the positive moral values associated with a good Christian life as a reason for wanting their child to be a good Christian. For example, Julie Choi, who attended an English-language congregation in a Korean immigrant church while teaching in its Sunday school, asserted that being a good Christian meant being a good student and more:

> Being a good Christian because that's how I was brought up, and being a good Christian helped me to be a good student. For example, what I learned as a Christian helped me to be a better person with better morals, so when you're in school you wouldn't cheat on your test.

We asked our younger-generation Indian Hindu informants two questions regarding their priority on religion for their child's socialization. Although these questions should have been asked of all informants, unfortunately they were asked of only those twenty informants who were married. One question was, "How important do you think it is that your children retain the Hindu religion? Why?" Only 26 percent of them said that it was very important for their children to retain the Hindu religion, and 37 percent said that it was somewhat important. A 35-year-old Indian woman who came to the United States from Telegu, India, at the age of 15 responded in reference to her son:

> This is to me one of the most important things. He will see one day how important it is for him to have a religion in his life. He knows already, but he is still young. When he gets old, I want him to realize how much religion will help him. I cannot force this on him. You let them live and learn. He will surely see how important it is to be a Hindu . . . to live with love in your heart and just be a good person with a good heart.

This comment indicates that she believes it important for her child to be a good Hindu mainly because of the religion's moral values.

Another 37 percent of the married informants said that Hinduism was not important or not at all important to their children. In chapter 6, I noted that the vast majority of the Indian Hindu immigrants considered it very important that their children practice the Hindu religion. Because several younger-generation Hindu informants did not accept Hinduism as a religion because of their distaste for any organized religion and because Hinduism strongly opposes proselytism, it is not difficult to understand why many second-generation Americans of Indian Hindu ancestry do not believe it very important for their children to be observant Hindus. Vijay Gupta expressed his unwillingness to raise his children as a religious Hindu mainly because of his concern about organized religions. When asked whether he thought it was important for his children to be good Hindus, he said,

> Religiously, I don't want them to maintain Hinduism, because I have an inherent distaste for organized religions and because Hinduism is an organized religion. I would want them to identify with Hinduism from a cultural point of view. You can isolate religion and culture, so yes, I would want them to identify with Hinduism, but not as a Hindu. I wouldn't want them to go to someone and say "I am a Hindu."

Although this secular, cultural Hindu did not want his children to be religious Hindus, he did want his children to learn Indian cultural traditions from Hinduism. Responding to another question, he said:

> I would plan to take them to temples in India and I would take them to temples here. I would take them to some cultural events and stuff. Enough that they understand what was a part of me, but is clearly less a part of me than [it] was for my parents.

Another secular informant indicated that her children would benefit from going to temple to learn Indian cultural traditions. Rupam Sinha, a self-identified agnostic, rarely went to temple because of her aversion to organized religions. But when asked whether she planned to take her children to temple, she said that parents should take their children to temple to expose them to Indian culture and extended families.

> I think I would only do that, again, if we were with my larger extended family. Umm because ... I think it will become an important part of sharing that whole family experience and exposing them to the culture since neither my husband nor I am religious. I don't really identify so much as Hindu any more. I identify more as agnostic and we feel very strongly about not raising our children in any particular religion. But we also feel strongly about exposing them to religion and particularly religious ideas. So from that point of view, part of their understanding of their relatives, particularly their grandparents and aunts and uncles, would come from going to temple and seeing what it's all about.

Some younger-generation Hindu informants who believed it somewhat important or very important for their children to maintain their Hindu religion noted that regardless of their wishes, their children should ultimately decide their religion. The following remark by a second-generation Indian woman best reflects this viewpoint: "I think when I have children they will be able to choose whatever religion they want." There is no doubt that the younger-generation Indian Hindu informants' readiness to allow their children to choose their own religions has derived from the pluralistic worldview of Hinduism, its openness to all other religions and values. We can see the connection between Hinduism' openness to different religions and second-generation Hindus adults' respect for their children's own choice of religion in the following comment by Rani Ambany, a 32-year-old Indian pediatrician:

> I think it is very important for my future children to maintain Hinduism in a
> certain form. It is good to learn life values from Hinduism. Hinduism allows you
> to open to different values. Also, they can preserve Indian cultural traditions and
> identity through Hinduism. But if my children want to go to church, it is all right.

We also asked younger-generation Hindu informants whether being a good Hindu or being a good student was more important for their child. Half the twenty informants who answered this question chose the good-student answer, and only one informant chose the good-Hindu one. Four informants said that both were equally important, and five informants wanted their child to become "a good person" first. Thirty-eight percent of Indian Hindu immigrant informants chose the good-Hindu answer; 22 percent chose being a good student; and 40 percent put equal weight on both. The younger-generation sample was so small that a generalization based on these findings would be difficult. But the huge intergenerational drop in the percentage of the informants who chose the good-Hindu and "equally important" answers indicates a significant reduction in religious faith among younger-generation Indian Hindus.

Eighty-eight percent of younger-generation Korean Protestant informants wanted their child to become a good Christian first, and only three informants chose the good-student answer. The intergroup differential between younger-generation Korean Protestants and Indian Hindus in the percentage of informants who put more weight on religious education is as significant as the intergenerational differential in personal identity. These findings suggest that there may be a further drop in retaining Hindu religion among third-generation Indian Hindu Americans, whereas most third-generation Korean children of Protestant parents are likely to retain their parents' religion. Indian Hindu immigrants have a disadvantage, compared with Korean Protestant immigrants, in transmitting their religion to their children and grandchildren in this Christian country because of the traditional and noncongregational nature of religious rituals conducted in Sanskrit. Another factor that makes it difficult for Indian Hindus to transmit their religion to their descendants, compared with Korean evangelical Protestants, is their pluralistic worldview that accepts other religions and values and considers evangelism inherently dangerous. Second-generation Korean Protestants who consider evangelism as a central component of Christian life believe that their children must retain their religion. But many religious younger-generation Indian Hindus who embrace the Hindu pluralistic worldview consider it wrong to impose their religion even on their own children. Many other younger-generation secular Indians of Hindu parents try to keep their children away from any religion because of their misgivings about religious dogma.

Younger-generation Korean children of Catholic parents have a much lower rate of retention of childhood religion than do those of Protestant parents because of Korean Catholics' greater tolerance of other religions and other values. Buddhism also emphasizes a pluralistic worldview. Suh's study of a Korean Buddhist temple (2004, 88) reveals that Korean Buddhist immigrant women believe their children should choose their own religion. The social science literature on immigrants' religious practices focuses on institutional mechanisms, such as Sunday school and ethnic language schools, as facilitating the intergenerational transmission of religion (Ebaugh and Chafetz 2000, 431–45) but neglects the role of theology.

## The Importance of Religion for Social Boundaries

Younger-generation Korean Protestants' strong commitment to their religious faith suggests that their close friends were likely to be Korean Christians and that they preferred non-Korean Christians to non-Christian Koreans as close friends. To test this hypothesis, we asked younger-generation Korean informants to indicate the racial and religious backgrounds of their five best friends. The findings show that as expected, most of their five best friends were Korean Christians. For about 70 percent of the informants, three or more of their best friends were Korean Christians, and for 38 percent, all five of their best friends were Korean Christians. Only four informants had no Korean Christian as one of their five best friends. The majority of other best friends were non-Korean Christians, most of them Chinese and white Christians. These findings support our expectations about younger-generation Korean Christians' strong subethnic social boundaries and their preference for non-Korean Christian friends over non-Christian Korean friends.

The great tendency of younger-generation Korean Protestants to choose coethnic and coreligious close friends is based on their exceptionally frequent participation in congregations. Results of the 2003 survey of Korean English-language congregations show that most second-generation congregations had two or more extra meetings a week for Bible study, prayer, discipleship, and/or social activities. Nearly half of them went to small-group meetings regularly, each week or month, for the Bible study and fellowship at someone's home, at church, or at a restaurant. No doubt, these small-group meetings and weekly Sunday services influenced younger-generation Korean Christians' friendship networks.

Younger-generation Korean Christians' active involvement in their friendship networks also was influenced by their strict evangelical moral boundaries. We noted earlier that members of New York's Shin Kwang Church tried to limit their close friendship to fellow church members in order to avoid drinking and other types of secular entertainment activities that, they believe, are prohibited by the Bible. So-Young Park (2004, 189–90) also found that freshmen Korean evangelical Christian college students usually did not join the Korean students' club because of its involvement in drinking, smoking, and hip-hop dances. Those second-generation Korean evangelical Christian informants who had completed college and who identified as born-again Christians were more likely to emphasize their Christian moral values than other college students were. A 28-year-old female informant stated that her five best friends were Korean Christians and added: "If you don't have common values, how can you be friends? You won't get to a level where you can really share." Another informant said: "Korean Christians won't make other non-Christian friends, like Indian Hindus."

We asked our informants about the religious and racial backgrounds of their dating partners. Their responses showed that a majority of their dating partners were Korean Christians. During their high school and college, when they were not very religious, many informants dated non-Christians, but they said that they now tried to date Christians. A 30-year-old informant who worked as a system administrator said that in order to follow the biblical rules he had never dated: "I made sure I did not date. It's like a biblical thing. I waited until, I guess, God showed me what the signs were, who the woman was." We asked the informants how important it was to them to marry a Korean Christian. The majority said it was very important. But they put more priority on selecting a Christian partner than on finding a Korean partner, as the following comment by a 28-year-old man indicates: "I would prefer a Korean Christian. But my main priority is to marry a Christian. But I would also prefer someone who is Korean, because of my parents. They would be more comfortable."

When asked how important it was to marry a Korean Christian, 42 percent said that it was very important for them to have a marital partner who shared both the same religious and ethnic backgrounds. Another 41 percent said having a Christian spouse was very important but that they preferred a Korean. As John Lee stated: "Very important. Choosing a Korean person is a preference. Choosing a Christian is an absolute and definite choice." Seven informants (11%) chose a Korean as necessary and preferred a Christian, and only six informants (9%) reported that neither a Christian nor a Korean background mattered much.

**TABLE 9.3**

*Korean Protestants' Choice between Non-Christian Korean and Non-Korean Christian as Desirable Marital Partners, by Generation*

| | Generation | |
|---|---|---|
| More Desirable Marital Partner[a] | Immigrant | 1.5 and 2d |
| Non-Korean Christian | 39% | 71% |
| Non-Christian Korean | 46% | 26% |
| Korean Christian a necessity | 2% | 3% |
| Neither matters | 13% | 0% |
| Total | 100% $(n = 55)$ | 100% $(n = 66)$ |

Source: Personal interviews with 55 Korean Protestant immigrants and 66 1.5- and 2d-generation Korean Protestants.

Note: [a]Which is more desirable as your marital partner, a non-Christian Korean or a non-Korean Christian?

These figures suggest that the vast majority of younger-generation Korean Protestants believe it very important for them to marry a Christian, and they overwhelmingly prefer a Korean. They prefer a Korean for the convenience of their family life and the preservation of their ethnic heritage, such as "to make my parents happy," "to share the same cultural heritage," and "because we can raise our children effectively." But because of their deep religious faith, they believe it very important to have a Christian spouse.

We asked the Koran Protestant immigrant informants which was a more desirable marital partner for their child, a non-Korean Christian or a non-Christian Korean. As shown in table 9.3 and noted previously, 46 percent of Korean Protestant immigrant informants chose a non-Korean Christian as a more desirable marital partner for their child, compared with 39 percent who chose a non-Christian Korean partner. We also asked younger-generation Korean Christian informants the same hypothetical question to see the change in attitudes across generations. We expected the younger-generation informants to put more weight on a Christian background than the immigrant informants did. As expected, 71 percent of the younger-generation informants, a much higher proportion than of Korean immigrant informants, chose a non-Korean Christian partner, compared with only 26 percent of them who chose a non-Christian Korean partner. Two informants insisted that their marital partners be both Korean and Christian.

Although younger-generation informants were far more open to accepting non-Korean marital partners than their parents were, they more strongly preferred marrying a Christian. We asked them why they chose one or the other category of answers. Many informants provided interesting arguments to justify their choices. Rebecca Shin, a 29-year-old optometrist, said: "Non-Korean Christian. Marriage is something in which the two support one another. You need that emotional and spiritual support system, prayer system. That's more important than cultural interactions." She added that finding a Korean partner was important only because she wanted to honor her parents' wishes. David Jung, another male informant who was already cited in regard to his strong Christian identity, explained why he wanted a Christian wife: "Non-Korean Christian. I want to meet my wife in heaven as well. I believe being a Christian leads to heaven."

Those who chose a non-Christian Korean partner were not very religious in their personal lives, although they may have attended church regularly or irregularly. Some of those who were somewhat religious said that they would make their non-Christian partner convert to Christianity but that they would not be able to change a non-Korean Christian partner's physical characteristics. Soon-Mi Kwon, a 30-year-old single woman who came to the United States at the age of 12, attended a Korean English-language congregation twice a week and prayed at home almost every day. These religious practices indicate that she was deeply religious, but she chose a non-Christian Korean as a more desirable partner. She explained why:

> I would have to go with Korean non-Christian. I think it'll be easier, being that we're from the same background. They'll be so much more understanding if he's Korean. Him being not Christian, it will be easier to change him and convert him. It will be easier changing non-Christian to Christian than a non-Korean to Korean.

But a few female informants pointed out that it would be very difficult to convert their husband to Christianity. For example, Jenny Park stated, "A non-Korean Christian. I want to stay Christian. My mom went crazy because my dad didn't let her go to church. I don't want that to happen to me. Christianity is something I strongly believe in and the most important thing in my life." Interestingly, we noted earlier that responding to a similar question some female Korean immigrant informants indicated the difficulty of converting their non-Christian husband to Christianity.

We previously found that for 38 percent of younger-generation Korean informants, all five of their best friends were Korean Christians and that for 70 percent, three of their five best friends were Korean Christians. Given that there are more than twice as many native-born Indian Americans of Hindu ancestry in the New York / New Jersey area than native-born Korean Protestants,[5] Indian Hindus have a much greater chance of having coethnic and coreligious close friends than Korean Protestants do. But younger-generation Indian Hindus' responses to the same question show that they select close friends from outside their own group far more than Korean Protestants do. All five best friends of only 13 percent of fifty-five Indian Hindu informants were Indian Hindus, and three of the five best friends of 52 percent were Indian Hindus. The Indian informants had more coethnic friends with different religions and also more nonethnic friends with different religions than the Korean informants had. More significantly, nine informants (16%) had one or more South Asian or Indo-Caribbean Muslims as close friends.

Not surprisingly, the less religious Indian Hindu informants had more non-Hindus as close friends than did those who were more religious. Since Indian Hindu informants, as a group, were much less committed to their religious faith than were Korean Protestant informants, more Indian Hindu informants had close friends from outside their religious group. Younger-generation Indian Hindus accept people with other religions as their close friends far more easily than do their Korean Protestant counterparts because they generally accept Hinduism as their own personal worldview and Indian cultural heritage. By contrast, younger-generation Korean evangelical Protestants, like other evangelicals, accept the inerrancy of the Bible and evangelism as the central components of their Christian lives, and Jesus Christ as the savior of the world. Therefore, they have difficulty in making close friends with those who do not share their religious beliefs. An overwhelming majority of younger-generation Korean Protestant informants are what Robert Wutnow calls "exclusive Christians," who restrict their social networks largely to other Christians (Wuthnow 1995, chap. 6).

While the majority of Korean Protestant informants' dating partners were Korean Christians, the majority of Indian Hindu informants' dating partners were Indians with other religions or non-Indians with other religious backgrounds. Some informants who had dated mostly non-Indian partners in earlier years tried to date Indian Hindus or at least Indian partners as young adults when they were looking for marital partners. They realized that having Indian Hindu or Indian marital partners was important for raising their children and sharing cultural values. Three Indian Hindu informants dated Muslim partners, and one of them was married to a Muslim. Several informants dated Sikh or Jain partners.

In regard to the importance of marrying an Indian Hindu, 28 percent of younger-generation Indian Hindu informants reported that it was very important and another 34 percent said that it was somewhat important. Isha Sen, a 30-year-old Indian woman who worked as a computer programmer, married an Indian Hindu man. She explained why it was very important to choose an Indian Hindu husband:

It was very important because you know I always wanted to get married to somebody who was from my own culture so we could always get along well. There is no problem getting married to someone from a different caste or religion. But you know in the long run we need some compatibility among two partners, so I've always wanted somebody from my religion so we can be more compatible and we can celebrate the same festivals and we can pray to the same God, and then maybe our kids will also do that because we have the same level of things.

Many of the second group who said "somewhat important" expressed the view that their partner's Indian background was more important than his or her Hindu background. Vasudha Dhingra, a native-born Indian college senior, said that because she had lost much of Indian cultural traditions, she needed to marry an Indian partner of any religion, except for a Muslim: "I would prefer that the person I marry is Indian so that I can gain some of the culture back. It wouldn't matter if he is a Sikh or Jain. It would matter if he is a Muslim."

The remaining 38 percent said that it was not important or not at all important for them to have an Indian Hindu partner. Many of them also preferred to have an Indian partner, with the exception of a Muslim. But many others said that they were open to members of any racial and ethnic group with any type of religion if only the other partner accepted Hinduism. Rani Ambani, who was dating an Indian Sikh at the time of the interview, emphasized that she was open to anyone as long as the other partner accepted Hinduism: "He does not have to be an Indian. But he should be open to Hinduism. I can accept a white partner as long as he accepts Hinduism."

In fact, six Indian Hindu informants were married to non-Indians: one to a Pakistani Muslim, two to white Protestants, two to white Catholics, and one to a white partner with no religion. Two more informants were married to non-Hindu Indians, one to a Sikh and the other to a Jain. Before the interview started, I did not instruct the interviewers to interview intermarried Indians. But we ended up interviewing many Indian Hindus in interfaith marriages because we interviewed many professionals, especially professors. By contrast, only twelve of the sixty-six Korean Protestant informants were married, with none intermarried. But this does not mean that younger-generation Indian Hindus have a higher intermarriage rate than their Korean Protestant counterparts. We simply stopped interviewing younger-generation Korean informants without interviewing intermarried persons. On the contrary, an analysis of the 2001–2006 American Community Surveys shows that only 32 percent of native-born Indian Americans born after 1965 are married to non-Indian partners, compared with 54 percent of Korean counterparts (Min and C. Kim 2009). Native-born Indians have the lowest intermarriage rate of all six major Asian groups, whereas the intermarriage rate of native-born Korean Americans (53%) is very close to that of native-born Asian Americans as a whole (55%). Native-born Indians' non-Christian religious background seems to be the major contributing factor to their much lower intermarriage rate. By contrast, native-born Koreans' Christian background seems to facilitate their marriage to white Americans.

The fact that only a small proportion of younger-generation Indian Hindus intermarry does not mean that they are strongly opposed to interfaith or interracial marriage. Of course, Indian Hindu immigrants, as well as Indian immigrants of other religious faiths, emphasize the importance of endogamous marriage, and many still have arranged marriages (Khandelwal 2002, 154–55). But younger-generation Indian Hindus are usually liberal enough to consider interfaith or interracial marriage if their partner accepts their religion. Their commitment to religious pluralism permits them to accept an exogamous marriage in which both partners keep their premarital religion.

How interfaith couples negotiate with religious authorities to arrange weddings and how they socialize their children are important issues (Wuthnow 1995, 264–76). Although our interviews with several intermarried Indian Hindus did not provide any information about these issues, they reveal their views about how living with someone with a different religion. In regard to the importance of marrying an Indian Hindu, Geeta Anand, who married a white Episcopalian, explained, "Most second-generation Hindus do not know much about Hinduism. My husband[, however,] not only accepts Hinduism but also knows a lot about Hinduism." Sunita Patel, who married a Pakistani Muslim, added, "Well, I fell in love with a guy who's not a Hindu, but he respects my culture and my religion. That's what matters."

These Indian Hindu informants maintained their Hindu traditions while accepting their partners' religious practices. Priyanka Jain, a 39-year-old, second-generation Indian woman who was married to a Portuguese American Catholic, went to the Sai Center every week from September to May and prayed at home almost every night. Although she did not perform many rituals, she was very spiritual. When asked whether her marriage to a white Catholic had changed her Hindu beliefs, she replied:

> It hasn't changed anything about my belief system and sense of spirituality. I knew I would still baptize my children whether or not he wanted to because I believe all religions have a universal truth. One thing is that we both came to the same conclusions from different paths. Also, I didn't feel uncomfortable with him because I was exposed to it from the Sai Center. . . .
>
> With my husband, we both do our things together and that's fine. I would never want to impose and never want to have anything imposed upon me. I would never want to be involved with someone who wants me to convert.

The wife of Sandeep Karthick, a 39-year-old Indian professor of media studies, was born in Germany and had no religion. Karthick regularly did yoga and meditation at home and was a strict vegetarian. He visited his parents about four times a year to celebrate major Hindu holidays. He said that his wife "silently participated in the *pujas*" performed at his parents' home. Sunita Patel also did not stop her Hindu religious practices after getting married, attending temple once a month and praying twice every day.

Although younger-generation Indian Hindu informants are generally open to non-Hindu and even non-Indian partners, they acknowledged that marrying an Indian Muslim was the most difficult thing. When asked if they would marry an Indian Muslim, all but seven of the informants said that it would be almost impossible for them to marry an Indian Muslim; some even said that it would be easier to marry a white Christian. Two factors made it difficult for them to marry a Muslim. First, their family would reject a Muslim owing to past and present conflicts between Hindus and Muslims in India. A few even said that it was taboo for an Indian Hindu to marry an Indian Muslim partner. The following response by Pallavi Mosumder, a 23-year-old graduate student, shows this concern: "It would create too much tension in my family even to begin to have relations on a personal level with a Muslim. So, no. It would create tension because grandparents fled from Pakistan during partition and lost everything. I know my parents remember what that was like for them."

In addition, according to our informants, Muslims are not open to marrying people of another faith. Several informants said that Muslims are so religious that they will not marry a Hindu unless that person converts to Islam. When asked whether she would marry a Muslim, Sunita Patel, who is married to a Portuguese Catholic, said, "Yes, but I would be cautious of the cultural differences. I haven't come across a Muslim guy who wasn't hard-edged and into conversion. I don't believe in conversion, so I wouldn't if one had to be picked." A Hindu woman married to a Muslim reported that she had not had any serious problem with her interfaith marriage because she and her husband accepted each other's religion.

We found no Korean Protestants who had married someone of a different religion, because Korean Protestants' strong commitment to their religion does not allow them to marry someone of a different religion. Korean evangelical Christians would marry someone of a different religion only if that person converted to Christianity. Many younger-generation Korean Protestants marry non-Korean, often white, Christians. But they are likely to have a stronger Christian identity than other Korean Christians, and they often attend English-language Korean congregations. Nonetheless, evangelical English-language Korean congregations include few Korean cultural elements. By contrast, younger-generation Indian Hindus marry non-Hindus and maintain their religious practices while accepting their partners' religion because they are strongly committed to religious pluralism. Indian Hindu immigrants would have difficulty marrying a non-Hindu because of their religious rituals at home, including eating vegetarian foods and fasting. But we found that younger-generation intermarried Indian Hindus maintain the spiritual and value components of Hinduism, which involve few rituals.

# 10 A Summary of Major Findings and Their Theoretical Implications

## A Summary of Major Findings

Religious organizations help both Korean Protestant and Indian Hindu immigrants preserve ethnicity, but in different ways. First, Korean Protestant immigrants have a huge advantage over Indian Hindu immigrants in maintaining ethnic fellowship and networks through their frequent participation in religious institutions. Korean Protestant immigrants probably attend church more frequently and spend more hours a week in church than any other Christian group in the United States. This and various other congregation-related small-group activities, along with their cultural homogeneity, help them maintain strong friendship networks and ethnic ties rarely found in other religious groups. The Shin Kwang Church of New York is a medium-size church with about 550 members, and members of various committees, age-based groups, and district groups interact with other members both inside and outside the church. No doubt, these strong friendship and fellowship networks help them cope with alienation from the larger society. These friendship ties and communal bonds are the main reason that new, non-Christian Korean immigrants go to Korean immigrant churches.

By contrast, Indian Hindus' irregular temple attendance and the noncongregational nature of their worship services do not help create fellowship and ethnic networks. Indian Hindu immigrants visit religious institutions much less frequently and spend much less time on each visit than Korean Protestant immigrants do. Moreover, Indian Hindu immigrants visit different temples to participate in their cultural functions without necessarily being affiliated with a particular temple. Thus they have little personal connection with particular temples and the attendees at each temple. In addition, Hindu temples provide few activities and programs that enhance participants' fellowship and social networks. Our interviews with immigrants reveal that few Indian Hindu immigrants go to temple for fellowship and friendship networks, whereas most Korean Protestant immigrants do so.

The Hindu temple helps immigrants preserve their Indian cultural traditions and subethnic and ethnic identities. The Korean church, too, helps Korean Protestant immigrants and their children preserve their cultural traditions. The temple helps Indian Hindus maintain their ethnic culture and identity mainly because its architectural design, religious rituals, and other sociocultural activities are based on Indian ethnic and subethnic cultural traditions. By contrast, the Korean church helps Korean immigrants preserve their cultural traditions mainly because it gives them a context for practicing and teaching their children Korean, especially Confucian, culture.

The Hindu temple displays its ethnic culture to the American public much better than the Korean church does because of the visibility of its architectural design, the Diwali festival, and other cultural activities and because of the "authenticity" of its cultural components. The cultural authenticity of Hindu temples and religious faith and rituals reinforce Indian Hindu immigrants' ethnic identity and pride, especially because all immigrant and minority groups are encouraged to offer something different to the U.S. multicultural table (Kurien 1998). Korean Protestants cannot display Korean customs and values practiced inside the church to the American public. Also, Americans do not regard the Korean Protestant church as a repository of Korean culture, but they do consider the Hindu temple as representing Indian or South Asian culture.

The temple helps Indian Hindu immigrants and their children preserve their religious rituals, such as those for holidays, weddings and funerals, and fasting and dietary rules. By contrast, the Korean church mainly helps preserve the Korean language and Korean Confucian customs and values, including respect for parents and other adults. The same two factors that contribute to the Korean church's fellowship (Koreans' cultural homogeneity and the strong congregational orientation) also enhance ethnic education. The Korean church is more effective than the Hindu temple in teaching the second generation the ethnic language and core ethnic values. But the Hindu temple may have a longer-term impact on the second and later generations' cultural retention than the Korean church does because its value-neutral rituals, such as ethnic festivals and weddings, usually last longer than the ethnic language and values (Alba 1990; Waters 1990).

The most significant difference in the effects of religion on ethnic retention is their preservation of ethnic culture through religious practices at home. Indian Hindu immigrants perform at home religious rituals that are also Indian cultural traditions, such as celebrating several holidays, eating vegetarian food, and fasting on many religious holidays. Most Korean Protestant immigrants, too, practice their religion at home, praying daily, reading the Bible a few times a week, and regularly singing and listening to hymns and gospel songs. But these do not contribute to the retention of Korean cultural traditions mainly because of the dissociation between their religion and Korean secular culture.

Because Hinduism is a religion indigenous to India, Hindu rituals are closely related to the holidays, food, music, and other elements of Indian folk culture. Korean immigrants have adopted Christianity plus some Korean traditions, such as a strong congregational orientation, regular district meetings, and a strict gender hierarchy in the congregation's organization. But their Christian religion is disconnected from Korean folk culture. In addition, over many centuries different forms of Hinduism that incorporate local cultural traditions have gradually developed in the Indian states. Thus observing religious holidays and performing ceremonies on auspicious family occasions with traditional foods and flowers are central—more important than reading and interpreting sacred texts—to Hindu immigrants' religious practices. But Protestantism, especially the Korean version of evangelical Christianity, puts far more emphasis on reading the Bible and listening to the pastor's sermons (interpretations of the Bible) than on practicing informal rituals at home. Regardless of the extent of linkage between their religion and Korean culture, Korean evangelical Protestants, like other evangelical Protestants, do not often practice religious rituals at home.

These analyses suggest that the relationship between religious and ethnic identities is close for Hindus but full of tension for Korean Protestants. Indian Hindu and Korean Protestant immigrants' responses to several key questions further highlight the differences in this relationship. Significantly, more than one-third of Korean Protestant immigrant informants chose Christian over Korean as their primary identity and preferred non-Korean Christian to non-Christian Korean marital partners for their children. As evangelical Christians, they support Christian universalistic values over ethnic particularistic values. Conversely, Indian Hindus do not have to choose between religious and ethnic identities because the two are complementary. Thus Indian Hindu immigrants have a huge advantage over Korean Protestant immigrants in using their religion to enhance their ethnic identity.

Indian Hindus appear to have a slight advantage over Korean Protestants in maintaining ethnic traditions through religion. But it is difficult to determine with data based only on immigrants which group is more successful in transmitting its ethnicity through religion to subsequent generations. Major findings from the second-generation data show different levels of inheritance of religion and ethnicity through religion among 1.5- and second-generation Korean Protestants and Indian Hindus. About 60 percent of the younger-generation Korean young adults who attended Korean Protestant immigrant churches during their childhood and adolescence retained their childhood religion, meaning that they were affiliated with a church. As evangelical Christians, they are active participants in their congregations. Most of them are affiliated with Korean English-language congregations and are more active than they were in their immigrant church during their childhood.

Our interviews with younger-generation informants confirm these findings pertaining to the important role of Korean immigrant churches in teaching younger-generation children the Korean language and Confucian etiquette.

However, Korean English-language congregations, which are heavily evangelical, have eliminated many Korean cultural traditions in worship services and other sociocultural activities typical of Korean immigrant churches. As a result, their participation in Korean congregations does not help them preserve Korean cultural traditions. While other Protestant groups' second-generation congregations usually provide bilingual and bicultural services (Mullins 1987), Korean congregations for 1.5- and second-generation Koreans are entirely in English.

Korean English-language congregations do contain some ethnic elements. First, owing to their sense of racial marginalization, younger-generation Korean Protestants prefer Korean or Asian American congregations or at least multiracial congregations, such as the Redeemer Presbyterian Church in Manhattan, to predominantly white American congregations. Moreover, as Rebecca Kim pointed out (2006), young, socially active Korean American Christians in a Korean church reflect a recreated Korean ethnic culture based on their similar professional lifestyles and shared immigrant family experiences. In addition, Korean American Christians' frequent participation in a Korean congregation in a Korean immigrant church helps them maintain ties with their parents and friendships with fellow Korean Christians.

Mainly or partly owing to their experiences with racial prejudice and discrimination, most younger-generation Korean Christians choose Korean congregations rather than white American churches. For this reason, Rebecca Kim (2006) used the revised theory of "emergent ethnicity" associated with Yancy and his associates (1976) to explain the reconstructed form of ethnicity found in Korean English-language congregations. But we should not overemphasize the ethnic elements—whether inherited or emergent—of the Korean English-language ministry because of its basis on Christian universalistic values. The worship styles and overall congregational culture of Korean evangelical English-language congregations are more similar to those of white American evangelical congregations than Korean immigrant congregations. Moreover, the Korean Christian subculture of Korean English-language congregations is very different from the ethnic culture of second-generation non-Christian Koreans. In addition, Korean Christians have created a Korean Christian subethnic boundary within second-generation Korean congregations rather than an all-encompassing Korean ethnic boundary. Because of the salience of their Christian identity, second-generation Korean evangelical Christians' ethnic identity is much less important to them than it is to their non-Christian counterparts.

Given the great differences in congregational culture between Korean immigrant and second-generation congregations, more and more second-generation Korean evangelical congregations are likely to become independent as they become financially secure. As they become independent, they are likely to draw more and more non-Korean, especially Chinese American, Christians. One independent Korean English-language evangelical congregation in New York City has a significant number of younger-generation Chinese members and thus is turning into a Pan-East Asian church. Younger-generation Korean and Chinese Christians make up nearly half the members of Manhattan's Redeemer Presbyterian Church, a large, multiracial church. Although Korean and Chinese members have not established a separate Pan-East Asian congregation there, they have frequent interactions through separate "home fellowship groups" and a separate monthly praise night (Chai 2005, 274). Accordingly, I believe that more English-language Korean congregations will become multiracial or Pan-East Asian churches in the future. But some evangelical Korean English congregations are likely to continue to maintain some ties with immigrant congregations mainly because of their intergenerational coordination in foreign missionary activities. Nonetheless, a few mainline second-generation Korean congregations will remain as ethnic congregations within Korean immigrant churches that emphasize their ethnic components.

Younger-generation Indian Hindus are more apt than their Korean counterparts to retain their childhood religion (identify themselves as Hindus) simply because the Hindu religion is very flexible. But they go to temple substantially less frequently than Indian Hindu immigrants, who attend much less frequently than do Korean Protestant immigrants. This contrasts with younger-generation Korean Protestants, who go to church as often as, or even more often than, Korean Protestant immigrants. Three factors have contributed to younger-generation Indian Hindus' going to temple less: (1) their difficulty in learning how to perform rituals at the temple, since many are conducted in Sanskrit, (2) their concern about "too excessive rituals" performed in temples for deities that they consider superstitious and even materialistic, and (3) their increasingly liberal and secular worldview and distaste for organized religions. But even their reduced temple attendance helps younger-generation Indian Hindus preserve their ethnic heritage and identity because the temples' architecture and rituals are part of Indian cultural and philosophical traditions. Many younger-generation Korean Protestants claim that a Korean American congregation is not an "ethnic congregation" but a spiritual community with no room for Korean culture. By contrast, many second-generation Indian Hindus occasionally visit a temple. especially for the cultural benefits.

Indian Hindu immigrants practice their religion mainly through their rituals at home, whereas Korean Protestant immigrants practice their religion mainly through their participation in congregations. As such, their religious practices at home are likely to have a more significant impact on younger-generation Indian Hindus' retention of their childhood religion and ethnic traditions. Our interviews with younger-generation Indian Hindu informants support this conclusion. Most of them reported that during their childhood and adolescence, their daily observations of and occasional participation in family rituals, often involving parents' relatives and friends, had a greater effect on their religious and ethnic heritage than did their irregular attendance at a temple.

Not surprisingly, younger-generation Indian Hindus perform religious rituals much less often than do their immigrant parents. But the data also indicate that younger-generation Indian Hindus are more religious than the existing literature may lead us to believe. A vast majority of the informants accepted the spiritual components of Hinduism while also recognizing its cultural and philosophical values. The others accepted Hinduism only as a source of Indian cultural heritage or as a philosophy involving moral values such as nonviolence, humility, and compassion. Even spiritual Hindus tend to put more emphasis on the rational aspects of Hindu religious practices such as meditation and reading scriptures as a way of finding peace of mind and put less emphasis on complicated rituals involving belief in a supernatural power. Since Hinduism has many different deities, beliefs, and core values, with no one central scripture comparable to the Bible for Christianity, American-educated younger-generation Indians of Hindu parents observe those aspects of Hinduism useful to their adaptation to American society. But no matter what form of Hinduism younger-generation Indian Hindus accept, it enhances their ethnic heritage and identity because Hinduism is a uniquely Indian religion.

Younger-generation Korean Protestant informants recollected that their parents actively practiced their religion at home, mostly praying and reading the Bible regularly. But their parents' religious practices at home did not affect their children's ethnic retention, mainly because these practices were not Korean ethnic traditions. The younger-generation Korean Protestant informants practiced their religion slightly more at home than their parents did during their childhood. But these practices did not contribute to their preservation of ethnic traditions. For example, many younger-generation Korean informants observed Easter as the most important religious holiday. But what they did on Easter—fasting, reading the English-language Bible, and having quiet time—had little to do with Korean cultural traditions. Rather, they learned how to observe Easter and other Christian religious holidays from Christian books written by American evangelical organizations.

Younger-generation Korean Protestants are much more strongly committed to their religious faith than younger-generation Indian Hindus are, as reflected in their personal identity, child socialization, and social relations. Qualitative data based on personal interviews show that an overwhelming majority of younger-generation Korean Protestants identify as Christian first and as Korean second.

Since most Korean Protestants' religious and ethnic identities have a zero-sum relationship, as their religious identity becomes stronger, their ethnic identity becomes weaker. The tension between the two becomes clear when younger-generation Korean Christians criticize Korean immigrant churches for being too ethnic and un-Christian. By contrast, the loosening of faith among younger-generation Indian Hindus leads them to have a weaker religious identity than their parents do. But their embrace of Hinduism in any form enhances their ethnic identity, as the majority of them identify first as Indian.

The different levels of their religious faith also are reflected in their child socialization and social relations. Younger-generation Korean Protestants, who accept three or four commandments in the Bible as absolute truths, consider it a life-or-death issue for their children to inherit their religion. Thus an overwhelming majority of them put priority on making their children good Christians over making them good students. By contrast, younger-generation Indian Americans of Hindu parents who adopt some elements of Hinduism as useful to their adaptation to the United States choose the good-student over the good-Hindu option. Not surprisingly, Korean Protestants who are highly committed to Christianity choose Korean Christians as their close friends and prefer non-Korean Christians to non-Christian Koreans as their close friends and marital partners. Younger-generation Indian Hindus put less stress on religion in choosing close friends and selecting marital partners than Korean Protestants do. Moreover, because they are tolerant of different religions and different value systems, many Indian Hindus are open to choosing nonethnic and non-Hindu marital partners if they accept Hinduism. Members of other religious faiths, especially Christians and Muslims, will not marry Hindus unless they convert to their religion. The aversion of Indian Hindus to convert to other religions and the rejection of white Christians to accept their marital partners' non-Christian religion seem to be the main reasons why second-generation Indian Hindus are less apt to marry white Americans than second-generation Korean Protestants are (Min and C. Kim 2009). We consistently found that some second-generation Indian Hindu informants in interfaith marriages continued to practice Hinduism while recognizing their partner's religion.

## Theoretical and Other Contributions

The extremely frequent participation of Korean immigrant Protestants in the church has helped them preserve their ethnicity mainly through their coethnic fellowship and friendship networks and by helping them retain Korean cultural traditions. By contrast, Indian Hindu immigrants' occasional attendance at temple and active performance of religious rituals at home have helped them preserve their ethnic traditions and identity mainly because their Hindu religious practices themselves symbolize Indian ethnic traditions and identity.

Whether Korean Protestant immigrants' congregation-oriented religion or Indian Hindu immigrants' indigenous noncongregational religion better preserves their ethnicity is determined by the intergenerational transmission of ethnicity through religion. Korean Protestant immigrants are more successful than Indian Hindu immigrants in transmitting religion to their children. Younger-generation Korean Protestants are as active as or even more active in both their participation in congregations and their religious practices at home than their parents are. By contrast, younger-generation Indian Hindus go to temple substantially less often and perform religious rituals at home less often than their parents do. Korean Protestant immigrants are more successful in transmitting their religion to their children, partly because of their advantage in religious education deriving from the congregational nature of their Christian religion, but mainly because of their stronger commitment to their religious faith. Indian Hindu immigrants have difficulty teaching their Americanized children traditional Hindu religious rituals. Moreover, because of the tolerant nature of Hinduism, they also respect their children's voluntary choice of their own religion to a greater extent than do Korean evangelical Christians.

However, ironically, Indian Hindu immigrants are more successful in transmitting their cultural traditions and identity through their religion than Korean Protestant immigrants are. Although younger-generation Korean Christians are very active in both congregational and domestic religious practices, these practices have little to do with Korean cultural traditions, because of the short history of Protestantism in Korea and the heavily evangelical orientation of second-generation Korean Protestant churches. A few second-generation Korean mainline congregations have absorbed many Korean cultural traditions in their services and other sociocultural activities. But a majority of second-generation Korean congregations are evangelical. Because of their strong evangelical Christian identity, both young-generation Korean pastors and lay members minimize Korean cultural components in their worship services and other sociocultural activities. By contrast, younger-generation Indian Hindus' adoption of Hinduism in any form has enhanced their ethnic traditions and identity mainly because the religion itself represents Indian cultural and philosophical traditions.

When I started working on this book about eight years ago, some of my colleagues wondered why I wanted to compare two very different religious groups. I hope most of the readers of this book now understand why comparing the Korean evangelical Protestant and Indian Hindu immigrants' intergenerational transmission of ethnicity through religion is theoretically significant. The major findings of this study have important theoretical implications for understanding the relationship between religion and ethnicity. They show the limitations of the traditional theory that emphasizes participation in the congregation as the major contributing factor to ethnic preservation. They show the significance of domestic religious rituals and the strong association between religion and ethnic culture for the preservation of ethnicity, which previous studies have neglected. As many researchers documented (Dolan 1985; Herberg 1960; Ostergren 1981), no one can deny that congregational activities indeed helped the earlier white immigrant/ethnic groups preserve their ethnic traditions. Yet, even many earlier non-Protestant immigrant/ethnic groups were able to preserve their ethnic traditions over generations because their religious rituals practiced in the congregation were strongly tied to their cultural traditions. Not only ethno-religious groups, such as the Jews and the Amish, but also several Catholic and Eastern Orthodox groups (Irish, Italian, Polish, Greek, and Hungarian) came from countries where Catholicism or Eastern Orthodoxy was the dominant religion. Their religious rituals, including the celebration of religious holidays, foods, weddings and other life-cycle events, were inseparable from their ethnic traditions (Greeley 1971, 1972; Waters 1990).

Because their religious rituals were more often practiced in family and community settings than in congregations, the exclusive focus of the earlier studies on congregations failed to capture the effects of religious rituals, practiced outside congregations, on ethnic retention. The methodological advantage of this book is that it combines a congregational study with survey research and personal interviews with Indian Hindu and Korean Protestant immigrants and the second generations. This book systematically examined the effects of both participation in congregations and domestic religious practices on the preservation of ethnicity for both groups over generations. A congregational study that did not combine personal interviews conducted outside congregations would have concluded that Korean Protestant immigrants have advantages over Indian Hindu immigrants in preserving ethnicity through religion. A comparative study of Korean Protestant and Indian Hindu immigrants that used the two different data sources but did not include the second generation would have concluded that Korean Protestant and Indian Hindu immigrants were equally successful in preserving ethnicity through religion, albeit in radically different ways.

This book also contributes to Asian American studies by examining religious practices of two major Asian groups. The religious practices of Korean Protestants and Indian Hindus have received a great deal of scholarly attention. But there has been no systematic study of younger-generation Indian Hindus' religious practices. This book provides detailed information about younger-generation Indian Hindus' retention of religion and ethnicity through religion and their adoption of different elements of Hinduism. More research has been conducted on younger-generation Korean Protestants than on any other younger-generation religious group in the United States, but nearly all these studies are congregational studies. As such, they do not show younger-generation Korean Protestants' retention of childhood religion, the prevalence of Korean English-language evangelical congregations, the incorporation of Korean culture in Korean English-language evangelical congregations, and the position of younger-generation clergy on women's ordination as elders and pastors. To answer these questions, I have used two types of survey data in this book. Since second-generation Korean Protestants have emerged probably as the largest second-generation Christian evangelical group, I have also tried to systematically explain their heavily evangelical orientation itself using multiple data sources. I believe the major findings about these issues are useful not only to social science researchers, but also to Korean immigrant and second-generation pastors and theologians. Many Korean immigrant pastors want to see second-generation Korean evangelical churches infuse Korean cultural traditions in services and other congregational activities. But reading this book will help them understand that a strong evangelical church and a strong ethnic church do not go together.

This book contributes not only to the social science studies, but also religious and theological studies, of post-1965 immigrants' and their children's religious practices in that it paid special attention to the importance of theology for the intergenerational transmission of religion and ethnicity through religion. The social science literature has emphasized the extent to which other non-Christian religious institutions have adopted the Christian style Sunday school as a primary mechanism of religious education for transmitting their religion to the second generations (Ebaugh and Chafetz 2000, 432). But the extent to which immigrant parents transmit their religion to their children also depends upon the theological position of each religion. Evangelical Christians who accept a set of religious dogmas as absolute truths put priority on transmitting their religion to their children in child socialization. But Buddhists and Hindus, who tolerate other religions and values, are more open to their children's own choice of religion. This book shows that Indian Hindu immigrants are less successful in transmitting their religion to their children than Korean Protestant immigrants partly because theologically they consider proselytizing other people, including their children, as inherently dangerous. Although I did not realize it before starting this book project, the Korean version of evangelical Protestantism and Indian Hinduism also represent the two extremes in the degree of "dogmatic authority," as we have discussed.

Finally, the finding about the salience of religious identity among younger-generation Korean Protestants and other religious groups (Indian and other South Asian Muslims to be discussed in the next section) contributes to studies of ethnic identity among younger-generation Asian Americans. Given that about 25 percent of second-generation Koreans are evangelical Christians and that they have strong religious identity with a weak ethnic identity, no researcher can examine second-generation Koreans' ethnic and racial identities adequately without examining the role of their religious identity. But previous studies have analyzed patterns of their ethnic and racial identities with no attention to the role of religious identity (Kibria 2002; S. Lee 2006). Studies of 1.5- and second-generation Indians and other South Asians' identity and youth culture (Joshi 2006; Maira 2002; Purkayastha 2005) have paid some attention to the role of religion, as almost all of South Asians are affiliated with a religion. But none of the studies has pointed out that religious identity will enhance younger-generation Indian Hindus' ethnic identity whereas it may weaken Indian Christians' and South Asian Muslims' ethnic identity.

## Speculations about Other Religious-Immigrant Groups Using the Same Theoretical Frameworks

Based on our findings about Korean Protestants and Indian Hindus, we can speculate about how well the other major religious-immigrant groups between these two extremes are likely to preserve religion and ethnicity through religion in their own and subsequent generations.

Table 10.1 compares the association between religion and ethnicity of seven contemporary religious immigrant groups in their participation in religious institutions, dogmatic authority, and intergenerational transmission of religion and ethnicity. In regard to the association between religion and ethnicity, owing to the long history of their religion in their country, Thai Buddhists, Pakistani Muslims, and Mexican Catholics have similarly close associations, and more than 80 percent of their populations subscribe to their home country religion.[1] Thai Buddhist immigrants have a slightly closer association than either Pakistani Muslims or Mexican Catholics do, partly because Buddhism has a more nationalistic religious hierarchy and theology than does Islam in Pakistan or Catholicism in Mexico. Thus I assign a "high" value to Thai Buddhists and a "medium" value to Pakistani Muslims and Mexican Catholics, and a "very high" value to Indian Hindus.

The history of Syrian Christianity in India goes back to the first century (George 1998), and thus its rituals have incorporated many Indian cultural components. But since members of this religious group comprise only a tiny minority in India, they have maintained a strong Christian subethnic identity and are regarded as a separate social group in India (Kurien 2004). Accordingly, their Christian minority status in India does not enhance their Indian ethnic identity,

TABLE 10.1

A Comparison of Seven Religious Immigrant Groups in
the Three Independent and Two Dependent Variables

| | Indian Hindus | Thai Buddhists | Pakistani Muslims | Mexican Catholics | Indian Syrian Christian | KMP[a] | KEP[b] |
|---|---|---|---|---|---|---|---|
| Religion-ethnicity association | Very high | High | Medium | Medium | Low | Low | Very low |
| Participation in religious institutions[c] | Low | Low | Medium | Medium | High | High | Very high |
| "Dogmatic authority" | Low | Low | High | Medium | High | High | Very high |
| Intergenerational transmission of religion | Medium | Low | High | Medium | High | High | Very high |
| Intergenerational transmission of ethnicity through religion | High | Medium | Low-medium | Medium | Low-medium | Low-medium | Low |

Notes: [a]Korean mainline Protestants.
[b]Korean Evangelical Protestants.
[c]Scores for level of participation in religious institutions are largely based on the 2003 New Immigrant Survey conducted by Gillemina Jasso, Douglass Massey, Mark Rosenzweig, and James Smith.

so we assign a "low" value to this group in the religion-ethnicity association variable. Because Protestantism has a short history in Korea, it has not incorporated Korean folk culture, and Protestants comprise only a small proportion of the Korean population. Therefore, for Korean Protestant immigrants, the association between religion and ethnicity is low or very low. But Korean mainline Protestant immigrant churches put more emphasis on Korean cultural and nationalistic components than Korean evangelical churches do. So Korean mainline immigrant churches are rated "low," but Korean evangelical churches are rated "very low."

Not only Indian Hindus but also the other three non-Protestant religious groups with a high or medium association between religion and ethnicity use family and individual rituals more extensively in their religious practices than in their participation in religious institutions (Gasi 2000; Sullivan 2000). Family religious practices included preparing ethnic foods and celebrating religious-ethnic holidays and life-cycle events, which are important ways of reinforcing ethnicity (Ebaugh and Chafetz 2000, 391–92). Non-Protestant religious groups practice more family rituals than do Protestant groups because their religious practices have incorporated to a much greater extent their national or regional cultures in the form of food, life-cycle rituals, and religious holidays. By contrast, Protestants are highly scripture oriented and thus practice family and life-cycle rituals less often than do the other religious groups.

The next row in table 10.1 shows the level of participation in religious institutions. Korean evangelical Protestant immigrants participate in religious institutions most frequently, followed by Korean mainline Protestants and Indian Syrian Christians (Kurien 2004, 168).[2] The other four groups, including Mexican Catholics (Sullivan 2000), with a high association between religion and ethnicity, have a low or medium level of participation in religious institutions. Because these religious immigrant groups practice their religion largely through family and individual rituals, they participate in religious institutions less frequently than Protestant groups do. Our observation of these seven cases suggests a high negative correlation between the religion-ethnicity association and participation in religious institutions.

Because of the fairly high negative correlation between the two religious mechanisms of ethnicity, the seven religious-immigrant groups are able to maintain their ethnicity through religion almost equally well, especially the preservation of ethnicity in the immigrant generation. Studies of Indian Syrian Christian churches show that their members retain their Keralan Christian and subcultural traditions through their regular participation in congregations (George 1998; Kurien 2004). Thai Buddhists, Pakistani Muslims, and Mexican Catholics, as well as Indian Hindus, benefit much less from participating in religious institutions than Protestant groups do simply because most participate irregularly and less congregationally. Moreover, Pakistani Muslims and Mexican Catholics have a disadvantage in ethnic preservation compared with Indian Hindus and Thai Buddhists in that they often participate in multiethnic or multiracial religious institutions.

In regard to the intergenerational transmission of ethnicity through religion, the association between religion and ethnicity is more effective than congregational participation, especially for Indian Syrian Christians and Korean mainline and evangelical Protestants. Korean mainline immigrant churches are slightly more ethnic than Korean evangelical immigrant churches. However, many Korean English-language congregations are evangelical congregations, although their mother churches belong to a mainline denomination. This suggests that regardless of the denomination of their childhood Korean church, many younger-generation Korean Protestants become evangelical Christians through their involvement in campus ministry at college. Interestingly, Kurien (2004, 178) indicates that children of Indian Syrian Christian immigrants also emphasize being born-again Christians and evangelists and criticize their parents for having no born-again experience and avoiding evangelism.[3]

When we consider the level of "dogmatic authority" in table 10.1, we can better understand younger-generation Asian evangelical Protestants' separation of religion and ethnicity. Korean evangelical Christian immigrants generally accept the Bible as absolutely true and thus have the strongest commitment to their religious dogma. Many evangelical Christian and Pentecostal immigrants from other Asian and Latin American countries (Balmer 2003; Chen 2008; Cook 2000) belong to the same category of very high dogmatic authority. Korean mainline Protestant and Indian Syrian Christian immigrants follow Korean evangelical Protestant immigrants in the rating of "high" for dogmatic authority. Of the remaining four non-Protestant religious groups, the level of dogmatic authority for Pakistani Muslims is as high as that of the two Asian Christian groups.

Mexican Catholics stand between the three Asian Christian groups (with a very high or high level of dogmatic authority) and Asian Hindus/Buddhists (with a low level of dogmatic authority), so they are rated "medium" in dogmatic authority. Donald Smith (1970, 75) regarded Indian Hindus as having a lower level of dogmatic authority than Asian Buddhists. My review of the literature on Asian Buddhist immigrants (Kniss and Numrich 2007, 135; Suh 2004; Yang 2000b), however, suggests that their low level of dogmatic authority is similar to that of Indian Hindus. For example, according to Yang's interviews (2000b, 86), many Chinese Buddhist immigrant parents "would not object to their children becoming Christian or having no religion at all, although they hope that they will become committed Buddhists." Accordingly, both Thai Buddhists and Indian Hindus are rated "low" in dogmatic authority.

The fourth row in table 10.1 compares the seven religious immigrant groups' intergenerational transmission of religion. The three Asian Christian immigrant groups and Pakistani Muslim immigrants should be highly successful in transmitting their religion to their children because they are very highly or highly committed to their religious dogma. Pakistani and other Muslim immigrants are at a disadvantage compared with the Asian Christian groups in intergenerationally transmitting their religion because of their less congregationally oriented religious practices in a predominantly Christian society. But the strong commitment of most Muslim immigrant groups to their Islamic religious values[4] is likely to enable them to transmit their religion to their children as successfully as Asian mainline Christian immigrants do. For example, in her ethnographic study of Muslim college students, Peek (2005, 222–23) found that almost all the Muslim students observed Islamic religious rituals and more than

90 percent of the women wore *hijab*. She also discovered that almost all had Muslim given names and surnames and abstained from religiously prohibited activities.

Although Indian Hindu immigrants have a low level of dogmatic authority equal to that of Thai Buddhist immigrants, they are more successful in transmitting their religion to their children than Thais are because of the close association between their religion and ethnic traditions. The groups with indigenous religions, such as Indian Hindus and American Jews, have an advantage in maintaining their religious traditions over generations because their members are highly motivated to teach their children religious rituals as a means of preserving their ethnic heritage. But Thai and other Asian Buddhist immigrant groups have great difficulty transmitting their religion to their children (Cadge 2005; Suh 2004; Yang 2000a, 86) partly because they have a low level of dogmatic authority and partly because, unlike Indian Hindus, their religion is not indigenous to their home country. Thailand and other Asian countries have developed their own versions of Buddhism, but it is not their indigenous religion, as Hinduism is for Indians. Although this puts Asian Buddhist immigrants at a disadvantage for transmitting the religion to their children, the same factor helps them propagate it to other Americans. Buddhism is very popular, more popular than Hinduism, with white Americans. The opposite is true for Indian Hindus. Although the very strong association between their religion and ethnicity enables them to maintain their ethnic traditions, Hinduism, like Judaism, discourages other Americans from practicing it because of its close association with its country of origin.

The last row in table 10.1 shows the levels of the seven religious immigrant groups' intergenerational transmission of ethnicity through religion, the central focus of this book. Indian Hindu immigrants transmit their ethnicity through religion most successfully because of the extremely high association between the two. Because of their high level of dogmatic authority, Pakistani Muslims and Korean evangelical Protestants are far more successful in transmitting their religion to their children than the other religious groups are. But because of their emphasis on universalistic religious values and strong religious identity associated with high dogmatic authority, their 1.5- and second-generation children have difficulty maintaining their ethnic culture and identity. Research reveals that American-born second-generation Muslims, like second-generation Korean Protestants, have a stronger religious identity than ethnic identity and are likely to accept interethnic and interracial marriages more easily (Bagby 2006; Ebaugh and Chafetz 2000, 403–4; Kniss and Numrich 2007, 132–33; Leonard 2003; Peek 2005). Muslim immigrants and their children have a strong religious identity because Islam emphasizes core religious values. Their strong religious identity in the United States and Europe has also been enhanced by the hostile anti-Islamic environment (Haddad 1998). Only black immigrant Muslims, like African American Muslims, are less likely to accept their religion as their primary identity, because blacks in the United States are still defined in terms of the master status of their race (Merton 1967; Waters 1999, 5). Korean Protestant immigrants have greater difficulty transmitting ethnicity through religion than Pakistani Muslim immigrants do because of the lower association between their religion and ethnicity. The other two Asian Christian groups have a slight advantage in the intergenerational transmission of ethnicity through religion over Korean evangelical Protestant immigrants because fewer of their children become evangelical Christians.

Indian Syrian Christian and Korean mainline Protestant immigrant churches put more emphasis on ethnic culture than do Korean evangelical Protestant churches. But their children preserve their ethnicity less well through religion than Thai Buddhists or Mexican Catholics do, because they are more likely to be born-again evangelical Christians through their exposure to their college's campus evangelical ministry. Thus not only the association between religion and ethnicity but also the influence of the evangelical campus ministry are important to the level of ethnic retention through religion. Although both Thai Buddhists and Mexican Catholic immigrants have a majority religious status in their home country, the origin of Buddhist and Catholic immigrants from multiple countries puts them at a level of intergenerational transmission of ethnicity lower than that of Indian Hindus. Thai Buddhism and Mexican Catholicism are part of the ethnic culture. Second-generation Thai Buddhists and Mexican Catholics, however, cannot associate their practices with their ethnic heritage because both Buddhist and Catholic immigrants come from different countries.

# Appendix 1

Description of Data Collections

## Survey of Indian Hindu and Korean Protestant Immigrants' Participation in Religious Institutions

A telephone survey of Indian and Korean immigrants in New York City provided data on their self-reported premigrant and current religions and frequency of participation in a religious institution. The survey was conducted as part of a larger study comparing Indian, Chinese, and Korean immigrants in New York City in ethnic attachment and solidarity. For survey research on the three major Asian groups, I used the surname-sampling technique, a technique often used for research on ethnic and new immigrant groups (Bozorgmehr 1997; Min 1997; Shin and Yu 1984).

Using seventeen prominent Indian surnames,[1] we randomly selected eight hundred Indian households from the five boroughs' 2004 telephone directories. Through the initial screening, Caribbean Indian immigrants were eliminated from the telephone interview because they usually do not identify as Indians. For a survey of Korean immigrants I used the Kim sample technique, which I had used in my previous survey studies (Min 1996, 1997). The Kim sample technique is useful for sampling Korean immigrant households because (1) Kims comprise as much as 22 percent of the population of South Korea; (2) Kims represent the Korean population socioeconomically; and (3) Kim is a uniquely Korean name (Shin and Yu 1984). U.S.-born Indian and Korean Americans and 1.5-generation Koreans who immigrated before or at the age of 12 were not interviewed.

The telephone interview was conducted at Queens College on eight Sundays between March and May 2005. The questionnaire contained thirty-two to fifty-four items, depending on the respondents' category of work. Three questions were about religion: (1) the respondents' premigrant religious background, (2) their religion at the time of the interview, and (3) the frequency of their participation in a religious institution. The examination of Korean and Indian immigrants' frequency of participation in a religious institution, as well as their premigrant and current religious backgrounds, is based on the responses to these three questions.

We interviewed 277 Korean and 213 Indian immigrants in the spring of 2005. Indian Muslim immigrants, all with Muslim names, were not included in the

Indian sample based on the prominent Indian surnames. We interviewed separately forty-two Indian Muslim immigrants found through personal channels. The Indian respondents did not include any Christian, since Indian Christians also have Christian names, which I did not consider at the time of sampling. Thirty-two Indian Christians we interviewed were contacted mainly through several Indian Christian churches. These additional interviews increased the sample size of Indian respondents to 287.

### Ethnographic Research on a Selected Korean Church and a Hindu Temple

I conducted ethnographic research on a Korean Protestant church in Queens for four months in 2003 and a Hindu temple in Queens between February 2001 and December 2003. There are approximately 550 Korean churches in the New York / New Jersey metropolitan area with about 200,000 Koreans as of 2005. Most Korean churches are small, with fewer than 200 members. The Shin Kwang Church of New York is a medium-size church located in Bayside, with about 550 participants at the Sunday worship services. I chose this church for my study because it is located very close to my home and because I personally knew the senior pastor well. Like most other Korean Presbyterian churches in New York, this church is theologically conservative, with emphasis on church participation and missionary activities. It was established in 1985 during the peak of Korean immigration. I selected a Presbyterian church because Presbyterian churches account for about half of all Korean immigrant churches in the United States (P. Min 1992, 2008).

There are approximately thirty-five Indian Hindu temples in the New York / New Jersey metropolitan area with about 480,000 people of Asian Indian ancestry in 2005.[2] The Hindu Temple Society of North America (Sri Maha Vallabha Ganapati Devasthanam), located in the southern part of Flushing, a heavily Indian residential center, was selected for this study. It is one of nine large temples in the United States affiliated with the Council of Hindu Temples of North America. This temple, commonly called the Ganesh Temple, is the oldest Hindu temple in New York City, established in 1977, and the second largest temple in the area. Hindu temples do not have members, but according to a temple staff member, it had about 25,000 devotees on three weekend days in 2001.

My ethnographic research covered (1) participant observations of services and other sociocultural activities in the two selected religious institutions, (2) personal interviews with religious leaders and lay participants, and (3) a review of documents and weekly and monthly newsletters. In the first four months of 2003, I observed the Sunday worship services, Wednesday services, the Sunday lunch service and fellowship in the dining room, the Korean-language class, and other sociocultural activities in the Shin Kwang Church of New York. I also interviewed the senior pastor, two associate pastors, two elders, the principal and teachers of the Korean-language school, and several lay members. I reviewed the church's annual directory, newsletters, and other documents. When I had questions about the church's worship services and other sociocultural activities while writing the book manuscript, I called the senior pastor and associate pastors for more information. I also visited the church several times in the next few years to update my information.

Between the summer of 2001 and the fall of 2003, I also made participant observations of devotions and sociocultural activities in the selected temple. I observed worshippers in the main worship room where about twenty images of gods and goddesses are housed. I usually went on the weekend when thousands of Hindus attended. I also observed a few *puja* ceremonies prepared for life-cycle events for particular families, a Hindu wedding ceremony conducted at the wedding hall, a few meetings at the senior citizens center, annual parades during the Sri Ganesh Chaturthi festival, meals at the canteen, dance performances, lectures, music discourses, youth group meetings, and Indian dance/music, language, and various other Saturday classes for Indian children and adolescents.

I also interviewed the president and the public relations officer several times, usually on weekdays when the temple was not busy, as well as two vice presidents and three other staff members of the temple, a priest, the coordinator of the youth program, and about twenty lay participants. I reviewed the temple's monthly newsletter (*Ganesanjali*), many fliers, and other published materials. I put my name on the temple's mailing list in 2002 and have often participated in its activities, both for my research and because of my personal interest in its rituals and various cultural activities. From January through March 2006, I interviewed two staff members and several participants to update my information.

Most of the other ethnographic studies of immigrant religious institutions, including those in *Gatherings in Diaspora* (Warner and Wittner 1998) and *Religion and the New Immigrants* (Ebaugh and Chafetz 2000), involved more intensive participant observations for longer periods of time than my ethnographic research. I could not devote a great deal of time and energy to gathering the ethnographic component of data sources, partly because, unlike other ethnographic studies, I used many other data sources for this book. In fact, I used ethnographic research on the selected Korean church and the Hindu temple for only chapters 4 and 5. But I also thought I did not need to spend a lot of time on ethnographic research on the Korean church because, first, many other studies had already examined the cultural, social, economic, and/or social status functions of Korean immigrant churches (Dearman 1982; Hurh and Kim 1990; I. Kim 1981; Kim and Kim 2001; Kwon 2003; Kwon, Ebaugh, and Hagan 1997; Min 1992; K. Park 1997). Second, I am familiar with the sociocultural functions of Korean immigrant churches in New York because I conducted two survey studies of Korean immigrant churches, in 1988/1989 (Min 1992) and in 1997 (Queens Historical Society 1998), to examine their sociocultural functions. Third, I am familiar with worship and other sociocultural activities in Korean immigrant churches because I myself attended a Korean church for several years in Atlanta and in New York City. I also taught an Asian American course for the Korean doctor of ministry class at New York Theological Seminary between 1988 and 1992. Most of the students in the class were pastors of Korean immigrant churches in the New York / New Jersey area.

### Interviews with Korean Protestant and Indian Hindu Immigrants

Interviews with fifty-six Korean Protestant immigrants and fifty-nine Indian Hindu immigrants in the New York / New Jersey metropolitan area were conducted between December 2000 and November 2001 (see appendix 2). I interviewed fifteen Korean Protestants and twenty Indian Hindus, and three Korean and two Indian students, all bilingual, conducted the other eighty interviews. The interviewees were selected to maintain a balance in socioeconomic status and sex. As a result, Korean interviewees were equal numbers of men and women, and Indian interviewees consisted of thirty-two men and twenty-seven women. Seventy-one percent of Indian and 66 percent of Korean interviewees had completed four years of college.

To examine how they taught their children religious and cultural values at home, I interviewed Korean Protestants and Indian Hindus with one or more children. The vast majority of Indian ($n = 55/59$) and Korean ($n = 52/56$) interviewees were married, and almost all had one or more school-age children. To make the results of the personal interview more generalizable to the Indian Hindu and Korean Protestant immigrants in New York City, the interviewees were located outside the two selected religious institutions. But several Indian Hindu informants attended the selected Hindu temple because there were only twenty-five Hindu temples in the New York / New Jersey area in the early 2001. The Korean Protestant respondents were selected in such a way that no more than three respondents attended the same Korean church.

The questionnaire included eighty, mostly open-ended, items. The interview items were related to the interviewees' background and their participation in the congregation and its cultural and fellowship activities, observance of religious faith and rituals at home, teaching of religious and cultural values to children, and relative importance of religion versus ethnic background for their identity. The Indian Hindus were interviewed in English, and the Korean Protestants were interviewed in Korean. To examine family practices of religious rituals and religious decorations, I tried to interview as many informants at home as possible. Most of the others were interviewed in a place of worship, a store, or an office. Completing one tape-recorded personal interview took approximately thirty to ninety minutes.

## Younger-Generation Koreans' Religious Affiliations and Frequency of Participation in Congregation

A closed-ended telephone survey of 202, 23 to 35-year-old 1.5- and second-generation Korean Americans in the New York / New Jersey metropolitan area, conducted by Dae Young Kim in 1997, provided information about their religious affiliation and participation in religious institutions.[3] This survey used random sampling of twenty prominent Korean surnames included in the 1997 telephone directories in the New York / New Jersey metropolitan boroughs and counties.[4]

Although a majority (166, or 82%) of 1.5 or second-generation Korean American respondents were directly located from screened households, close to a fifth (36, or 18%, were eligible second generation living away) were found through parents in screened households who willingly gave out their children's contact numbers. The questionnaire contained 108 items about 1.5- and second-generation Korean Americans' socioeconomic adjustment and four questions about their religious experiences. Although the sample is small, it is the only survey data on 1.5- and second-generation Korean adults based on random sampling.

## Telephone Survey of Korean English-Language Congregations

When I was doing research on second-generation Korean Protestants in 2003, studies focusing on second-generation Korean congregations (Alumkal 1999, 2001, 2003; Chai 1998, 2001a; Chong 1998; S. Park 2001) revealed that second-generation Korean Protestant congregations, mostly evangelical, eliminated many Korean cultural components from services and other sociocultural activities. I decided to conduct a survey of younger-generation Korean congregations to see whether these findings could be generalized to other English-language Korean congregations.

Large Korean immigrant churches have recently established English-language congregations for second-generation Korean adults. In March 2003, Young Oak Kim called all the Korean immigrant churches (about 550) in the New York / New Jersey area to see whether they had English-language congregations for adults. This initial screening found thirty-eight English-language congregations in Korean immigrant churches. In addition, I found five physically separate Korean English-language churches. Between March and June 2003, I conducted a telephone survey of second-generation Korean congregations, talking with the pastors of thirty-five second-generation congregations, thirty-three congregations established in Korean immigrant churches, and two independent congregations (see appendix 2).

The questionnaire had fifty-five items, most of which were open-ended. The items asked about the general characteristics of each congregation, fellowship and ethnic friendship networks, Korean cultural elements, and ethnic identity. All but four of the congregations had non-Korean members, between 2 percent and 19 percent. The majority of non-Korean members were Chinese, with others being Asian Indians, Filipinos, Vietnamese, whites, Latinos, and blacks. Emerson and Kim defined (2003) a multiracial congregation "as one in which less than eighty percent of the members share the same racial background." According to this definition, none of the surveyed Korean English-language congregations in New York in my study could be considered multiracial. Rather, it means that all the surveyed congregations could be considered Korean ethnic congregations.

## Interviews with Younger-Generation Korean Protestants and Indian Hindus

Interviews with 1.5- and second-generation Korean Protestant and Indian Hindus were my third data source. Fifty-five interviews with 1.5- and second-generation Indian Hindu adults (twenty-four years and older) and another sixty-six interviews with Korean Protestant counterparts were completed between September 2002 and November 2003 (see appendix 2). Three Korean American graduate students interviewed fifty-four second-generation Korean Protestants, and three second-generation Indian Hindu students (two graduate students and one undergraduate student) interviewed forty-two second-generation Hindus. I interviewed the remaining twelve Korean Protestants and thirteen Indian Hindus. I selected one very religious, another moderately religious, and a third not-so-religious interviewer for each group so that they could select informants with different levels of religious faith. Most of the interviews were taped at the interviewees' workplaces or religious institutions, and the remaining interviews were conducted at the interviewees' homes. Each interview took twenty-five to ninety minutes.

Men made up 48 percent of Korean Protestant informants and 53 percent of Hindu informants. Korean informants were aged 24 to 33, and Indian Hindu informants were aged 23 to 39, and one was 55. All but five of Korean informants had completed college, and 35 percent were completing or had completed graduate school. Two of Indian Hindu informants were in college at the time of the interview, and all the others had completed college. Forty percent of Indian Hindu informants were completing or had completed graduate school, and several were in medical or dental school. Only 12 percent of the sixty-six Korean Christian informants ($n = 8$) were married, and 36 percent of the Indian Hindu informants ($n = 20$) were married. Thirty-eight percent of the Korean Christian informants did not live with their parents, compared with 63 percent of the Indian Hindu informants.

The questionnaires had eighty-five items, mostly open-ended. The items were related to their (1) personal background, (2) participation in religious institutions during childhood, (3) practice of religious rituals at home during childhood, (4) participation in religious institutions at the time of the interview, (5) practice of religious rituals at home at the time of the interview, (6) affiliation with and participation in ethnic and panethnic organizations, and (7) identity and social relations.

# Appendix 2

## Questionnaires

1. **Background information**
   Sex:
   Age:
   Family members:
   Marital status:
   Number of school-age children:
   Length of residence (years) in the U.S.:
   Education:
   Occupation:

2. **Premigrant religious background:**
   What was your religion in Korea?
   If you were a Christian, how often did you attend church in Korea?
   When did you start attending a Korean immigrant church?
   Why or how did you decide to attend a Korean church?
   Did you attend another Korean church before the current one? How
      many?
   Why did you switch churches?

3. **Affiliation with and participation in the current church**
   What is the name of your current church? What denomination?
   What is the membership of your church? How many members?
   How far is it from your house? (Miles)
   How long have you been affiliated with the current church? (Years)
   How often do you go to church? (Three times a week, twice a week, once a
      week, every other week, etc.)
   Do all of your family members go to the same church on Sunday?
   What religious position do you hold in the church? (Elder, exhorter, dea-
      con, or other position)

What other nonreligious positions do you hold, and what role do you play
in your church? (Principal of Korean-language school, treasurer, organist, children's group teacher, head of your district, etc.)

Approximately how much money did you donate to your church in 2000
or 2001?

What are the reasons you attend a Korean church regularly? (To meet
Korean friends, to belong to a Korean group, for children's ethnic education, for religious purposes, for peace of mind, for information, for
my elderly parents, etc.)

If service is the only reason, why don't you attend an American church?

4. **Church-related social and cultural activities and functions**

What time do you usually go to church, and what time do you return
home on Sunday?

How long does the Sunday service last?

How long do you stay in church for fellowship after the service on Sunday?

What do you usually do during the fellowship hour? (Talk with friends,
eat snacks or lunch)

What else do you do in church on Sunday? Do you sometimes go to a restaurant with your church friends and/or relatives for lunch or dinner
after the Sunday service?

How many hours do you spend on church affairs each week?

How many church picnics and retreats did you go to last year?

How often do you attend your church's district meeting? (Usually once
per month)

How many members usually go to the district meeting?

Is the district meeting held at a different district member's home each
time?

Does the host family serve dinner at the district meeting?

How long does the district meeting last?

What do you do at the district meeting?

How many of your relatives attend your church regularly?

How are they related to you?

How many of your five best friends belong to your church?

Do your church members play *yoot* at a member's home on lunar New
Year's Eve?

What kinds of cultural activities does your church offer each year?

Do you think attending a Korean church is helpful to maintaining Korean
culture? In what ways?

If the informant has one or more children who attend school now or attended school in the past:

Do you think attending a Korean church is helpful to teaching your children Korean cultural traditions? In what ways?

Do (did) your children attend a Korean-language program at your church?

5. **Affiliations with and participation in other Korean ethnic organizations**

What other ethnic organizations are you affiliated with?

What activities do they offer?

How often do you go to the organizations' meetings?

6. **Observance of religious faith and rituals at home**

How often do you read the Bible each week at home?

How often do you pray, and at what time?

How often do you sing and/or listen to hymns?

How many hours do you spend each week at home reading the Bible, praying, singing hymns, and/or holding religious services?

What do you do at home to celebrate Korean traditional holidays (lunar New Year and Chuseok)?

How do you celebrate Easter and Christmas at home?

What decorations do you put up at your home to signify your Christian identity?

7. **Teaching Christian religious and Korean cultural values to children**

How important is it to you that your children remain Christian?

How do you teach your children Christian values and rituals at home?

How important is it to you that your children retain Korean cultural traditions?

How do you teach your children Korean cultural values and customs at home?

Which is more important for your child, being a good student or being a good Christian?

Who would be a better marital partner for your child, a non-Christian Korean or a non-Korean Christian?

8. **Identity and Christian attitudes**

Which is more important to your personal identity, your Christian religion or your Korean ethnic background? Why?

Do you think being a good Christian means being a good Korean?

How many close non-Christian Korean friends do you have?

How many close non-Korean Christian friends do you have?

How many non-Korean friends do you have?

1. **Background information:**

   Sex:

   Age:

   Marital status:

   Family members:

   Number of children:

   Number of school-age children:

   Number of children who completed school:

   Length of residence in the U.S.:

   Education:

   Occupation:

   Birthplace in India:

   Regional language:

2. **Affiliation with and participation in a Hindu temple**

   Were you a Hindu in India?

   If so, how often did you attend temple and other Hindu organizations?
   What were the Hindu organizations' activities?

   Do you go to a Hindu temple [name] in New York?

   Do you always go to the same temple or two or more different temples?

   What are the names of these temples?

   What regional languages does the temple use?

   How often do you go to temple? About once a week, every other week,
   once a month, or a few times a year?

   On what occasions do you go? On what holidays?

   Do you go with your family members, including your children?

   How far (miles) is the temple from your home?

   How long (years) have you been affiliated with the temple?

   What position do you hold, and what role do you play in the temple?

   Approximately how much money have you donated to the temple in the
   past year?

   What are the main reasons you go to temple regularly or irregularly? (For
   worship services, for religious purposes, for peace of mind, to meet
   Indian friends, to belong to an Indian group, for information, for children's ethnic education, for my elderly parents, etc.)

3. **Temple-related social and cultural activities and functions**

On what days of the week do you usually go to temple?

How long do you stay for fellowship after the service?

What do you usually do during the fellowship hour? (Talk with friends and/or eat snacks or lunch)

How many hours each week do you spend on temple affairs?

How many picnics and retreats does your temple organize for its members per year?

How many of your relatives attend the same temple regularly?

How are they related to you?

How many of your five best friends are Indians who attend the same temple?

What kinds of cultural activities does your temple offer each year?

Do you think attending an Indian Hindu temple is helpful to maintaining your Indian cultural traditions? In what ways?

---

If the informant has one or more children who attend school now or attended in the past:

Do you think attending an Indian Hindu temple is helpful to teaching your children Indian cultural traditions? In what ways?

Do (did) your children attend a language program offered by a temple?

How many times a year do you perform a Hindu ritual for your family members at the temple?

4. **Affiliation with and participation in local Hindu and Pan-Hindu organizations**

Do you belong to any local Hindu organizations (Satsang, Balavihar, etc.)?

How many members do they have?

When did you and other members start organizing it (them)?

How many people regularly go to the meetings?

How often do you go to the meetings?

What are the organization's major goals and activities?

Do you belong to any national or international Hindu organizations?

How many members do they have?

How often do you go to the meetings?

What are the major activities of the Pan-Hindu organizations?

Do you go to any other Hindu religious meetings and/or festivals? How often?

Do you belong to any nonreligious Indian regional or linguistic associations?

How many members do they have?

How often do you go to their meetings?

What are the associations' major goals and activities?

5. **Observance of religious faiths and rituals at home**

Do you have a family shrine at home?

How often do you pray at home, and at what time?

How many times do you fast each year?

How many Hindu holidays do you celebrate, and how do you celebrate them?

What nonreligious Indian holidays do you celebrate at home?

Are you a vegetarian?

What other Hindu rituals do you perform at home by yourself and/or with family members?

How often do you sing or listen to Hindu songs at home?

What decorations do you put up at home to signify your Hindu identity?

Have you ever visited India for religious purposes? (Pilgrimage)

6. **Teaching Hindu religious and Indian cultural values to children**

How important is it to you that your children remain Hindu? Why?

How do you teach your children Hindu values and rituals at home? How often?

Have you ever sent your children to India for religious education?

How important is it to you that your children retain Indian nonreligious cultural traditions?

How do you teach your children nonreligious cultural values and customs at home?

Do you encourage your children to have non-Indian, non-Hindu friends?

Which is more important for your child, being a good student or being a good Hindu?

Who would a better marital partner for your child, a non-Hindu Indian (e.g., Christian or Muslim) or a non-Indian Hindu (Bangladeshi or Guyanese Indian)?

7. **Identity and social relations**

Which is most important to your personal identity, your Hindu religion, Indian national background or gender? Why?

Do you think being a typical (authentic) Hindu means being a typical Indian?

How many close non-Hindu Indian friends do you have?

How many close non-Indian Hindu friends do you have?

How many close non-Indian friends do you have?

Background information about the congregation:
Participation in congregation and congregational
culture and sociocultural activities:

1. n what part of New York City is your church located?
   (1) Flushing　　(2) Bayside　　(3) Other parts of Queens
   (4) Manhattan　(5) Brooklyn　　(6) Bronx　　(7) Staten Island
   (8) Long Island　(9) New Jersey　(10) Upstate New York

2. When did your English-language congregation start? Year_____

3. What are ages of your members? Age range_____

4. How many members are affiliated with your congregation?

5. How many members are not Korean, and what are their racial backgrounds?

6. Is your congregation in a Korean immigrant church, or is it an independent church?
   (1) In a Korean immigrant church　　(2) An independent church

7. What is the denomination of your congregation?

8. Is it a mainline or evangelical congregation?

9. How many staff members work for your congregation, and what are their positions?

10. What time does the main service on Sunday start?

11. In addition to the main service, how many meetings does your church have each week for Bible study and other religious and sociocultural activities?

12. If your congregation is in a Korean immigrant church, how often do you have Sunday's main service with the immigrant congregation?

13. How often do your members sing hymns or praise songs in Korean?
    (1) About half the verses each Sunday　(2) Some verses each Sunday
    (3) One verse each Sunday　　　　　　(4) Never

14. Do you use gospel songs, instruments, and an overhead projector for the Sunday main service?

15. How often do you give a sermon in Korean?

16. How many Korean words or phrases do you use in your sermons?

17. How many times have you mentioned Korea in your sermons over the past year?

18. How many times have you mentioned the Korean American community in your sermons over the past year?

19. How often do you give a prayer in Korean?

20. Does your congregation provide lunch or snacks after Sunday main service?

    (1) No         (2) Yes, snack         (3) Yes, full lunch

21. How often do you serve Korean food at your church?

22. Do you have district meetings?

    (1) Yes              (2) No

23. If yes, how often?

24. How many times do your congregation members go on a retreat per year?

25. What other social activities over the past year has your congregation organized to increase its members' fellowship and social interactions?

26. Do you celebrate lunar New Year in your congregation? How do you celebrate it?

27. Do you celebrate Korean Thanksgiving day (Chooseok) in your congregation? How do you celebrate it?

28. Do you observe March First Independence Movement Day in your congregation? How do you observe it?

29. Do you observe August 15th Independence Day in your congregation? How do you observe it?

30. What other Korean cultural activities have you organized over the past year?

31. Approximately what proportion of leadership positions do women hold in your congregation?

32. How many elders are there in your congregation? How many of them are women?

**Respondent's personal background and theological philosophy:**

33. What is the title of your position at your congregation?

    (1) Head pastor     (2) Associate pastor     (3) Other: specify

34. What is your racial/ethnic background?

35. What is your educational background?

36. If you have an MDV or doctor of ministry degree, from what school did you get the degree?

37. What generation do you belong to?

    (1) First immigrant generation     (2) 1.5 generation

    (3) Second generation         (4) Multigeneration

38. How important is it to you for a second-generation Korean church to preserve Korean cultural traditions? Why?

39. Many second-generation Christians complain that Korean immigrant churches are too Korean, like Korean clubs. What do you think?

40. Do you think a second-generation Korean church should recruit Chinese and other members too?

41. Do you intend to keep your congregation a Korean ethnic congregation?

42. Do you think women should be able to serve as elders and pastors?

## D. QUESTIONNAIRE FOR INTERVIEWS WITH SECOND-GENERATION KOREAN PROTESTANTS

1. **Background information:**
   Sex:
   Age:
   Marital status:
   Type of residence:   (1) Live with parents   (2) Live independently
   Family members:
   Number of children:
   Birthplace:   (1) United States   (2) Korea
   Length of residence (years) in the U.S.:
   Education:
   Occupation:

2. **Affiliation with and participation in Korean church during childhood**
   Where did you grow up during your childhood and adolescence? (In New York City or other part of the U.S.)
   What were your parents' religions during your childhood?
   If they were Protestants, how often did they attend church during your childhood? (Once a week, once every two weeks, once a month, a few times a year)
   How often did you attend a Korean church with your parents during your childhood/or adolescence?
   If you did not attend church every week, when did you go? (On what holidays)
   Why do you think your parents took you to a Korean church during your childhood/adolescence?
   Do you think going to a Korean church during your childhood helped you retain Korean cultural traditions and identity? If so how?
   Did you attend a Korean-language or other Korean cultural program at a Korean church during your childhood/adolescence?
   Did you belong to a Korean or Christian club during high school and/or college?
   What other Korean or Pan-Asian clubs did you belong to in college?

3. **Performance of religious rituals at home during childhood/adolescence**

How often did (do) your parents read the Bible at home during your
   childhood?

How often did (do) your parents pray at home?

How many Korean traditional or Christian holidays did (do) your parents
   celebrate at home?

What other Christian rituals did (do) your parents perform at home?

4. **Current church attendance**

Are you currently affiliated with a Protestant church? Is it a Korean immigrant, second-generation Korean, Pan-Asian, or predominantly white
   American church?

How often do you go to church?

If you do not go to church every week, when (holidays) do you go?

Why did you choose to attend this type of Christian church? (Korean
   immigrant, second-generation Korean, Pan-Asian, or white American)

Do you hold a position in the church?

How long do you usually stay in church on each visit for religious services
   and sociocultural activities?

How many picnics and retreats does your church organize for its members
   per year?

How many of your relatives attend the same church regularly?

How are they related to you?

How many of your five best friends are Koreans who attend the same church?

What kinds of Korean cultural activities does your church offer each year?

If you attend a Korean church, does it celebrate any traditional Korean
   holidays such as lunar New Year's Day and Chuseok (Korean Thanksgiving Day)?

What are the reasons you go to a Korean church regularly

or occasionally? (For worship services, to meet Korean friends, to belong
   to a Korean group, for Korean cultural retention, for religious purposes, for peace of mind, for information, for my elderly parents, etc., in
   order of priority)

Do you think attending a Korean Christian church is helpful to maintaining Korean cultural traditions? In what ways?

How important is it to you that a second-generation Korean church maintains Korean cultural traditions through various programs?

---

If the informant has one or more children:

Do you usually take your child(ren) to church with you?

Do you plan to take your children to church when you go?

Do (did) your children attend a language class at church?

Do you think attending a Korean church is helpful to teaching your children Korean cultural traditions? In what ways?

5. **Religious practices at home**

How often do you read the Bible at home?

How often do you pray at home?

Do you often sing or listen to Christian music at home?

How many Christian holidays do you celebrate at home, and how do you celebrate them?

How many Korean traditional holidays do you celebrate at home?

What decorations do you put up at your home to signify your Christian religion?

What other Christian rituals do you perform at home?

What do you do at home to teach your children Christian faith and rituals?

Which is more important for your child, being a good student or being a good Christian?

6. **Affiliations with Christian and Non-Christian organizations other than church**

Do you belong to any Christian organizations?

How many members do they have?

How often do you go to the meetings?

What are the organizations' major activities and goals?

Do you belong to any Korean or Asian American organizations?

How many members do they have?

How often do you participate in the organizations?

What are their major activities?

7. **Identity and Christian values**

How important is Christianity to your personal identity? Is it more important than your Korean national background, your Asian American background, or your gender status? Why?

Do you think your practice of Christianity symbolizes your Korean identity?

How many of your five best friends are Korean Christians? What are the other best friends' ethnic or religious backgrounds?

Have you usually dated Korean Christians? If not, what are ethnic and religious backgrounds of your dating partners?

How important is it to you to marry a Korean Christian? Why?

Which is a more desirable marital partner for you, a non-Christian Korean or a non-Korean Christian? Why?

Do you think you have been discriminated against because of your Christian background? Give examples.

Do you think you have been discriminated against because of your Korean/Asian American background? Give examples.

## E. QUESTIONNAIRE FOR INTERVIEWS WITH SECOND-GENERATION INDIAN HINDUS

1. **Background information:**
   Sex:
   Age:
   Marital status:
   Family members:
   Number of children:
   Birthplace:          (1) United States          (2) India (Province)
   Regional language:
   Length of residence (years) in the U.S.:
   Education:
   Occupation:
   Type of residence:    (1) Live with parents    (2) Live independently

2. **Affiliation with and attendance at Hindu temple during childhood**
   Where did you grow up during your childhood and adolescence? (New York City or other part of the U.S.)

   What are your parents' religions?

   If they are Hindus, how often did they go to temple during your childhood? (Once a week, once every two weeks, once a month, a few times a year)

   How often did you attend a Hindu temple with your parents?

   On what occasions (holidays) did you go?

   Why do you think your parents took you to a temple during your childhood/adolescence?

   Do you think going to temple during your childhood helped you retain your Indian cultural traditions and identity? If so, how?

   Did you attend an Indian-language class or other Indian cultural program at the temple during your childhood/adolescence?

   Did you belong to any Hindu club during high school and/or college?

3. **Performance of Hindu rituals at home during childhood/adolescence**
   Did your parents have a family shrine at home during your childhood/
       adolescence?
   How often did they pray at home?
   How many Hindu holidays did they celebrate at home?
   What other Hindu rituals did your parents perform at home?
   How many times did your parents invite a Hindu priest to perform rituals
       for you and your brothers/sisters during your childhood/adolescence?
   Were your parents vegetarians?
   How often did your parents cook traditional Hindu food for Hindu holi-
       days?

4. **Current temple attendance**
   How often do you go to temple?
   What temple(s) do you usually attend?
   On what occasions (holidays) do you go to temple?
   What days of the week do you usually go to temple?
   What position do you hold, and what role do you play in the temple?
   Approximately how much money did you donate to temples in 2000 or
       2001?
   How long do you usually stay at the temple on each visit for religious
       services and sociocultural activities?
   How many picnics and retreats does your temple organize for its devotees
       each year?
   How many of your relatives attend the same temple regularly?
   How are they related to you?
   How many of your five best friends are Indians who attend the same
       temple?
   What kinds of cultural activities does your temple offer each year?
   What are the reasons you go to temple regularly or occasionally? (For
       worship services, to meet Indian friends, to belong to a Indian group,
       for Indian cultural retention, for religious purposes, for peace of mind,
       for information, for my elderly parents, etc.)
   Do you think attending an Indian Hindu temple is helpful to maintaining
       Indian cultural traditions? In what ways?

---

   If the informant has children:
   Do you usually take your child(ren) with you to temple?
   Do you plan to take your children with you to temple?

Do (did) your children attend a language class at the temple?

Do you think attending an Indian Hindu temple is helpful to teaching your children Indian cultural traditions? In what ways?

How many times do you perform a Hindu ritual for your children at the temple each year?

5. **Religious practices at home**

Do you have a family shrine at home?

How often do you pray at home, and at what time?

Do you have Hindu scriptures at home? How often do you read them?

How often do you sing or listen to Hindu songs at home?

How many Hindu holidays do you celebrate at home, and how do you celebrate them?

What nonreligious Indian holidays do you celebrate at home?

What decorations do you put up at your home to signify your Hindu religion?

What other Hindu rituals do you perform at home?

How many times do you invite a Hindu priest to perform rituals for your children?

Do you consider yourself a vegetarian?

How often do you cook traditional Hindu food for Hindu holidays?

How important is it to you that your children remain Hindu?

Why? (American individualism, dangerous youth culture associated with drugs and sex)

How do you teach your children Hindu values and rituals at home?

Which is more important for your child, being a good student or being a good Hindu?

6. **Affiliation with and participation in local Hindu and Pan-Hindu organizations**

Do you belong to any local Hindu organizations? (Satsang, Balavihar, etc.)

How many people regularly go to the meetings?

How often do you go to the meetings?

What are the organization's major goals and activities?

---

Do you belong to any national or international Hindu organizations?

How many members do they have?

How often do you go to the meetings?

What are the Pan-Hindu organizations' major activities?

Do you go to any other Hindu religious meetings and/or festivals? How often?

Do you belong to any nonreligious Indian regional/linguistic or professional associations?

How many members do they have?

How often do you go to the meetings?

What are the organizations' major goals and activities?

7. **Identity and Hindu attitudes**

How important is Hinduism to your personal identity? Is it more important than your Indian national background, South Asian background, or gender status? Why?

Do you think your practice of Hindu rituals symbolizes your Indian identity?

How many of your five best friends are Indian Hindus? What are the ethnic backgrounds of your other best friends?

Have you usually dated Indian Hindus? If not, what are your dating partners' ethnic and religious backgrounds?

How important is it to you to marry an Indian Hindu? Why?

If you could marry a non-Hindu Indian, could you also marry a Muslim?

How important is it to you to marry an Indian? Why?

Do you think you have been discriminated against because of your religious background? Give examples.

Do you think you have been discriminated against because of your Indian/South Asian background? Give examples.

# Notes

1. Before I started this book project eight years ago, I believed that Korean Protestant immigrants had a huge advantage over other Asian immigrant groups in transmitting their ethnicity through religion to the second generation because of their active participation in Korean churches and the latter's strong ethnic elements.
2. Swaminarayan Hinduism, the Gujarati form of Hinduism, usually organizes religious worship services for immigrants and second-generation children separately in the same temple. But only a small proportion of Indian Hindus, almost all from Gujarat, are affiliated with Swaminarayan Hinduism.

## CHAPTER I

1. But even some earlier white Catholic immigrant groups, such as Italian and Polish, did not attend church regularly. See Hirschman 2004, 1217–18.
2. The Second Ecumenical Council of the Vatican, commonly known as Vatican II, began in 1962 and ended in 1965. It approved sixteen documents, which led to radical changes in the liturgy and lay members' greater participation in services. The changes were a greater emphasis on Christian ecumenism (cooperation among different religious groups of Christianity) and interfaith pluralism and on the propagation of Catholicism without destroying local cultures.
3. Buddhism and Jainism are two other religions that originated in India and so share some similarities to Hinduism in rituals and religious values.
4. Korean Catholicism is far more liberal than Korean Protestantism. As chapter 3 explains, Catholics and Buddhists in Korea are far more similar in their theological position and considerably different from Protestants.
5. Although about 80 percent of Filipino immigrants are Catholics, most of them seem to participate in multiracial congregations. For example, according to a survey study (Mangiafico 1988, 174), only 17 percent of Filipino immigrants in Chicago are affiliated with Filipino ethnic congregations.
6. No information about second-generation Asian American Catholics is available because there has been no research on the group, but a number of studies shed light on second-generation Asian American Protestants, especially evangelical Protestants
7. Rebecca Kim's study (2006) shows that Korean evangelical college students prefer coethnic congregations to Pan-Asian, multiethnic, or white congregations, mainly because of their desire for community, homophily, and empowerment. But her study was conducted at a large, western, public university with a huge number of 1.5- and second-generation Korean Americans, and establishing a Korean ethnic congregation in a smaller university or college is very difficult.

## CHAPTER 2

1. At the end of the eighteenth and early nineteenth centuries, several Korean Catholic pioneers were martyred in Korea, mainly because they had violated the norm of ancestor worship.

2. In 1958, Korea Campus Crusade for Christ became the first overseas mission post for Campus Crusade for Christ, founded by Rev. Bill Bright in 1951.

3. The confinement of Buddhist temples to mountain areas far away from cities before 1970 was partly caused by the formal repression of Buddhism by the government during the Chosŏn dynasty and the Japanese colonial government.

4. In particular, the adoption of Western medical techniques has weakened the popularity of shamanistic rituals, which usually were performed when some one was seriously ill. Also, through the *saemaeul undong* (the new village movement) the Park Chung Hee government (1961–1979) required people to abolish shamanistic rituals in favor of the modernization and economic development of South Korea.

5. Women account for nearly 60 percent of Protestants in South Korea, so many must marry non-Protestant partners.

6. In January 2003, I visited Seoul to study the effects of Protestantism on Buddhism's modernization of its rituals and social services. I arranged a meeting with a Buddhist scholar at the School of Buddhism at Dong-Guk University, but when I asked him about the influence of Protestantism on Buddhism in South Korea, he got very angry and ended the conversation. When I went to two Buddhist temples and tried to talk with the abbots about the same issue, they also became angry about many Korean Protestants' evangelizing efforts to convert Buddhists to Protestantism.

CHAPTER 3

1. For example, according to Sung Joo Lee, editor of *Christian Herald in Los Angeles*, as of March 2002, there were approximately 15,000 Korean pastors for about 4,000 Korean churches in the United States, with about one thousand Koreans graduating from theological schools each year. There are no data indicating how many Korean pastors were in New York's Korean community in the 1970s. But according to senior Korean immigrant pastors, there were far more pastors than needed for Korean churches at that time.

2. For example, my conversations with both the former and current presidents of the Council of Korean Churches of Greater New York suggested that eight of the ten largest Korean immigrant Protestant churches in the New York / New Jersey are Presbyterian.

3. If pastors want to go a church affiliated with another denomination, they must obtain additional education from a theological school associated with that denomination.

4. The Korean immigrant community is socially segregated from the larger society to a greater extent than is any other Asian immigrant community. First, because they speak only one language, almost all Korean immigrants depend heavily on Korean ethnic media for news, information, and entertainment. Second, most Korean adult immigrants (more than 80%) are business owners or employees of coethnic businesses, which socially segregates them from the larger society. Third, the close affiliation of Korean immigrants with Korean immigrant churches (about 75%) and their exceptionally frequent attendance also socially segregate them from the larger society. For more detailed information on this issue, see Min 1991, 1998, 48–50.

5. Korean immigrants who are elected as elders in Korea or in another Korean immigrant church can keep their title and the attendant prestige in a new church with or without participating in the consistory (session) for decisions about church affairs.

6. Elders in most Korean immigrant churches offer one-tenth of their earnings to their church as a tithe. Since most elders are successful business owners, they contribute large amounts of money, without which many Korean churches could not survive financially.

7. The largest Korean Catholic church, located in Flushing, has vans to pick up its members from major subway and bus stations.

8. Separated, divorced, and even old single women often are uncomfortable in Korean Protestant churches because pastors and many church members emphasize family ties and discriminate against them. Some of these single women switch to Korean Buddhist temples, and some Korean Christians switch to Buddhist temples because Korean immigrant churches want their members to donate large amounts of money. See Suh 2004, 127–30.

9. Korean Buddhist leaders told me that the New York City government would not allow another group to organize a Buddha's birthday parade in Manhattan.

10. According to the 2001 Census of India, the literacy rate of Christians in India is 90 percent, compared with 76 percent for Hindus (see http://en.wikipedia/wiki/Census_of_India).

11. According to the 2002 Census of India, the literacy rates of Muslims and Jains are, respectively, 60 percent and 90 percent, compared with 76 percent for Hindus (see htttp://en.wikipedia/wiki/Census_of_India).

12. Most Caribbean immigrants of Indian origin chose the category of Indian ancestry and thus are likely to be included in the Indian population of 400, 000 in the New York / New Jersey area in the 2000 census.

CHAPTER 4

1. At that time, to be ordained in Korea they needed to obtain an undergraduate degree from a theological college.

2. One church member told me that the church's elders, deacons, and other members who could afford it took turns donating the money for the Sunday lunch program.

3. Members of many other Korean churches in New York, including the one I attended in the early 1990s, go to a Korean restaurant with their relatives or friends after the Sunday service. But the senior pastor of this church discourages its members from eating out on Sundays in order to devote themselves to God.

4. *Janchijip* are stores that provide ready-made Korean dishes for parties and other group activities. Dozens of *janchijip* in New York City offer Korean food for such reasonable prices that Korean immigrant families often order Korean food from a *janchijip* instead of cooking it at home. *Janchijips* are busy especially on Sundays because many Korean church members order Korean food for their church.

5. This Christian organization, established by eight Korean women in 1974, is supposed to provide programs for all people, regardless of ethnic background, and its youth, women, and elderly programs have served largely Korean clients. Even now, all its board members are Korean women, and about 80 percent of its clients are Koreans.

6. American clergy have shown interest in this Korean-originated practice mainly as a means of increasing the church's membership, in connection with the Full Gospel Yoido Church in Seoul, the largest church in the world (see Brennan 1990).

7. Chinese immigrant churches also have "fellowship groups" similar to Korean "district groups," but the division of Chinese Protestants into different groups is based on language, first, and then on interest (Yang 2000a). However, it is not clear whether Chinese immigrants have brought this practice from their home countries.

8. Most Korean immigrants choose a church based on friendship/kin ties and/or the charisma of the main pastor rather than on distance. One major implication of Korean immigrants' choosing "commuter churches" rather than neighborhood churches is that Korean immigrant churches do not pay much attention to their non-church neighborhoods.

9. Following the Korean tradition, in the 1970s and early 1980s Korean immigrant churches in the United States celebrated the lunar New Year's Day. But this church, like most other Korean churches, celebrates New Year's Day according to the solar calendar, although in Korea they still observe the lunar New Year's Day.

10. On March 1, 1919, thirty-three Korean leaders announced Korea's declaration of independence at a major park in Seoul, thereby challenging the Japanese occupation. Sixteen of the leaders were Christian pastors and leaders, indicating the magnitude of the Korean Christian churches' contribution to the independence movement at that time. Many Korean churches in different cities mobilized their members to participate in the marches protesting the Japanese colonization.

11. In regard to Korean children's ethnic education, Korean educators prefer the term "Korean school" rather than "Korean-language school" because the school intends to teach Korean children Korean culture, history, arts, and *taekwondo* as well as the Korean language. Nevertheless, most Korean schools focus on teaching Korean children the Korean language.

12. The education pastor who runs the Korean school said exactly the opposite: "English-language ministry is far more effective than Korean-language ministry for enhancing second-generation Korean children's religious belief because their mother tongue can touch their hearts."

13. The activities include purchasing gifts for parents, taking them to a good restaurant for lunch or dinner, and organizing and funding trips for them.

14. Later in his book, Alumkal (2003, 162) maintains that both Korean Confucianism and evangelical Christianity are responsible for barring women from serving as pastors in second-generation Korean churches.

15. U.S. Protestant churches do not have the position of "exhorters." Protestant churches in Korea seem to have created this position for the women members who are qualified to be elders in religious faith and services to the church but who are not qualified simply because of their sex.

CHAPTER 5

1. Korean and Vietnamese Buddhist temples have memberships (Huynh 2000; Suh 2004), but Chen says that Taiwanese Buddhists in California "did not exclusively join one temple, but worshipped and practiced in multiple temples" (Chen 2008, 93).

2. This suggests that proportionally more Gujarati Indians are settled in New Jersey than in New York City.

3. The temple's annual calendar gives information about daily and hourly religious activities and lists addresses and phone numbers of several hotels in the Flushing area for Hindu visitors from other states.

4. A Hindu myth led to the origin of Diwali: That is, after a fourteen-year exile, the legendary king Rama returned home victorious on this day after slaying Ravana. The festivities mark the joy of his homecoming.

5. Indian Hindus cremate bodies when people die, and in the United States, if requested, Hindu priests perform funerals at the crematorium.

6. According to a Hindu priest, when second-generation Indians marry whites, they often have two wedding ceremonies, one following the Hindu ritual and the other following the ritual observed by the white partner. The wedding is more apt to be held in a hotel than at a temple.

7. For example, in the summer of 2004 the temple dance school presented a beautiful dance program in celebration of Holi (a Hindu holiday celebrating the onset of summer) organized by the Queens borough president, Helen Marshall, and the Caribbean Hindu Society of York College.

8. Vedanta or Vedantic philosophy is a school of theological interpretation based on the Upanishads, the Bhagavad Gita, and the Brahma sutra.

CHAPTER 6

1. Portions of this chapter have appeared as Pyong Gap Min, "Religion and Maintenance of Ethnicity among Immigrants: A Comparison of Indian Hindus and Korean Protestants," *Immigrant Faiths: Transforming Religious Life in America*, edited by Karen Leonard, Alex Stepick, Manuel A. Vasquez, and Jennifer Holdaway, 99–122 (Walnut Creek, CA: Altamira Press, 2006).

2. Many Korean Catholics in Korea and Korean Catholic churches practice ancestor worship at home, but few Korean Protestants do.

3. He apologized, "I am sorry as a Christian that I have to play this hymn before I play the American and Korean national anthems."

4. Some Korean immigrant churches organize Korean-language plays for adults or children, based on Bible stories. When second-generation Korean children stage Korean-language plays based on Bible stories in church, it contributes to their ethnicity.

5. A middle-aged Gujarat immigrant with five children said: "Generally no children in my family eat meat. I never touch it and my kids never touch it. So that rule is very important."

6. It is understandable, because Korean immigrants work outside the home for long hours and most Korean children are extremely busy with extracurricular activities after school.

CHAPTER 7

1. About one-fourth of nearly six hundred Korean immigrant churches in the New York / New Jersey area have a Korean (language) school, which makes an important contribution to ethnic education in the Korean community.

2. The survey results regarding second-generation Koreans' religious affiliation and frequency of attendance at religious institutions are valuable, especially because the PUMS of the 2000 U.S. Census do not provide information about religion.

3. I heard a similar comment by a leader of the Korean Christian Club at New York University when I visited the campus to give a talk to the Asian Christian organization in December 2004.

4. I have often been asked by native-born white Americans, "Can you speak English?" Although I have a strong Korean accent, this question irritates me, and it is not surprising that native-born Korean Americans with no accent regard this kind of question as a sign of prejudice against them.

5. The flow of Indian immigrants has exploded during recent years. Before 1995, about thirty thousand Indians became formal immigrants in the United States annually, but in the 2000s, the annual number of Indian immigrants has increased to about seventy thousand. The huge increase in the number of Hindu temples is not a problem because of the concomitant increase in the annual number of Indian immigrants. But Vijay Patel's concern about what will happen to many Hindu temples in twenty or thirty years will be an important issue if the current size of the annual Indian immigrant flow is drastically reduced in the future.

6. As discussed in chapter 9, many of the informants took courses on Hinduism, Indian philosophy, and/or South Asian history in college.

CHAPTER 8

1. One informant said that her parents had taught her that she could be a good religious Hindu without being a vegetarian.

2. They celebrated Diwali with parents or friends with vegetarian dishes, listened to Hindu songs now and then, and/or kept images of gods and goddess at home. But they never prayed. They went to temple either a few or several times a year to enjoy Hindu cultural activities and foods.

3. As noted in chapter 5, the Ganesh Temple and many other Hindu temples, as well as many universities and colleges, offer courses to high school and college students on Hinduism, Indian philosophy, and Sanskrit. Fenton pointed out that about 150 students of South Asian ancestry at Emory University had already taken his comparative religious course which included Hinduism (Fenton 1992, 261).

### CHAPTER 9

1. In fall of 2002, when a U.S. military court acquitted two U.S. servicemen whose car had hit two Korean middle school students, Koreans organized large-scale anti-American demonstrations in several cities that lasted for a few months.

2. *Hyungboo & Nolboo* is a popular classic Korean novel about two brothers with contrasting personalities, which tries to teach its readers that good people ultimately become successful and bad people fail.

3. Eighteen percent of the informants stated that being Hindu was their primary identity and another 20 percent considered their Indian national origin and the Hindu background equally important to their identity. Two informants cited their South Asian background as their primary identity.

4. Other studies also show that younger-generation Korean Christians consider their parents' overemphasis on children's educational success as un-Christian (Alumkal 2003, 113; Chai 1998).

5. The Integrated Public Use Microdata Sample of the 2000 census counted 19,173 1.5-generation and native-born Indians twenty-five to sixty-four years old and 16,159 younger-generation Korean adults. About 70 percent of these younger-generation Indians were Hindus (13,412), but only 35 percent of these Koreans were Protestants (5,655).

### CHAPTER 10

1. American Jews also have a perfect or extremely high association between religion and ethnicity. But I have not included them because contemporary Jewish immigrants are less religious than American Jews because of their experience with religious oppression in their countries of origin.

2. Kurien (2004, 168) indicates that Syrian Christians from Kerala usually attend church every Sunday. My data also show that about 65 percent of Indian Christian immigrants in New York City go to church once a week or more.

3. Citing Raymond Williams's book (Williams 1996), Kurien points out that Indian Syrian Christians have traditionally avoided active evangelism in order to maintain peaceful relations with their Hindu neighbors (Kurien 2004, 178).

4. Of course, Muslim immigrants' commitment to Islamic religious values and religious practices is variable. For example, a survey of Iranian immigrants in Los Angeles found that only 5 percent of Iranian Muslims are religiously observant Muslims (Bozorgmehr and Sabagh 2000).

### APPENDIX I

1. Only two Indian names, Patel and Singh, are prominent, each taking up several pages of New York City's telephone directory. But unlike Kim for the Korean group, neither name statistically represents the Indian immigrant population. That is, many Patels are Hindus from Gujarat, and

Singhs are usually Sikhs. Therefore, we added the following fifteen Indian surnames: Das, Dhar, Dhillon, Ghosh, Gupta, Jain, Kumar, Mehta, Pal, Prashad, Rao, Roy, Sen, Singh, Srivastava, and Sinha. But none was a prominent Indian name taking up several pages of the telephone directory.

2. People of Asian Indian ancestry include Guyanese and other Caribbean immigrants of Indian ancestry who remigrated to the United States. Caribbean Indians in New York City are heavily concentrated in Queens.

3. I thank Dae Young Kim for allowing me to use his data set.

4. As a rough proxy for the Metropolitan New York / New Jersey boroughs and counties, Korean surnames were obtained from the following area codes: New York: 718, 212, 516, and 914; New Jersey: 201, 908, and 973.

# References

Abusharaf, Rogaia Mustafa. 1998. Structural Adaptations in an Immigrant Muslim Congregations in New York. In R. Stephen Warner and Judith G. Wittner, eds., *Gatherings in Diaspora: Religious Communities and the New Immigration*, 235–64. Philadelphia: Temple University Press.

Alba, Richard D. 1990. *Ethnic Identity: The Transformation of White America*. New Haven, CT: Yale University Press.

Alumkal, Antony. 1999. Preserving Patriarchy: Assimilation, Gender Norms, and Second-Generation Korean American Evangelicals. *Qualitative Sociology* 22 (1):129–40.

———. 2001. Being Korean, Being Christian: Particularism and Universalism in a Second-Generation Congregation. In Ho-Youn Kwon, Kwang Chung Kim, and R. Stephen Warner, eds., *Korean Americans and Their Religions: Pilgrims and Missionaries from a Different Shore*, 181–92. University Park: Pennsylvania State University Press.

———. 2003. *Asian American Evangelical Churches: Race, Ethnicity, and Assimilation in the Second Generation*. New York: LFB Scholarly Publishing LLC.

Ammerman, Nancy Tatom. 2001. *Congregation and Community*. New Brunswick, NJ: Rutgers University Press.

Badr, Hoda. 2000. Al-Noor Mosque: Strength through Unity. In Helen Rose Ebaugh and Janet Saltzman Chafetz, eds., *Religion and New Immigrants: Continuities and Adaptations in Immigrant Congregations*, 193–229. Walnut Creek, CA: Altamira Press.

Bagby, Ihsan. 2006. "Second-Generation Muslim Immigrants in Detroit Mosques: The Second Generation's Search for Their Place and Identity in the American Mosque." In J. L. Heft, ed., *Passing on the Faith: Transforming Traditions for the Next Generation of Jews, Christians, and Muslims*, 218–46. New York: Fordham University Press.

Baker, Donald.. 1997a. Buddhism. In John H. Koo and Andrew Nam, eds., *An Introduction to Korean Culture*, 155–78. Elizabeth, NJ: Hollym.

———. 1997b. Christianity. In John H. Koo and Andrew Nam, eds., *An Introduction to Korean Culture*, 179–200. Elizabeth, NJ: Hollym.

Balmer, Randall. 2003. Crossing the Borders: Evangelicalism and Migration. In Yvonne Yazbeck Haddad, Jane I. Smith, and John L. Esposito eds., *Religion and Immigration: Christian, Jewish, and Muslim Experiences in the United States*, 53–70. Walnut Creek, CA: Altamira Press.

Bankston, Carl III, and Min Zhou. 1995. The Ethnic Church, Ethnic Identification, and Adaptation of Vietnamese Adolescents in an Immigrant Community. *Sociological Quarterly* 36 (2):523–34.

Bansal Named Chair of Commission on International Religious Freedom. 2004. *India Abroad*, July 9, A4.

Bellah, Robert, R. Madsen, W. M. Sullivan, A. Swindler, and S. M. Tipton. 1985. *Habits of the Heart: Individualism and Commitment in American Life*. Berkeley: University of California Press.

Bhachu, Parminder. 1985. *Twice Migrants: East African Sikh Settlers in Britain*. London: Tavistock.

Bhardwaj, Surinder M., and Madhusudana N. Rao. 1998. The Temple as a Symbol of Hindu Identity in America. *Journal of Cultural Geography* 17:19–31.

Bhattacharjee, A. 1992. The Habit of Ex-Nomination: Nation, Women and the Indian Immigrant Bourgeoisie. *Public Culture* 5 (1):19–44.

Bozorgmehr, Mehdi. 1997. Internal Ethnicity: Iranians in Los Angeles. *Sociological Perspectives* 40 (3):387–408.

———. 2000. Does Host Hostility Create Ethnic Solidarity? The Experience of Iranians in the United States. *Bulletin of the Royal Institute of Inter-Faith Studies* 2:159–78.

Bozorgmehr, Mehdi, and Any Bakalian. 2005. Discriminatory Reactions to September 11 Terrorist Attacks. In Pyong Gap Min, ed., *Encyclopedia of Racism in the United States*, 557–64. Westport, CT: Greenwood Press.

Bozorgmehr, Mehdi, and Georges Sabagh. 2000. Secular Immigrants: Religiosity and Ethnicity among Iranian Muslims in Los Angeles. In Yvonne Haddad and Jane Smith, eds., *Muslim Communities in North America*, 445–73. Albany: State University of New York Press.

Brennan, Patrick J. 1990. *Re-imagining the Parish: Base Communities, Adulthood, and Family Consciousness*. New York: Crossroad.

Burghart, Richard, ed. 1987. *Hinduism in Great Britain: The Perpetuation of Religion in an Alien Cultural Milieu*. London: Tavistock.

Busto, Rudy. 1996. The Gospel According to the Model Minority? Hazarding an Interpretation of Asian American Evangelical College Students. *Amerasia Journal* 22 (1):133–48.

Cadge, Wendy. 2005. *Heartwood: The First Generation of Theravada Buddhism in America*. Chicago: University of Chicago Press.

Caldarola, C., ed. 1982. *Religions and Societies: Asia and the Middle East*. Berlin: Mouton.

Carnes, Tony, and Fenggang Yang, eds. 2004a. *Asian American Religions: The Making and Remaking of Borders and Boundaries*. New York: New York University Press.

———. 2004b. Introduction to *Asian American Religions: The Making and Remaking of Borders and Boundaries*, ed. Tony Carnes and Fenggang Yang, 1–37. New York: New York University Press.

Cha, Peter. 1994. Toward a Vision for Second Generation Korean American Ministry. Paper presented at Katalyst, Sandy Cove, MD, August.

Chai, Karen. 1998. Competing for the Second Generation: English-Language Ministry at a Korean Protestant Church. In R. Stephen Warner and Judith Wittner, eds., *Gatherings in Diaspora: Religious Communities and the New Immigration*, 295–332. Philadelphia: Temple University Press.

———. 2001a. Beyond "Strictness" to Distinctiveness: Generational Transition in Korean Protestant Churches. In Ho-Youn Kwon, Kwang Chung Kim, and R. Stephen Warner, eds., *Korean Americans and Their Religions: Pilgrims and Missionaries from a Different Shore*, 157–80. University Park: Pennsylvania University Press.

———. 2001b. Intra-Ethnic Religious Diversity: Korean Buddhists and Protestants in Greater New York. In Ho-Youn Kwon, Kwang Chung Kim, and R. Stephen Warner, eds., *Korean Americans and Their Religions: Pilgrims and Missionaries from a Different Shore*, 273–94. University Park: Pennsylvania University Press.

———. 2005. Chinatown or Uptown? Second-Generation Chinese American Protestants in New York City. In Philip Kasinitz, John H. Molenkoph, and Mary C. Waters eds., *Becoming New Yorkers: Ethnographies of the New Second Generation*, 257–87. New York: Russell Sage.

Chen, Carolyn. 2002. The Religious Varieties of Ethnic Presence: A Comparison between a Taiwanese Immigrant Buddhist Temple and an Evangelical Christian Church. *Sociology of Religion* 63:215–38.

————.2008. *Getting Saved in America: Taiwanese Immigration and Religious Experience*. Princeton, NJ: Princeton University Press.

Cho, Dong-Ho. 2002. Intimate Alien: An Immigrant Critique of Korean Pentecostalism. PhD diss., City University of New York.

Choe, Sang-Hun. 2007a. Freed Koreans Are Contrite amid Growing Criticisms. *New York Times*, September 3, A5.

————.2007b. Shamanism Enjoys Revival in Techno-Savvy South Korea. *New York Times*, July 7.

Chong, Kelly. 1998. What It Means to Be Christians: The Role of Religion in the Construction of Ethnic Identity and Boundary among Second-Generation Korean Americans. *Sociology of Religion* 58:258–86.

Chung, C. 1982. Korea. In C. Caldarola, ed., *Religions and Societies: Asia and the Middle East*, 606–28. Berlin: Mouton.

Conzen, Kathleen Neils. 1991. Mainstreams and Side Channels: The Localization of Immigrant Culture. *Journal of American Ethnic History* 10:5–20.

Cook, David. 2000. Iglesia Cristina Evangelica: Arriving in the Pipeline. In Helen Rose Ebaugh and Janet Saltzman, eds., *Religion and the New Immigrants: Continuities and Adaptations*, 171–92. Walnut Creek, CA: Altamira Press.

Cornell, Stephen, and Douglas Hartman. 1998. *Making Identities in a Changing World*. Thousand Oaks, CA: Sage.

Crane, Ken R. 2003. *Latino Churches: Faith, Family, and Ethnicity in the Second Generation*. New York: RFB Scholarly Publishing LLC.

DasGupta, Sayantani, and Shamita Das DasGupta. 1996. Women in Exile: Gender Relations in the Asian Indian Community in the U.S. In Sunaina Maria and Rajini Srikanth, eds., *Contours of the Heart: South Asians Map North America*, 381–400. New York: Asian American Writers Workshop.

Davis, Richard. 1995. Introduction to *Religions of India in Practice*, ed. Donald S. Lopez, 3–52. Princeton, NJ: Princeton University Press.

Dearman, Marion. 1982. Structure and Function of Religion in the Los Angeles Korean Community. In Eui-Young Yu, Earl H. Phillips, and Eun Sik Yang, eds., *Koreans in Los Angeles*, 165–83. Los Angeles: Center for Korean-American and Korean Studies, California State University at Los Angeles.

Dhingra, Pawan. 2007. *Managing Multicultural Lives: Asian American Professionals and the Challenge of Multiple Identities*. Stanford, CA: Stanford University Press.

Diaz-Stevens, Ana Maria. 1994. Analyzing Popular Religiosity for Socio-Religious Meaning. In Anthony M. Stevens-Arroyo, and Ana Maria Diaz-Stevens, eds., *An Enduring Flame: Studies of Latino Popular Religiosity*, vol. 1, 17–36. New York: Bildner Center for Western Hemisphere Studies.

Dolan, Jay. 1985. *The American Catholic Experience: History from Colonial Times to the Present*. Garden City, NY: Doubleday.

Ebaugh, Helen Rose, and Janet Saltzman Chafetz, eds. 2000. *Religion and the New Immigrants*. Walnut Creek, CA: Altamira Press.

Ecklund, Elaine Howard. 2005. Models of Civil Responsibility: Korean Americans in Congregations with Different Ethnic Compositions. *Journal for the Scientific Study of Religion* 44:15–28.

————.2006. *Korean American Evangelicals: New Models for Civic Life*. New York: Oxford University Press.

Eid, Paul. 2007. *Being Arab: Ethnic and Religious Identity Building among Second Generation Youth in Montreal*. Montreal: McGill–Queens University Press.

Emerson, Michael O., and K. C. Kim. 2003. Multiracial Congregations: An Analysis of Their Development and a Typology. *Journal of the Scientific Study of Religion* 29:19–34.

Espiritu, Yen Le. 1992. *Asian American Panethnicity: Bridging Institutions and Identities*. Philadelphia: Temple University Press.

Farber, Bernard, Bernard Lazerwitz, and Charles Mindel. 1998. The Jewish-American Family. In Charles Mindel, Robert Habenstein, and Roosevelt Wright Jr., eds., *Ethnic Families in America: Patterns and Variations*, 422–49. Upper Saddle River, NJ: Prentice Hall.

Fenton, John. 1988. *Transplanting Religious Traditions: Asian Indians in America*. New York: Praeger.

———.1992. Academic Study of Religion and Asian Indian-American College Students. In Raymond Williams, ed., *A Sacred Thread: Modern Transmissions of Hindu Traditions in India and Abroad*, 258–79. Chambersburg, PA: Anima.

Finker, Roger, and Rodney Stark. 1988. Religious Economies and Sacred Canopies: Religious Mobilizations in American Cities, 1906. *American Sociological Review* 53:41–50.

———.1992. *The Church of America 1776–1990: Winners and Losers in Our Religious Economy*. New Brunswick, NJ: Rutgers University Press.

Frankenberg, Ruth. 1993. *White Women, Race Matters: The Social Construction of Whiteness*. Minneapolis: University of Minnesota Press.

Frykenberg, Robert Eric. 1993. Constructions of Hinduism at the Nexus of History and Religion. *Journal of Interdisciplinary History* 23:53–550.

Gallagher, Sally K. 2003. *Evangelical Identity and Gendered Family Life*. New Brunswick, NJ: Rutgers University Press.

Gans, Herbert. 1994. Symbolic Ethnicity and Symbolic Religiosity: Towards a Comparison of Ethnic and Religious Acculturation. *Ethnic and Racial Studies* 17:577–92.

Gasi, Maria V. 2000. St. Nicholas Greek Orthodox Church: Maturing through the Generations. In Helen Rose Ebaugh and Janet Saltzman Chafetz, eds., *Religion and the New Immigrants*, 153–70. Walnut Creek, CA: Altamira Press.

George, Sheba. 1998. Caroling with the Keralites: The Negotiation of Gendered Space in an Indian Immigrant Church. In R. Stephen Warner, and Judith Wittner, eds., *Gatherings in Diaspora: Religious Communities and the New Immigration*, 265–94. Philadelphia: Temple University Press.

Gibson, Margaret A. 1989. *Accommodation without Assimilation: Sikh Immigrants in an American High School*. Ithaca, NY: Cornell University Press.

Gillis, Chester. 2003. American Catholics: Neither Far out nor in Deep. In Yvonne Yazbeck Haddad, Jane I. Smith, and John L. Esposito, eds., *Religion and Immigration: Christian, Jewish, and Muslim*, 31–55. Walnut Creek, CA: Altamira Press.

Goodstein, Laurie. 2004. Catholics in America: A Restive People. *New York Times*, April 3, 5.

Gordon, Milton. 1964. *Assimilation in American Life: The Role of Race, Religion, and National Origins*. New York: Oxford University Press.

Goren, Arthur. 1982. *The American Jews*. Cambridge, MA: Harvard University Press.

Greeley, Andrew. 1971. *Why Can't They Be Like Us? America's White Ethnic Groups*. New York: Dutton.

———.1972. *The Denominational Society: A Sociological Approach to Religion in America*. Glenview, IL: Scott Foresman.

Guest, Kenneth J. 2003. *God in Chinatown: Religion and Survival in New York's Evolving Immigrant Community*. New York: New York University Press.

Guillermina, Jasso, Douglass S. Massy, Mark R. Rosenzweig, and James P. Smith. 2003. Exploring the Religious Preferences of Recent Immigrants to the United States: Evidence from the New Immigrant Survey Pilot. In Yvonne Yazbeck Haddad, Jane I. Smith, and John L. Esposito, eds., *Religion and Immigration: Christian, Jewish, and Muslim Experiences in the United States*, 217–53. Walnut Creek, CA: Altamira Press.

Gupta, Himanee. 2003. Staking a Claim on American-ness: Hindu Temples in the United States. In Jane Naomi Iwamura and Paul Spickard, eds., *Revealing the Sacred in Asian & Pacific America*, 193–208. New York: Routledge.

Gupte, Praynay. 1978. Stamp of India Heavier in the City. *New York Times*, June 4, R1.

Haddad, Yvonne Yazbeck. 1998. The Dynamics of Islamic Identity in North America. In Yvonne Yazbek Haddad and John L. Esposito, eds., *Muslims on the Americanization Path?* 19–46. New York: Oxford University Press.

Haddad, Yvonne Yazbeck, and Jane I. Smith, eds. 1994. *Muslim Communities in North America*. Albany, NY: State University of New York Press.

———. 2002. *Muslim Minorities in the West: Visible and Invisible*. Walnut Creek, CA: Altamira Press.

Hammond, Philip E. 1988. Religion and the Persistence of Identity. *Journal fort the Scientific Study of Religion* 27:1–11.

Hammond, Philip E., and Kee Warner. 1993. Religion and Ethnicity in Late-Twentieth Century America. *Annals of the American Academy of Political and Social Science* 527:55–66.

Han, Gil Soo. 1994. *Social Sources of Church Growth: Korean Churches in the Homeland and Overseas*. Lanham, MD: University Press of America.

Handlin, Oscar. 1979. *The Uprooted*. 2nd ed. Boston: Little, Brown.

Haniffa, Aziz. 2004. Diwali Awaits Stamp of Approval. *India Abroad*, October 22.

———. 2005. Hindu Group Moves Court for Religious Freedom. *India Abroad*, October 7, A8.

———. 2007. Rajan Zed Creates History. *India Abroad*, July 20, A1, A12.

———. 2008. Hindu Group Files Suit against Christian Number Plates. *India Abroad*, August 15, A10.

Harris, Michael S. 1997. Bangladeshis. In David Levinson and Melvin Ember, eds., *American Immigrant Cultures: Builders of a Nation*, vol.1, 56–62. New York: Macmillan Reference USA.

Hasan, Asma Gull. 2002. *American Muslims: The New Generation*. New York: Continuum.

Herberg, Will. 1960. *Protestant, Catholic, and Jew: An Essay in American Religious Sociology*. 2nd ed. Garden City, NJ: Doubleday.

Hindu American Foundation. 2005. Issues with California Textbooks. Available at http://www.hinduamericanfoundation.org.

———. 2006. Hindu American Foundation Sues California State Board of Education. Available at http://www.hinduamericanfoundation.org.

Hirschman, Charles. 2004. The Role of Religion in the Origins and Adaptation of Immigrant Groups in the United States. *International Migration Review* 38:1206–33.

Hunter, James Davison. 1983. *American Evangelicalism: Conservative Religion and the Quandary of Modernity*. New Brunswick, NJ: Rutgers University Press.

———. 1987. *Evangelicalism: The Coming Generation*. Chicago: University of Chicago Press.

Huntington, Gertrude Enders. 1998. The Amish Family. In Charles H. Mindel, Robert W. Habenstein, and Roosevelt Wright Jr., eds., *Ethnic Families in America: Patterns and Variations*, 450–79. New York: Elsevier.

Hurh, Won Moo, and Kwang Chung Kim. 1984. *Korean Immigrants in America: A Structural Analysis of Ethnic Confinement and Adhesive Adaptation*. Rutherford, NJ: Fairleigh Dickenson University Press.

———. 1990. Religious Participation of Korean Immigrants in the United States. *Journal for the Scientific Study of Religion* 29:19–34.

Huynh, Thuan. 2000. Center for Vietnamese Buddhism: Recreating Home. In Helen Rose Ebaugh and Janet Saltzman Chafetz, eds., *Religion and the New Immigrants: Continuities and Adaptations in Immigrant Congregations*, 45–66. Walnut Creek, CA: Altamira Press.

Iwamura, Jane Naomi, and Paul Spickard, eds. 2003. *Revealing the Sacred in Asian and Pacific America*. New York: Routledge.

Iype, George. 2002. Forced Religious Conversions Banned in Tamil Nadu. *India Abroad*, October 18.

Jacob, Simon, and Pallavi Thaku. 2000. Jyothi Hindu Temple: One Religion, Many Practices. In Helen Rose Ebaugh and Janet Saltzman Chafetz, eds., *Religion and the New Immigrants: Continuities and Adaptations in Immigrant Congregations*, 229–42. Walnut Creek, CA: Altamira Press.

Jaret, Charles. 1995. *Contemporary Racial and Ethnic Relations*. New York: HarperCollins.

Jensen, Joan M. 1988. *The Passage from India: Asian Indian Immigrants in North America*. New Haven, CT: Yale University Press.

Jeung, Russell. 2002. Asian American Pan-Ethnic Formation and Congregational Culture. In Pyong Gap Min and Jung Ha Kim, eds., *Religions in Asian America: Building Faith Communities*, 214–44. Walnut Creek, CA: Altamira Press.

———. 2005. *Faithful Generations: Race and New Asian American Churches*. New Brunswick, NJ: Rutgers University Press.

Joseph, George. 2006. Incumbents Sweep Hindu Temple Election. *India Abroad*, March 24, A27.

Joshi, Khyati Y. 2007. *New Roots in American Sacred Ground: Religion, Race, and Ethnicity in Indian American*. New Brunswick, NJ: Rutgers University Press.

Joshi, Monika. 2005. NYC Council Approves Diwali Parking Plan. *India Abroad*, October 7, C2.

———. 2006. Diwali Makes It to NYC Festival List Despite Mayor Bloomberg's Veto. *India Abroad*, January 6, C3.

Kennedy, R. J. R. 1944. Single or Triple Melting Pot? Intermarriage Trends in New Haven, 1870–1940. *American Journal of Sociology* 49:331–39.

Khandelwal, Madhulika. 2002. *Becoming American, Being Indian: An Immigrant Community in New York City*. Ithaca, NY: Cornell University Press.

Kibria, Nazli. 2002. *Becoming Asian American: Second Generation Chinese and Korean Identities*. Baltimore: Johns Hopkins University Press.

———. 2006. South Asian Americans. In Pyong Gap Min, ed., *Asian-Americans: Contemporary Trends and Issues*, 206–27. New York: Pine Forge.

Kim, Ae Ra. 1996. *Women Struggling for a New Life: The Role of Religion in the Cultural Passage from Korea to America*. Albany, NY: State University Press of New York.

Kim, Andrew. 2000. Korean Religious Culture and Its Affinity to Christianity in South Korea. *Sociology of Religion* 61 (2):117–34.

Kim, Bok In. 2001. Won Buddhism in the United States. In Ho-Youn Kwon, Kwang Chung Kim, and Stephen R. Warner, eds., *Korean Americans and Their Religions: Pilgrims and Missionaries*, 259–71. University Park: Pennsylvania State University Press.

Kim, Chan-Hee. 1982. Christianity and Modernization of Korea. In Earl H. Phillips and Eui-Young Yu, eds., *Religions in Korea: Beliefs and Cultural Values*, 117–27. Los Angeles: Center for Korean-American and Korean Studies, California State University at Los Angeles.

Kim, Dae Young. 2004. Leaving the Ethnic Economy: The Rapid Integration of Second-Generation Korean Americans in New York. In Philip Kasinitz, John M. Mollenkoph, and Mary C. Waters, eds., *Becoming New Yorkers: Ethnographies of the New Second Generation*, 154–188. New York. Russell Sage Foundation.

Kim, Henry H., and Ralph E. Pyle. 2004. An Exception to the Exception: Second Generation Korean Church Participation. *Social Compass* 51 (3):321–33.

Kim, Illsoo. 1981. *New Urban Immigrants: The Korean Community in New York*. Princeton, NJ: Princeton University Press.

Kim, Jung Ha. 1996. The Labor of Compassion: Voices of "Churched" Korean American Women. *Amerasia Journal* 22: 93–105.

———. 2002. Cartography of Korean American Protestant Faith Communities in the United States. In Pyong Gap Min, ed., *Religion in Asian America: Building Faith Communities in the United States*, 185–214. Walnut Creek, CA: Altamira Press.

Kim, Kwang Chung, and Shin Kim. 2001. The Ethnic Role of Korean Immigrant Churches in the United States. In Ho-Youn Kwon, Kwang Chung Kim, and Stephen R. Warner, eds., *Korean Americans and Their Religions: Pilgrims and Missionaries*, 71–94. University Park: Pennsylvania State University Press.

Kim, Rebecca Y. 2003. Second-Generation Korean American Evangelicals: Ethnic, Multiethnic, or White Campus Ministries. *Sociology of Religion* 65:19–34.

———. 2004. Negotiation of Ethnic and Religious Boundaries by Asian American Campus Evangelicals. In Tony Carnes and Fenggang Yang, eds., *Asian American Religions: The Making and Remaking of Borders and Boundaries*, 141–59. New York: New York University Press.

———. 2006. *God's New Whiz Kids: Korean American Evangelicals on Campus*. New York: New York University Press.

Kim, Sharon. 2008. Replanting Sacred Spaces: The Emergence of Second-Generation Korean American Churches. In David K. Yoo and Ruth H. Chung, eds., *Religion and Spirituality in Korean America*, 151–70. Urbana: University of Illinois Press.

Kim, Shin, and Kwang Chung Kim. 2000. Korean Immigrant Churches: Male Domination and Adaptive Strategy. *Korean and Korean American Studies Bulletin* 11:53–67.

King, Ursula. 1989. Some Reflections on Sociological Approaches to the Study of Modern Hinduism. *Numen* 36:72–97.

Kini, M. D. 2006. God Isn't in the Details: There Is No Point of Conversion. *India Abroad*, May 5, M12.

Kniss, Fred, and Paul D. Numrich. 2007. *Sacred Assemblies and Civic Engagement: How Religion Matters for America's Newest Immigrants*. New Brunswick, NJ: Rutgers University Press.

Korea National Statistical Office. 1992. *1992 Social Indicators in Korea*. Seoul: Korea National Statistical Office.

———. 2002. *2002 Social Indicators in Korea*. Seoul: Korea National Statistical Office.

———. 2005. *2005 Social Indicators in Korea*. Seoul: Korea National Statistical Office.

Korean Association of New York. 1985. *The History of the Korean Association of New York*. New York: Korean Businessmen's Association of New York.

Korean Christian Institute for the Study of Justice and Development. 1982. *A Comprehensive Research Report on Korean Churches in Commemoration of the One Hundred Years' Anniversary*. Seoul: Korean Christian Institute for the Study of Justice and Development.

Korean Church of New York. 1992. *Gangbyon-e Anza Ulotnora [We Wept Sitting by the River]*. Seoul: Gipeun Saem.

Kurien, Prema. 1998. Becoming American by Becoming Hindu: Indian Americans Take Their Place at the Multicultural Table. In R. Stephen Warner and Judith Wittner, eds., *Gatherings in Diaspora: Religious Communities and the New Immigration*, 37–70. Philadelphia: Temple University Press.

———. 1999. Gendered Ethnicity: Creating a Hindu Indian Identity in the United States. *American Behavioral Scientist* 42:648–70.

———. 2001. Religion, Ethnicity, and Politics: Hindu and Muslim Indian Immigrants in the United States. *Ethnic and Racial Studies* 24:263–93.

———. 2002. "We Are Better Hindus Here": Religion and Ethnicity among Indian Americans. In Pyong Gap Min and Jung Ha Kim, eds., *Building Faith Communities: Religions in Asian America*, 99–121. Walnut Creek, CA: Altamira Press.

———. 2004. Christian by Birth or Rebirth: Generation and Difference in an Indian American Christian Church. In Tony Carnes and Fenggang Yang, eds., *Asian American Religions: The Making and Remaking of Borders and Boundaries*, 160–81. New York: New York University Press.

———. 2007. *A Place at the Multicultural Table: The Development of American Hinduism*. New Brunswick, NJ: Rutgers University Press.

Kwon, Ho-Youn, Kwang Chung Kim, and Stephen Warner, eds. 2001. *Korean Americans and Their Religions*. University Park: Pennsylvania State University Press.

Kwon, Okyun. 2003. *Buddhist and Protestant Korean Immigrants: Religious Beliefs and Socioeconomic Aspects of Life*. New York: LFB Scholarly Publishing LLC.

Kwon, Victoria Hyonchu, Helen Rose Ebaugh, and Jacqueline Hagan. 1997. The Structure and Functions of Cell Group Ministry in a Korean Christian Church. *Journal for the Scientific Study of Religion* 36:247–56.

Lee, Helen. 1996. Silent Exodus—Can the East Asian Church in America Reverse Flight of Its Next Generation? *Christianity Today*, August 12.

Lee, Kwang Kyu. 1997. Folk Beliefs and Shamanism. In John H. Koo and Andrew C. Nahm, eds., *An Introduction to Korean Culture*, 121–34. Elizabeth, NJ: Hollym.

Lee, Sara. 2006. Class Matters: Racial and Ethnic Identities of Working- and Middle-Class Second Generation Korean Americans in New York City. In Philip Kasinitz, John H. Mollenkopf, and Mary Waters, eds., *Becoming New Yorkers: Ethnographies of the New Second Generation*, 313–38. New York: Russell Sage.

Lee, Won Kyu. 2000. *Hanguk kyohe erdiro gago itna? [Where Are Korean Churches Going?]* Seoul: Christian Literature Society of Korea.

Leonard, Karen Isaksen. 1992. *Making Ethnic Choices: California's Punjabi Mexican Americans*. Philadelphia: Temple University Press.

———. 2003. *Muslims in the United States: The State of Research*. New York: Russell Sage.

Lessinger, Jonathan. 1995. *From the Ganges to the Hudson: Indian Immigrants in New York City*. Boston: Allyn & Bacon.

Levitt, Peggy. 1999. Local-Level Global Religion: The Case of U.S. Dominican Migration. *Journal for the Scientific Study of Religion* 37:74–89.

———. 2001. *The Transnational Villagers*. Berkeley: University of California Press.

———. 2004. Redefining the Boundaries of Belonging: The Institutional Character of Transnational Religious Life. *Sociology of Religion* 65 (1):1–18.

————.2007. *God Needs No Passport: Immigrants and the Changing American Religious Landscape.* New York: New Press.

Liang, Zai, and Naomi Ito. 1999. Intermarriage of Asian Americans in the New York City Region: Contemporary Patterns and Future Prospects. *International Migration Review* 33 (4):876–900.

Lin, Irene. 1996. Journey to the Far West: Chinese Buddhism in America. In David Yoo, ed., *New Spiritual Homes: Religion and Asian Americans*, 134–68. Honolulu: University of Hawai'i Press.

Lopez, David S., ed. 1995. *Religions of India in Practice.* Princeton, NJ: Princeton University Press.

Lowman, Pete. 1983. *The Day of His Power: A History of the International Fellowship of Evangelical Students.* Leicester: Intervarsity Press.

Lyman, Stanford, and William Douglass. 1973. Ethnicity: Strategies of Collective and Individual Impression Management. *Social Research* 40:344–65.

Lyu, Kingsley K. 1977. Korean Nationalist Activities in Hawaii and the Continental United States, 1990–1919. *Amerasia Journal* 4 (1):23–90.

Maira, Sunaina Marr. 2002. *Desis in the House: Indian American Youth Culture in New York City.* Philadelphia: Temple University Press.

Malik, Salahuddin. 1997. Pakistanis. In David Levinson and Melvin Ember, eds., *American Immigrant Cultures: Builders of a Nation*, vol. 2, 674–78. New York: Macmillan.

Mangiafico, Luciano. 1988. *Contemporary American Immigrants: Patterns of Filipino, Korean, and Chinese Settlement.* New York: Praeger.

Marsden, George M. 1991. *Understanding Fundamentalism and Evangelicalism.* Grand Rapids, MI: Eerdman.

Marshall, Paul. 2000. *Religious Freedom in the World: A Global Report on Freedom and Persecution.* Nashville, TN: Broadman and Holman.

Mayer, Egon, Barry Kosmin, and Ariela Keysar. 2003. American Jewish Identity Survey 2001: The Religious and the Secular. New York: Center for Jewish Studies, Graduate Center of the City University of New York.

Mazumdar, Shampa, and Sanjoy Mazumdar. 2003. Creating the Sacred: Altars in the Hindu American Home. In Jane Naomi Iwamura and Paul Spickard, eds., *Revealing the Sacred in Asian & Pacific America*, 143–58. New York: Routledge.

McAlister, Elizabeth. 1998. The Madonna of 115th Street Revisited: Voodou and Haitian Catholicism in the Age of Transnationalism. In Stephen Warner and Judith Wittner, eds., *Gatherings in Diaspora: Religious Communities and the New Immigration*, 123–62. Philadelphia: Temple University Press.

McLeod, W. H. 1976. *The Evolution of the Sikh Community.* Oxford: Clarendon Press.

Menjivar, Cecilia. 2000. *Fragmented Ties: Salvadorian Immigrant Networks in America.* Berkeley: University of California Press.

Merton, Robert. 1967. *Social Theory and Social Structure.* New York: Free Press.

Michell, George. 1988. *The Hindu Temple: Its Meaning and Forms.* Chicago: University of Chicago Press.

Min, Anselm Kyongsuk. 2008. Korean American Catholic Communities: A Pastoral Reflection. In David K. Yoo and Ruth H. Chung, eds., *Religion and Spirituality in Korea America*, 21–39. Urbana: University of Illinois Press.

Min, Kyong Bae. 1988. *Hanguk Kidokgyohesa* [A History of Korean Christianity]. Seoul: Korean Christian Publishing.

Min, Pyong Gap. 1991. Cultural and Economic Boundaries of Korean Ethnicity: A Comparative Analysis. *Ethnic and Racial Studies* 14:225–41.

———.1992. The Structure and Social Functions of Korean Immigrant Churches in the United States. *International Migration Review* 26:1370–94.

———.1996. *Caught in the Middle: Korean Communities in New York and Los Angeles.* Berkeley: University of California Press.

———.1997. Korean Immigrant Wives' Labor Force Participation, Marital Power, and Status. In Elizabeth Higginbotham and Mary Romero, eds., *Women and Work: Exploring Race, Ethnicity, and Class,* 176–92. Thousand Oaks, CA: Sage.

———.1998. *Changes and Conflicts: Korean Immigrant Families in New York.* Boston: Allyn & Bacon.

———.2000. Immigrants' Religion and Ethnicity: A Comparison of Korean Christian and Indian Hindu Immigrants. *Bulletin of the Royal Institute for Inter-Faith Studies* 2:121–40.

———.2001. Koreans: An Institutionally Complete Community in New York. In Nancy Foner, ed., *New Immigrants in New York,* 2nd ed., 173–200. New York: Columbia University Press.

———.2002. A Literature Review with a Focus on Major Themes. In Pyong Gap Min and Jung Ha Kim, eds., *Religions in Asian America,* 15–36. Walnut Creek, CA: Altamira Press.

———.2004. A Comparison of Korean Immigrant Protestant, Catholic, and Buddhist Congregations in New York. Asian/American Center's Working Paper, Queens College, New York.

———.2006. Major Issues Related to Asian American Experiences. In Pyong Gap Min, ed., *Asian Americans: Contemporary Trends and Issues,* 80–107. Walnut Creek, CA: Altamira Press.

———.2008. Severe Under-representation of Women in Church Leadership in Korean Immigrant Churches in the United States. *Journal for the Scientific Study of Religion* 47:225–42.

Min, Pyong Gap, and Chigon Kim. 2009. Patterns of Intermarriage and Cross-Generational Intermarriage among Native-Born Asian Americans. *International Migration Review* 43:447–470.

Min, Pyong Gap, and Dae Young Kim. 2005. Intergenerational Transmission of Religion and Ethnic Culture: Korean Protestants in the United States. *Sociology of Religion* 66:263–82.

Min, Pyong Gap, and Jung Ha Kim, eds. 2002. *Building Faith Communities: Religions in Asian America.* Walnut Creek, CA: Altamira Press.

Min, Pyong Gap, and Young Oak Kim. 2009. Ethnic and Subethnic Attachments among Korean, Chinese, and Indian Immigrants in New York City. *Ethnic and Racial Studies* 32: 758–780.

Mohammad-Arif, Aminah. 2002. *Salam America: South Asian Muslims in New York.* London: Anthem Books.

Mozumder, Suman Guha. 2006a. HAF Retains Legal Counsel in Hindu Textbook Issue. *India Abroad,* January 20, A3.

———.2006b. More Groups Join Protest against Textbook Changes. *India Abroad,* January 20, A3.

———.2008. Religious Leaders Greet Pope with Gifts, Protests. *India Abroad,* April 25, 2008, A14.

Mullins, Mark. 1987. The Life Cycle of Ethnic Churches in Sociological Perspective. *Japanese Journal of Religious Studies* 14:320–34.

Nagel, Joane. 1994. Constructing Ethnicity: Creating and Recreating Identity and Culture. *Social Problems* 41:152–76.

New York City Department of City Planning. 2004. *Demographic Profiles—New York City Community Districts, 2000 Census.* New York: New York City Department of City Planning.

Noll, Mark A. 2001. *American Evangelical Christianity: An Introduction.* Malden, MA: Blackwell.

North American Jewish Data Bank. 2004. The National Jewish Population Survey 2000–2001: Strength, Challenge and Diversity in the American Jewish Population. Storrs: Center for Jewish Studies and Contemporary Jewish Life, University of Connecticut.

Numrich, Paul David. 1996. *Old Wisdom in the New World: Americanization in Two Immigrant Theravada Buddhist Temples*. Knoxville: University of Tennessee Press.

Orsi, Robert Anthony. 1996. *Thank You St. Jude: Women's Devotion to the Patron Saint of Hopeless Causes*. New Haven, CT: Yale University Press.

Ostergren, Robert. 1981. The Immigration Church as a Symbol of Community and Place in the Upper Midwest. *Great Plains Quarterly* 1 (1):225–38.

Ozorak, Elizabeth Weiss. 1996. The Power, but Not the Glory: How Women Empower Themselves through Religion. *Journal for the Scientific Study of Religion* 35 (1):17–29.

Padila, Felix. 1986. Latino Ethnicity in the City of Chicago. In Susan Olzak and Joane Nagel, eds., *Competitive Ethnic Relations*, 153–71. New York: Academic Press.

Pais, Arthur J. 2004. Temple Trouble: Opposition to Temples, Mosques and Gurdwaras Continues. *India Abroad*, November 10.

———. 2007. Hans Ucko. *India Abroad*, December 7.

Park, In-Sook Han, and Lee-Jay Cho. 1995. Confucianism and the Korean Family. *Journal of Comparative Family Studies* 26 (1):117–35.

Park, In-Sook Han, James Fawcett, Fred Arnold, and Richard Gardner. 1990. Koreans Immigrating to the United States: A Pre-Departure Analysis. Paper no. 114. Honolulu: Population Institute, East–West Center, University of Hawai'i.

Park, Kyeyoung. 1997. *The Korean American Dream: Immigrants and Small Business in New York City*. Ithaca, NY: Cornell University Press.

Park, So-Young. 2001. The Intersection of Religion, Race, Gender, and Ethnicity. In Ho-Youn Kwon, Kwang Chung Kim, and R. Stephen Warner, eds., *Korean Americans and Their Religions: Pilgrims and Missionaries from a Different Shore*, 193–209. University Park: Pennsylvania University Press.

———. 2004. Korean American Evangelicals: A Resolution of Sociological Ambivalence among Korean American College Students. In Tony Carnes and Fenggang Yang, eds., *Asian American Religions: The Making and Remaking of Borders and Boundaries*, 141–59. New York: New York University Press.

Park, Sung-bae. 1982. The Impact of Buddhism on the Axiological System Underlying Korean Culture. In Earl H. Phillip and Eui-Young Yu, eds., *Religions in Korea: Beliefs and Cultural Values*, 71–86. Los Angeles: Center for Korean-American and Korean Studies, California State University at Los Angeles.

Patterson, Wayne. 1988. *The Korean Frontier in America: Immigration to Hawaii, 1896–1910*. Honolulu: University of Hawai'i Press.

Peek, Lori. 2005. Becoming Muslim: The Development of a Religious Identity. *Sociology of Religion* 66:215–42.

Peterson, Mark. 1997. Confucianism. In John H. Koo and Andrew C. Nahm, eds., *An Introduction to Korean Culture*, 137–51. Elizabeth, NJ: Hollym.

Pew Forum on Religion and Public Life. 2008. *U.S. Religious Landscape Survey*. Washington, DC: Pew Forum Web Publishing and Communications.

Prebish, Charles S., and Kenneth K. Tanaka, eds. 1998. *The Faces of Buddhism in America*. Berkeley: University of California Press.

Purkayastha, Bandana. 2005. *Negotiating Ethnicity: Second-Generation South Asian American Traverse a Transnational World*. New Brunswick, NJ: Rutgers University Press.

Quebedeaux, Richard. 1978. *The Worldly Evangelicals*. Grand Rapids, MI: HarperCollins.

Rao, Samarth. 2003. The Role of Hindu Values in Global Understanding. *Ganesanjali* 26-03, 10.

Reitz, Jeffrey. 1980. *The Survival of Ethnic Groups*. Toronto: McGraw-Hill.

Rosenberg, S. 1985. *The New Jewish Identity in America*. New York: Hippocrene Books.

Rumbaut, Rubén. 1995. Origins and Destinies: Immigration, Race, and Ethnicity in Contemporary America. In Silvia Pedraza and Rubén Rumbaut, eds., *Origins and Destinies: Immigration, Race, and Ethnicity in America,* 21–42. Belmont, CA: Wadsworth.

Sabagh, George, and Mehdi Bozorgmehr. 1994. Secular Immigrants: Ethnicity and Religiosity among Iranian Muslims in Los Angeles. In Ivonne Y. Haddad and Jane I. Smith, eds., *Muslim Communities in North America,* 445–73, Albany, NY: State University of New York Press.

San Buenaventura, Steffi. 2002. Filipino Religion at Home and Abroad: Historical Roots and Immigrant Transformations. In Pyong Gap Min and Jung Ha Kim, eds., *Religions in Asian America: Building Faith Communities* 143–84. Walnut Creek, CA: Altamira Press.

Saran, Parmatma. 1985. *The Asian Indian Experience in the United States.* Cambridge, MA: Schenkman.

Schermerhorn, R. 1970. *Comparative Ethnic Relations.* New York: Random House.

Seeling, Holly A. 1997. Jains. In David Levinson and Melvin Ember, eds., *American Immigrant Cultures: Builders of a Nation,* vol. 1, 485–91. New York: Macmillan Reference USA.

Sheth, Manju. 1995. Indian Americans. In Pyong Gap Min, ed., *Asian Americans: Contemporary Trends and Issues,* 169–98. Walnut Creek, CA: Sage.

Shin, Eui Hang, and Hyung Park. 1988. An Analysis of Causes of Schisms in Ethnic Churches: The Case of Korean-American Churches. *Sociological Analysis* 49:234–48.

Shin, Eui Hang, and Eui-Young Yu. 1984. Use of Surname in Ethnic Research: The Case of Kim in the Korean American Population. *Demography* 21:347–59.

Singh, Pritam, and Shinder Singh Thandi, eds. 1999. *Punjabi Identity in a Global Context.* New York: Oxford University Press.

Smith, Christian. 1998. *American Evangelicalism: Embattled and Thriving.* Chicago: University of Chicago Press.

Smith, David. 2003. *Hinduism and Modernity.* Malden, MA: Blackwell.

Smith, Donald E. 1970. *Political Development: An Analytic Study.* Boston: Little Brown.

Smith, Timothy. 1978. Religion and Ethnicity in America. *American Historical Review* 83:1155–85.

Stepick, Alex. 1998. *Price against Prejudice: Haitians in the United States.* Boston: Allyn & Bacon.

Stevens, W. David. 2004. Spreading the Word: Religious Beliefs and the Evolutions of Immigrant Congregations. *Sociology of Religion* 65:121–138.

Stevens-Arroyo, Anthony M., and Ana Maria Diaz-Stevens, eds. 1994. *An Enduring Flame: Studies on Latino Popular Religiosity,* vol. 1. New York: Bildner Center for Western Hemisphere Studies.

Stout, Harry S. 1975. Ethnicity: The Vital Center of Religion in America. *Ethnicity* 2:204–24.

Stryker, Sheldon. 1980. *Symbolic Interactionism: A Social Structural Version.* Menlo Park, CA: Benjamin/Cummings.

Suh, Sharon. 2003. "To Be Buddhist Is to Be Korean": The Rhetorical Use of Authenticity and the Homeland in the Construction of the Post-Immigrant Identities. In Jane Naomi Iwamura and Paul Spickard, eds., *Revealing the Sacred in Asian and Pacific America,* 171–92. New York: Routledge.

———. 2004. *Being Buddhist in a Christian World: Gender and Community in a Korean American Temple.* Seattle: University of Washington Press.

Sullivan, Kathleen. 2000. St. Catherine's Catholic Church: One Church, Parallel Congregations. In Helen Rose Ebaugh and Janet Saltzman Chafetz, eds., *Religion and the New Immigrants: Continuities and Adaptations in Congregations,* 255–90. Walnut Creek, CA: Altamira Press.

Suziedelis, Antanas, and Raymond H. Potvin. 1981. Sex Differences in Factors Affecting Religiousness among Catholic Adolescents. *Journal for the Scientific Study of Religion* 30:381–94.

Takaki, Ronald. 1989. *Strangers from a Different Shore*. Boston: Little, Brown.

Tamney, Joseph B. 1993. Religion in Capitalist East Asia. In William H. Swatos Jr., ed., *A Future for Religion*, 92–108. Newbury Park, CA: Sage.

Tomasi, S. M., and H. M. Engel. 1971. *The Italian Experience in the United States*. New York: Center for Migration Studies.

Tong, Chee Kiong. 2007. *Rationalizing Religion: Religious Conversion, Revivalism, and Competition in Singapore Society*. Boston: Leiden.

Tweed, Thomas A. 1997. *Our Lady of Exile: Diasporic Religion at a Cuban Catholic Shrine in Miami*. New York: Oxford University Press.

United Jewish Communities. 2004. The National Jewish Population Survey 2000–2001. A United Jewish Communities Report in Cooperation with the Mandell L. Berman Institute. New York: United Jewish Communities.

Varshney, Ashutoshi. 2002. *Ethnic Conflict and Civic Life: Hindus and Muslims in India*. 2nd ed. New Haven, CT: Yale University Press.

Warner, R. Stephen. 1988. *New Wine in Old Wineskins: Evangelicals and Liberals in a Small-Town Church*. Berkeley: University of California Press.

———. 1993. Work in Progress toward a New Paradigm for the Sociological Study of Religion in the United States. *American Journal of Sociology* 94:1044–93.

———. 1994. The Place of Congregation in the American Religious Configuration. In James Wind and James Lewis, eds., *American Congregations*, 54–99. Vol. 2: *New Perspectives in the Study of Congregations*. Chicago: University of Chicago Press.

———. 1998. Immigration and Religious Communities in the United States. In R. Stephen Warner and Judith Wittner, eds., *Gatherings in Diaspora: Religious Communities and the New Immigration*, 3–36. Philadelphia: Temple University Press.

Warner, R. Stephen, and Judith Wittner, eds. 1998. *Gatherings in Diaspora: Religious Communities and the New Immigration*. Philadelphia: Temple University Press.

Warner, W. L., and Leo Srole. 1945. *The Social System of American Ethnic Groups*. New Haven, CT: Yale University Press.

Waters, Mary. 1990. *Ethnic Options*. Berkeley: University of California Press.

———. 1999. *Black Identities: West Indian Immigrant Dreams and American Realities*. Cambridge, MA: Harvard University Press.

Wellmeier, Nancy J. 1998. Santa Eulalia's People in Exile: Maya Religion, Culture, and Identity in Los Angeles. In R. Stephen Warner and Judith Wittner, eds., *Gatherings in Diaspora: Religious Communities in the New Immigration*, 92–112. Philadelphia: Temple University Press.

Williams, Raymond Brady. 1984. *A New Face of Hinduism: the Swaminarayan Religion*. Cambridge: Cambridge University Press.

———. 1988. *Religions of Immigrants from India and Pakistan*. New York: Cambridge University Press.

———, ed. 1992. *A Sacred Thread: Modern Transmissions of Hindu Traditions in India and Abroad*. Chambersberg, PA: Anima.

———. 1996. *Christian Pluralism in the United States: The Indian Immigrant Experience*. Cambridge: Cambridge University Press.

———. 1997. South Asian Christians. In David Levinson and Melvin Ember, eds., *American Immigrant Cultures*, 829–35. Vol. 2: *Builders of a Nation*. New York: Macmillan Reference USA.

Worth, Robert. 2003. A Hindu Temple of Discord; Amid Priests and Chants, a Bitter Campaigns for Leadership. *New York Times*, December 5.

————. 2004. Hindu Temple to Challenge State Judge on Religious Grounds. *New York Times*, August 4.

Wuthnow, Robert. 1995. *America and the Challenges of Religious Diversity*. Princeton, NJ: Princeton University Press.

————. 1999. Mobilizing Civic Engagement: The Changing Impact of Religious Involvement. In Theda Skocpol and Morris P. Fiorina, eds., *Civic Engagement in American Democracy*, 331–63. Washington, DC: Brookings Institution Press.

Yancy, William, Richard Juliani, and Eugene Erikson. 1976. Emergent Ethnicity: A Review and Reformulation. *American Sociological Review* 41:391–403.

Yang, Fenggang. 1999. *Chinese Christians in America: Conversion, Assimilation, and Adhesive Identities*. University Park: Pennsylvania State University Press.

————. 2000a. Chinese Gospel Church: The Sinicization of Christianity. In Helen Rose Ebaugh and Janet Saltzman Chafetz, eds., *Religion and the New Immigrants: Continuities and Adaptations*, 89–108. Walnut Creek, CA: Altamira Press.

————. 2000b. The His-Nan Chinese Buddhist Temple: Seeking to Americanize. In Helen Rose Ebaugh and Janet Saltzman Chafetz, eds., *Religion and the New Immigrants: Continuities and Adaptations*, 87–108. Walnut Creek, CA: Altamira Press.

Yang, Fenggang. 2002. Chinese Christian Transnationalism: Diverse Networks of a Houston Church. In Helen Rose Ebaugh and Janet Saltzman Chafetz, eds., *Transnational Religious Networks*, 129–48. Walnut Creek, CA: Altamira Press.

Yang, Fenggang, and Helen Rose Ebaugh. 2001a. Religion and Ethnicity among New Immigrants: The Impact of Majority–Minority Status in Home and Host Countries. *Journal for the Scientific Study of Religion* 40:367–78.

————. 2001b. Transformations in New Immigrant Religions and Their Global Implications. *American Sociological Review* 66:269–88.

Yinger, J. Milton. 1994. *Ethnicity: Source of Strength? Source of Conflict?* Albany, NY: State University of New York Press.

Yoo, David K. 2000. *Growing up Nisei: Race, Generation, and Culture among Japanese Americans of California, 1923–49*. Urbana: University of Illinois Press.

————. 2010. *Contentious Spirits: A Religious History of Korean America*. Stanford, CA: Stanford University Press.

Yoon, Young Hae. 2002. Hangook Bulgyo-eui Gidokgyo barabogi [Korean Buddhism's Perception of Christianity]. *Buddhist Review* 4:98–114.

Yu, Eui-Young. 2001. The Growth of Korean Buddhism in the United States with Special Reference to Southern California. In Ho-Youn Kwon, Kwang Chung Kim, and R. Stephen Warner, eds., *Korean Americans and Their Religions: Pilgrims and Missionaries from a Different Shore*, 211–26. University Park: Pennsylvania State University Press.

Zhou, Min, Carl Bankston III, and Rebecca Kim. 2002. Rebuilding Spiritual Lives in the New Land: Religious Practices among Southeast Asian Refugees in the United States. In Pyong Gap Min and Jung Ha Kim, eds., *Religions in Asian America: Building Faith Communities*, 37–70. Walnut Creek, CA: Altamira Press.

# Index

# About the Author

PYONG GAP MIN is Distinguished Professor of Sociology and Director of the Research Center for Korean Community, Queens College and the Graduate Center of the City University of New York, and the author of several books, including *Caught in the Middle: Korean Merchants in America's Multiethnic Cities* and *Ethnic Solidarity for Economic Survival: Korean Greengrocers in New York City*.